FOUNDATIONS
NEW TESTAMENT

A 260-DAY BIBLE READING PLAN FOR BUSY BELIEVERS

ROBBY & KANDI GALLATY
WITH GUS HERNANDEZ & TIM LAFLEUR

LifeWay Press® • Nashville, Tennessee

Laura Magness
Writer

Joel Polk
Editorial Team Leader

Reid Patton
Content Editor

Brian Daniel
Manager, Short-Term Discipleship

David Haney
Production Editor

Michael Kelley
Director, Groups Ministry

Jon Rodda
Art Director

Published by LifeWay Press® • © 2018 Replicate Ministries

ISBN 978-1-5359-3587-6 • Item 005810327

Dewey decimal classification: 225.07
Subject headings: BIBLE. N.T.—STUDY AND TEACHING /
DISCIPLESHIP / CHRISTIAN LIFE

To order additional copies of this resource, write to LifeWay Resources Customer Service; One LifeWay Plaza; Nashville, TN 37234; fax 615-251-5933; phone toll free 800-458-2772; email orderentry@lifeway.com; order online at LifeWay.com; or visit the LifeWay Christian Store serving you.

Printed in the United States of America

Groups Ministry Publishing • LifeWay Resources
One LifeWay Plaza • Nashville, TN 37234

Contents

ABOUT THE AUTHORS

ROBBY GALLATY is the senior pastor of Long Hollow Baptist Church in Hendersonville, Tennessee. He was radically saved from a life of drug and alcohol addiction on November 12, 2002. In 2008 he founded Replicate Ministries to educate, equip, and empower men and women to be disciples who make disciple makers (replicate.org). He's the author of *Growing Up: How to Be a Disciple Who Makes Disciples* (B&H, 2013), *The Forgotten Jesus: How Western Christians Should Follow an Eastern Rabbi* (Zondervan, 2017), *Rediscovering Discipleship: Making Jesus' Final Words Our First Work* (Zondervan, 2015), and *Here and Now: Thriving in the Kingdom of Heaven Today* (B&H, 2019). He's the coauthor with his wife, Kandi, of *Foundations: A 260-Day Bible Reading Plan for Busy Believers* (LifeWay, 2015).

KANDI GALLATY has been investing in the lives of women for over a decade. She believes there are three major sources to draw from when investing in the lives of others: God's Word, God's work in one's life, and God's Spirit. She's passionate about cultivating a biblical worldview from the truths of Scripture and about teaching women how to steward the life experiences and lessons God has allowed in their lives. Together Kandi and Robby lead Replicate Ministries. Kandi loves being a pastor's wife and serving alongside her husband at Long Hollow Baptist Church. Kandi and Robby are the proud, thankful parents of two boys, Rig and Ryder. Kandi is the author of *Disciple Her: Using the Word, Work, and Wonder of God to Invest in Women* (B&H, 2019) and the coauthor with Robby of *Foundations: A 260-Day Bible Reading Plan for Busy Believers* (LifeWay, 2015).

GUS HERNANDEZ JR. is the Spiritual Formation pastor at Long Hollow Baptist Church, where he serves on the executive team, providing direction and oversight for the church's disciple-making strategy. He also serves on the board of Replicate Ministries, equipping pastors and leaders to create a disciple-making culture in their churches by providing training, coaching, and resources. Before joining Long Hollow, Gus was the college pastor at Christ Fellowship Miami, where he was involved in planting and starting new college and young-adult ministries across Miami. Gus is passionate about equipping people to become disciples who make disciples.

TIM LAFLEUR served for twenty years as the campus minister at Nicholls State University in Thibodaux, Louisiana. He pastored churches for thirty years, many while at Nicholls State. Tim was the disciple-making pastor at Brainerd Baptist Church in Chattanooga, Tennessee, for four years. He assisted in expanding the discipleship ministry from twelve people the first year to more than twelve hundred in 2015. He currently serves as the equipping pastor at Long Hollow Baptist Church.

LAURA MAGNESS is the director of children's ministry at Trinity Church in Nashville, Tennessee. Originally from Lexington, Kentucky, she moved to Nashville by way of Samford University and Dallas Theological Seminary, where she received a BA in English and an MA in biblical studies, respectively. Previously, Laura spent ten years as an editor and a writer at LifeWay Christian Resources. Laura has contributed to several books and Bible-study resources, including *Foundations: A 260-Day Bible-Reading Plan for Busy Believers* and smallgroup.com. She and her husband, Nathan, are the parents of two boys.

INTRODUCTION

When I (Robby) was a new believer, I used the OPRA technique for reading the Bible: I randomly *opened* the Bible, *pointed* to a passage, *read* the verse, and tried to figure out a way to *apply* it to my life. Thankfully, I didn't land on the Scripture that says, "He [Judas Iscariot] went and hanged himself" (Matt 27:5). Reading random Scriptures won't provide solid biblical growth any more than eating random foods from your pantry will provide solid physical growth. An effective reading plan is required.

My wife, Kandi, and I, along with the help of Tim LaFleur and Gus Hernandez, have developed a reading plan called the Foundations 260 New Testament. The F-260 NT is a 260-day reading plan that follows the New Testament, covering one Gospel each quarter and moving chronologically through Acts and the Letters one chapter a day. Every chapter in the New Testament will be covered during the course of one year. After using the original Foundations reading plan, we wanted to create an alternative plan that would help provide variety and be more easily digested by new believers.

The plan expects believers to read one chapter a day for five days each week, with an allowance for weekends off. The two off days a week are built in so that you can catch up on days when you're unable to read. With a traditional reading plan of four to five chapters a day, unread chapters can begin to pile up, forcing you to skip entire sections to get back on schedule. It reduces Bible reading to a system of box checking instead of a time to hear from God. The required reading also makes it difficult to sit and reflect on what you've read for that day.

The F-260 NT encourages believers to digest more of the Word by reading less and by keeping a HEAR journal.

HOW DO I LOG A HEAR JOURNAL ENTRY?

The HEAR journaling method promotes reading the Bible with a life-transforming purpose. No longer will you focus on checking off the boxes on your daily reading schedule; instead, your purpose will be to understand and respond to God's Word.

The acronym HEAR stands for *highlight*, *explain*, *apply*, and *respond*. Each of these four steps helps create an atmosphere to hear God speak. After establishing a place and a time to study God's Word each day, you'll be ready to hear from God.

For an illustration let's assume that you begin your quiet time in the Book of 2 Timothy and that today's reading is chapter 1 of the book. Before reading the text, pause to sincerely ask God to speak to you. It may seem trite, but it's absolutely imperative that we seek God's guidance in order to understand His Word (see 1 Cor. 2:12-14). Every time we open our Bibles, we should pray the simple prayer that David prayed:

Open my eyes so that I may contemplate
wondrous things from your instruction [Word] (Ps. 119:18).

After praying for the Holy Spirit's guidance, open your notebook or journal and at the top left-hand corner write the letter H. This exercise will remind you to read with a purpose. In the course of your reading, one or two verses will usually stand out and speak to you. After reading the passage of Scripture, *highlight* each verse that speaks to you by copying it under the letter H. Record the following.
- The name of the book
- The passage of Scripture
- The chapter and verse numbers that especially speak to you
- A title to describe the passage

This practice will make it easier to find the passage when you want to revisit it in the future.

After you've highlighted the passage, write the letter E under the previous entry. At this stage you'll *explain* what the text means. By asking some simple questions, with the help of God's Spirit, you can understand the meaning of a passage or verse. Here are a few questions to get you started.
- Why was this text written?
- To whom was it originally written?
- How does this text fit with the verses before and after it?
- Why did the Holy Spirit include this passage in the book?
- What does the Holy Spirit intend to communicate through this text?

At this point you're beginning the process of discovering the specific, personal word God has for you from His Word. What's important is that you're engaging with the text and wrestling with its meaning.

After writing a short summary of what you think the text means, write the letter A below the letter E. Under the A write the word *apply*. This application is the heart of the process. Everything you've done so far culminates under this heading. As you've done before, answer a series of questions to uncover the significance of these verses to you personally, questions like:

- What does this text teach me about God?
- What does this passage mean today?
- What would the application of this passage look like in my life?
- Does the text identify an action or attitude to avoid or embrace?
- What is God saying to me?

These questions bridge the gap between the ancient world and your world today. They provide a way for God to speak to you from the specific passage or verse. Answer these questions under the A. Challenge yourself to write between two and five sentences about how the text applies to your life.

Finally, below the first three entries, write the letter R for *respond*. Your response to the passage may take on many forms. You may write a call to action. You may describe how you'll be different because of what God has said to you through His Word. You may indicate what you're going to do because of what you've learned. You may respond by writing a prayer to God. For example, you may ask God to help you be more loving or to give you a desire to give more generously. Keep in mind that this is your response to what you've just read.

Notice that all of the words in the HEAR formula are action words: *highlight, explain, apply,* and *respond*. God doesn't want us to sit back and wait for Him to drop truth into our laps. Instead of waiting passively, God wants us to actively pursue Him. Jesus said:

Keep asking, and it will be given to you. Keep searching, and you will find. Keep knocking, and the door will be opened to you (Matt. 7:7).

Think of the miracle of the Bible. Over centuries of time, God supernaturally moved in a number of men in an unusual way, leading them to write the exact words of God. He led His people to recognize these divine writings and to distinguish them from everything else that had ever been written. Next God's people brought these sixty-six books together. The preservation and survival of the Bible are as miraculous as its writing. Then God gave men, beginning with Gutenberg's printing press, technological knowledge to copy and transmit the Bible so that all people could have it. All because God has something to say to you.

MEMORIZING THE WORD

Each week the F-260 NT provides three options for Scripture memory. Options 1 and 2 come from Psalms and Proverbs, while option 3 is a one-year plan to memorize the Sermon on the Mount, a couple of verses a week. You (and your group if you're leading one) can choose one of the three options or mix them up as desired to best meet your needs.

While many plans for memorizing Scripture are effective, a simple system has been effective for me. All you need is a pack of index cards and a committed desire to memorize God's Word. It's easy. Write the reference of the verse on one side of the card and the text of the verse on the other. Focus on five verses at a time and carry your pack of Scripture cards with you.

Whenever you have a few minutes throughout the day, pull out your pack of Scripture cards and review them. Read the reference first, followed by the verse. Continue to recite the verse until you get a feel for the flow of the passage. When you're comfortable with the text, look only at the reference side of the card to test your recall.

It's important to recite the reference first, then the verse, finishing with the reference again. This will prevent you from becoming a concordance cripple. As a new believer, I was forced to look up every verse in the concordance at the back of my Bible. Sometimes when I quoted a Scripture while witnessing, the person asked me, "Where did you get that?" I could only respond, "Somewhere in the Bible." As you can imagine, that answer isn't effective when sharing with others! By memorizing the references, you'll speak with authority and gain the respect of your hearers when you quote Scripture.

After you master five verses, begin studying five more. Review all of the verses you've learned at least once a week. As your pack grows, you'll be encouraged to keep memorizing Scripture, and you'll experience its powerful effects in your life. For a sample HEAR entry, refer to page 270. For disciple-making resources, check out our website, replicate.org.

1//LUKE 1

The Bible is divided into two sections, the Old Testament and the New Testament. The Old Testament gives the accounts of God's creation of a perfect world; the corruption of that perfect world by sin (rebellion against God); and the redemptive relationship God established with the Israelites, whom God appointed as His chosen people. In the Old Testament God repeatedly promised that He would send a Savior to redeem His people from their sin. The Israelites clung to these promises, but four hundred years passed between the Old and New Testaments when God was silent. He made no promises; He offered no new hope. Thankfully, God didn't remain silent forever.

The Gospel of Luke begins with angelic announcements of two historic births—John the Baptist's and Jesus'. The birth stories of these two men were intricately linked. The angels' descriptions of both men reveal key information about who Jesus was and why He came. Jesus was the Son of God, and His name means "Deliverer" or "Savior." He came to save God's people from their bondage to sin. But for Jesus, that didn't mean saving just God's people, the Israelites. As Luke will show us, it meant offering His gift of salvation to anyone and everyone who would believe in Him as "the way of peace" (v. 79). This is the gospel, the good news with which the New Testament begins.

HIGHLIGHT · EXPLAIN · APPLY · RESPOND

2//LUKE 2

Luke 2 provides the account of Jesus' birth and childhood. Mary gave birth to Jesus in Bethlehem, an event that became a reason for all people to celebrate. An angel reported the good news to shepherds as a heavenly host sang God's praise. After Jesus' birth Mary and Joseph fulfilled the important Jewish rites of the circumcision and purification sacrifice at the temple in Jerusalem. At age twelve Jesus traveled with Mary and Joseph to the temple. He spent time speaking with the teachers, who were amazed by His wisdom. He then returned with His family to Nazareth.

From the beginning of Jesus' story, we learn that God's Son wouldn't fit people's expectations of the Messiah, the great Deliverer of the Jews. In fact, we quickly realize that the invitation to know Jesus extends to everyone, regardless of class, education, race, or position. God has limitless, unconditional, and equal love for all people. Likewise, we're called to have the same unconditional mindset as we obey His call to share the gospel.

HIGHLIGHT · EXPLAIN · APPLY · RESPOND

3//LUKE 3

MEMORY VERSES

OPTION 1: **Psalm 1:1-2**
OPTION 2: **Proverbs 1:7**
OPTION 3: **Matthew 5:1-2**

Luke began his Gospel with Gabriel's prediction of John the Baptist's birth and the critical role John would play in preparing people to meet Jesus, the Messiah. In Luke 3 we see the fulfillment of that prediction. John's ministry also fulfilled the prophet Isaiah's prophecy about one who would "prepare the way for the Lord" (v. 4) and help bring God's salvation into focus. The message John preached wasn't a pleasant one, but it was critical and life-changing. He called people to repentance, turning from their sin toward the right living God prescribed in the Old Testament law. Because of his bold call to repentance, people wondered whether John was the Messiah, but he quickly corrected them by drawing attention to Jesus.

The climactic moment of John's ministry came when he baptized Jesus. Unlike all the other baptisms John performed, this one set Jesus apart as God's chosen Son, the One whom He had sent to save the world from its sins. Through baptism Jesus initiated His earthly ministry, aligned Himself with the message of salvation and repentance John preached, and provided us with an example to follow.

This chapter ends with Jesus' genealogy, which Luke traced through David all the way back to Adam in order to highlight Jesus' authority to carry out God's mission of salvation.

HIGHLIGHT • EXPLAIN • APPLY • RESPOND

4//LUKE 4

OPTION 1: **Psalm 1:1-2**
OPTION 2: **Proverbs 1:7**
OPTION 3: **Matthew 5:1-2**

After validating Jesus' identity and establishing His authority as the Son of God, Luke began chapter 4 with Satan's temptation of Jesus in the desert. Before Jesus' earthly ministry even began, Satan called into question Jesus' divine nature and tried to convince Him to turn against His Heavenly Father. But because Jesus was "full of the Holy Spirit" (v. 1), the devil really stood no chance. Jesus' responses to Satan remind us that obedience to the Word of God and dependence on Him give us the power we need to withstand the temptations and accusations Satan levels against us.

Still "in the power of the Spirit" (v. 14), Jesus returned to Galilee from the desert and officially began His ministry of salvation. The quoted text from Isaiah 61 establishes key responsibilities God gave His Messiah, ones Jesus intended to fulfill. The responsibilities listed in Luke 4:18-19 center on the good news of the gospel and the freedom from sin's bondage that the gospel provides. Jesus makes new life available to all of us who are spiritually poor, captive, blind, and oppressed. Although not everyone appreciated Jesus' message of hope and ministry of healing, He was fully committed to His mission. The teachings in verses 31-32,42-44 highlight the unique authority of Jesus' words, and the healings in verses 38-41, the first of many the physician Luke recounted, back up His words with divine power. Jesus is the Messiah, and true freedom is found in Him alone.

HIGHLIGHT · EXPLAIN · APPLY · RESPOND

4//LUKE 4　13

5//LUKE 5

MEMORY VERSES

OPTION 1: **Psalm 1:1-2**

OPTION 2: **Proverbs 1:7**

OPTION 3: **Matthew 5:1-2**

Early in His ministry Jesus called disciples to join Him. He asked these men to give up their professions and become fully devoted followers who would learn from Him, travel with Him, and eventually continue His ministry by spreading the gospel throughout the world. After witnessing a miracle that revealed Jesus' power over the natural world, the first disciples "left everything, and followed him" (v. 11).

Near the end of Luke 5, Jesus made a critical statement about the goal of His ministry on earth: "It is not those who are healthy who need a doctor, but those who are sick. I have not come to call the righteous, but sinners to repentance" (vv. 31-32). Through the miracles recorded in this chapter, we learn that Jesus used physical healing to prove that He also had the power to forgive sins. Miraculous acts like the cleansing of a leper and the healing of a paralytic may seem more powerful to us, but the more important and much more costly miracle Jesus provides is to offer a way for people who are dead in their sins to find new life in God. Jesus' forgiveness and grace make that possible.

Jesus' encounter with the tax collector Levi (see vv. 27-32) reminds us that Jesus' grace has no limits. No one has sinned so greatly or wandered so far that God's love and forgiveness can't reach him or her. From the first disciples to the religious leaders that bookend this chapter, we're reminded that Jesus cares about every individual heart.

HIGHLIGHT · EXPLAIN · APPLY · RESPOND

6//LUKE 6

Luke 5 ends and Luke 6 begins with the first signs of tension between Jesus and the religious leaders of His day, the scribes and Pharisees. At issue in Luke 6 is obedience to observe the Sabbath, the day of holy rest God appointed in the Fourth Commandment. While the Pharisees elevated the law as most important, Jesus, the lawmaker Himself, taught that to love and care for others is true obedience to God. When Jesus healed the lame man's hand, He set Himself apart from the religious leaders in a conflict that would escalate until it ended at the cross.

From that scene Luke shifted to the calling and teaching of Jesus' disciples. The series of teachings recorded in verses 20-49 reveals the countercultural way of life to which Jesus calls His disciples. In a world that values riches, personal satisfaction, happiness, and acceptance, Jesus calls blessed those who are poor, hungry, sorrowful, and hated. Jesus called His disciples to adopt this blessed way of life, because with it comes a recognition of need and a dependence on God alone.

Jesus' teachings in this chapter highlight the character of a disciple, the chief quality being love. Among the marks of a disciple's love is the ability to love enemies and to extend forgiveness and generosity. The high standard of love to which Jesus calls His followers is made possible only through His love for us. The ability to love others as we've been loved sets us apart from the world.

HIGHLIGHT · EXPLAIN · APPLY · RESPOND

7//LUKE 7

MEMORY VERSES

OPTION 1: **Psalm 1:3-4**

OPTION 2: **Proverbs 2:6-7**

OPTION 3: **Matthew 5:3-4**

After teaching His disciples about Christlike love, Jesus took the opportunity to model it for them. The accounts in Luke 7 reveal Jesus' love and compassion for all people, from a powerful Roman centurion to a sinful, disgraced woman.

One of the major themes of Luke's Gospel is that Jesus came to save all people from their sins, not just the Jews. The centurion man at the center of the first story was a Gentile, not of Jewish ethnicity. However, his faith in Jesus' authority far surpassed that of even the Jewish leaders who were anxiously awaiting the Messiah. Jesus affirmed this man's faith and healed his servant, despite his ethnic heritage.

In the next encounter a poor, desperate widow received one of Jesus' greatest miracles. Widows were easy to overlook in Jesus' day, but Jesus saw the woman's grief and raised her son from the dead, a power reserved for God alone. It's no wonder people began to question who Jesus really was (see vv. 18-35). He had the authority of God's promised Messiah, but He didn't look or act anything like the militaristic ruler people expected. That contrast would deepen as His ministry continued. Luke 7 ends much as it began, with a reminder of the importance of love and grace in the kingdom of God.

HIGHLIGHT · EXPLAIN · APPLY · RESPOND

8//LUKE 8

MEMORY VERSES

OPTION 1: **Psalm 1:3-4**
OPTION 2: **Proverbs 2:6-7**
OPTION 3: **Matthew 5:3-4**

The early chapters in Luke follow a pattern that alternates between Jesus' miracles and His teachings, the two foundational aspects of His earthly ministry. Jesus' words taught people about the kingdom of God, and His miracles gave authority and power to His teaching. Because Luke's Gospel highlights the fact that Jesus' grace and forgiveness are available to all people, it repeatedly features women as the recipients of Jesus' teaching and healing. This positive attention to women would have been countercultural in the first century. The women in verses 1-3 responded to Jesus' work in their lives by supporting Him in His ministry.

This chapter of Luke also includes Jesus' well-known parable about the soil and the sower. The parable of the soil (see vv. 4-15), along with the parable of the lamp (see vv. 16-18) and Jesus' teaching in verses 19-21, calls followers of Jesus to actively listen and respond to God's Word. As if to prove why God's Word is worthy of being listened to and obeyed, Luke next included three miracles that show the power of Jesus' words over both the physical world (wind and waves and the human body) and the spiritual world (demons). In each of these miracles, Jesus intervened to save people in need, showing again His mercy and love. We're reminded that the only appropriate response to Jesus' love and power is to place our faith in Him: "Your faith has saved you. Go in peace" (v. 48).

HIGHLIGHT · EXPLAIN · APPLY · RESPOND

9//LUKE 9

MEMORY VERSES
OPTION 1: **Psalm 1:3-4**
OPTION 2: **Proverbs 2:6-7**
OPTION 3: **Matthew 5:3-4**

Luke 9 is a key passage of Scripture for understanding what it means to be a disciple of Jesus. The teachings and miracles in this chapter provide instruction and demonstrate Jesus' ministry in action. Jesus showed His concern for people's physical needs when He fed the hungry crowd. Later He also displayed His power over supernatural evil by healing a boy sickened by demon possession.

Through Jesus' conversations with His disciples in this chapter, we learn about His true identity and mission as the Son of God, the Messiah, who would die and be resurrected as the atonement for sin. Jesus' transfiguration with Moses and Elijah validated God's approval of His Son and the mission He was living out.

As Jesus' disciples, we're challenged to live a life of self-denial that focuses on selflessly serving others. Jesus didn't idealize discipleship; instead, He taught that following Him requires placing the needs of others—both physical and spiritual—ahead of our own.

HIGHLIGHT · EXPLAIN · APPLY · RESPOND

10//LUKE 10

MEMORY VERSES

OPTION 1: **Psalm 1:3-4**
OPTION 2: **Proverbs 2:6-7**
OPTION 3: **Matthew 5:3-4**

After Jesus commissioned the twelve disciples in Luke 9, Luke began to place greater emphasis on what discipleship and life on mission involve. The sending of the seventy-two teaches that the disciples' mission was to mirror Jesus' mission: "Heal the sick who are there, and tell them, 'The kingdom of God has come near you' " (10:9). In other words, disciples of Christ are to meet people's needs and preach the gospel, the good news of Jesus Christ. The way people respond to the gospel is never in the disciples' control, and many people will reject Jesus' disciples, just as He was rejected. The point, however, is that the disciples are obeying Jesus' command by preaching the gospel and giving people an opportunity to believe.

Jesus' interaction with the "expert in the law" (v. 25) and the teaching that follows help readers further understand what it means to follow Christ, who was the very fulfillment of the law. The expert's question was meant to put Jesus to the test by proving that Jesus' teachings stood in contrast to the Old Testament law. But Jesus' parable so perfectly summed up the law that no fault could be found. Obedience to God means wholeheartedly loving Him and loving others with the mercy and compassion the Samaritan showed to the desperate man in verses 30-37.

The brief narrative about Martha and Mary at the close of Luke 10 reminds us that only when we prioritize our love for Jesus over everything else will we be transformed into people who can love others as He loves us.

HIGHLIGHT · EXPLAIN · APPLY · RESPOND

11//LUKE 11

MEMORY VERSES

OPTION 1: **Psalm 1:5-6**
OPTION 2: **Proverbs 3:5-6**
OPTION 3: **Matthew 5:5-6**

Listening to Jesus and loving others are two foundational aspects of being a disciple of Jesus, as we saw in yesterday's reading. Another is prayer, which takes center stage at the start of Luke 11. Jesus' disciples asked Him to teach them how to pray, and He responded with an example that has become known as the Model Prayer or the Lord's Prayer. Jesus' example teaches His followers that prayer should include acknowledgment and praise of who God is (Father), requests for Him to continue working in our world (be holy and bring the kingdom), and petitions for Him to meet our daily needs (physical sustenance, forgiveness of sins, and the power to withstand temptation). This prayer emphasizes praying with God and His will as our focus. Verses 9-13 teach us that we pray to a God who greatly cares about the needs of His children and who loves to give them good gifts.

The remainder of Luke 11 returns to a theme that occurs throughout the Gospel: opposition to Jesus and His teaching. This opposition escalated as Jesus' influence spread. In this chapter the crowds, along with the scribes and the Pharisees, doubted Jesus. Opposition surfaced in the form of questions about Jesus' authority; was it from God or from Satan? Jesus' response to these doubts was to remind people, "Blessed are those who hear the word of God and keep it" (v. 28).

Over and over the scribes and the Pharisees missed the point of Jesus' teachings and clung to dead orthodoxy instead of the living God who stood in front of them. A relationship with God begins with believing Jesus is who He says He is—the Messiah, the One to whom the entire Old Testament pointed.

HIGHLIGHT · EXPLAIN · APPLY · RESPOND

12//LUKE 12

MEMORY VERSES

OPTION 1: **Psalm 1:5-6**
OPTION 2: **Proverbs 3:5-6**
OPTION 3: **Matthew 5:5-6**

Throughout His earthly ministry Jesus taught His followers truths to live by. Among the practical teachings in Luke 12, Jesus encouraged His followers to avoid hypocrisy by revering God and by boldly confessing Jesus before others. He also told a parable to warn them about greed and worry. The life of a child of God should be marked by trust in Him as the ultimate Provider and Protector. Throughout Scripture God proves time and again that He takes care of His children.

Jesus also reminds us that this world isn't our home, so temporary things shouldn't lead to fear or worry. The temporary nature of this world is the point of Jesus' parable on expectantly awaiting the Master's return. For disciples of Jesus, our task in this world is to anticipate and prepare for eternity. Our emphasis in the meantime should be on obeying Christ and participating in His gospel ministry.

HIGHLIGHT · EXPLAIN · APPLY · RESPOND

13//LUKE 13

MEMORY VERSES

OPTION 1: **Psalm 1:5-6**
OPTION 2: **Proverbs 3:5-6**
OPTION 3: **Matthew 5:5-6**

Two important themes of Jesus' ministry are the focus of Luke 13: God's judgment and the coming kingdom. When people questioned Jesus about a murderous act by Pilate, He used it as an opportunity to call them to repentance. Everyone will die, and no one can escape God's judgment. This is why repentance is such an important part of the gospel. People who repent of their sins (confess them to God and turn away from them) escape God's punishment and receive the gift of eternal life in His presence. The parable in verses 6-9 reminds us that God is patient with sinners, but a day will come when Jesus will return and the opportunity to repent will end.

Jesus' teachings about the kingdom of God use simple analogies to reveal important truths. God's earthly kingdom had a small, humble beginning with Jesus' birth in a manger in Bethlehem, but as the mustard seed and the yeast illustrate, it would eventually spread throughout the world. Also noteworthy is that like yeast, the kingdom's transformation begins from within. Jesus changes individual hearts, and then those changed by Him change the world. And although entrance into the kingdom is through a narrow door, meaning it's limited to people who believe in Jesus and repent of their sins, it's a door anyone can enter. No one is beyond the reach of God's kingdom and the reach of Jesus' saving grace.

HIGHLIGHT · EXPLAIN · APPLY · RESPOND

14//LUKE 14

MEMORY VERSES

OPTION 1: **Psalm 1:5-6**
OPTION 2: **Proverbs 3:5-6**
OPTION 3: **Matthew 5:5-6**

In Luke 14 Jesus told two parables in a banquet setting to teach the need for humility. Through these parables we learn that God values and honors a humble spirit that seeks to put others ahead of self. Jesus had grieved over Jerusalem at the close of Luke 13 because He knew the leaders of God's people, the Jews, had turned from Him and would ultimately be responsible for His death. Their lack of humility and elevated sense of self-importance had blinded them to Jesus' identity as their Messiah.

Jesus, on the other hand, modeled the humble spirit God values. He left His position with God the Father in heaven and came to earth to make a way for sinful humanity to be reunited with God. His actions required humility on many levels, culminating at the cross, where the Son of God died for us. Jesus is our model for a life of humble service in the kingdom of God.

A parable about a king going to battle anticipated disciples who count the cost before following Jesus. In order to be obedient to Jesus' call to discipleship, we must prioritize Him and His mission above everything else—even above life itself. Jesus made the ultimate sacrifice to restore humanity's broken relationship with God, and personal sacrifice is necessary for anyone who wants to be His disciple.

HIGHLIGHT • EXPLAIN • APPLY • RESPOND

15//LUKE 15

MEMORY VERSES
OPTION 1: **Psalm 1:5-6**
OPTION 2: **Proverbs 3:5-6**
OPTION 3: **Matthew 5:5-6**

In chapter 15 Luke included another series of parables that reveal important lessons about Jesus' relationship with us and how we're to live in response to Him. These three parables, often referred to as the lost parables, describe the joy associated with the repentance of sinners. They should be examined as a whole, teaching one truth. In Luke 4 Jesus had described the focus of His mission as being on the poor, captives, the blind, and the oppressed—people often rejected by society but in desperate need of help. The parables in Luke 15 came in response to the religious leaders' judgment of Jesus' association with those kinds of people—"tax collectors and sinners" (v. 1).

These parables remind us that all people matter to God and that their salvation should matter to us too. The parables of the lost sheep and the lost coin highlight God's love for sinners and the joy that repentance brings Him. In fact, He loves sinners so much that He actively goes in search of them to bring them back to Himself, just as the shepherd and the woman searched for their lost possessions. As the parable of the prodigal son demonstrates, no sin is so great that it can keep us out of reach of God's loving grace. The joy and celebration at the end of each parable illustrate that all of heaven rejoices when people turn to God through faith in Jesus. Once we experience salvation, everything changes, including the way we live day by day and the way we view the things of this world.

HIGHLIGHT • EXPLAIN • APPLY • RESPOND

16//LUKE 16

MEMORY VERSES

OPTION 1: **Psalm 3:3-4**
OPTION 2: **Proverbs 3:9-10**
OPTION 3: **Matthew 5:7-8**

Jesus' parables continue in Luke 16 with a series on money. In the kingdom of God, money can serve a good purpose when used properly. The first parable, the parable of the dishonest manager, emphasizes stewardship. Although this man is referred to as an "unrighteous manager" (v. 8), Jesus used him as an example of someone who made wise, calculated decisions in order to maximize his future opportunities. The manager deducted what was most likely his personal fees and commission from people's debts in order to be in their good graces if he needed a job in the future. Jesus used this parable to make the point that His disciples can make wise choices that maximize their money for the kingdom of God. As Jesus noted, "You cannot serve both God and money" (v. 13), so disciples must put their money to good use in serving God.

In contrast, when viewed from the wrong perspective, money can blind a person to what matters most—a right relationship with God. This truth is at the heart of the second parable, an indictment of the Pharisees, who were so focused on themselves that they failed to see Jesus as the fulfillment of Old Testament prophecy. We must be careful that we don't let greed keep us from knowing Jesus and serving Him.

HIGHLIGHT • EXPLAIN • APPLY • RESPOND

17//LUKE 17

MEMORY VERSES
OPTION 1: **Psalm 3:3-4**
OPTION 2: **Proverbs 3:9-10**
OPTION 3: **Matthew 5:7-8**

One theme that appears time and again in the Gospels is that salvation changes us. That change begins with the clean heart that comes from repentance. When a person experiences salvation through repentance, he or she becomes a disciple who joins Jesus' work of drawing people to Himself. Because disciples of Christ are assigned to help people see their sin and need for forgiveness, it's important that their hearts are motivated by love and not judgment (see vv. 1-4). The disciples requested greater faith to believe Jesus could turn even the darkest heart toward Him, but Jesus reminded them that as His followers, they already had that faith; they just needed to apply it.

Another story told in Luke 17 is about ten lepers whom Jesus healed. Only one of the ten returned to thank Him, demonstrating the truth that understanding the change Jesus has brought about in our lives should give us a heart of gratitude toward Him.

Another question from a Pharisee prompted Jesus to teach about the coming kingdom of God. The kingdom is often described as having both already and not-yet components. The teachings in chapter 17 focus on the not-yet aspect of the kingdom, most notably Jesus' second coming. Although no one can know when Jesus will return, one fact is certain: He's coming back, and He will find people who've surrendered their lives to Him and those who haven't. In the meantime His disciples should be busy telling people about Him.

HIGHLIGHT · EXPLAIN · APPLY · RESPOND

18//LUKE 18

MEMORY VERSES

OPTION 1: **Psalm 3:3-4**
OPTION 2: **Proverbs 3:9-10**
OPTION 3: **Matthew 5:7-8**

Prayer played a significant role in Jesus' life and teaching. At the beginning of Luke 18, Jesus told a story about a widow to highlight the need for persistence in prayer, even when it seems that God is slow to answer. This parable is connected to Jesus' teaching on His return at the end of chapter 17. As Luke noted in verse 1 of chapter 18, Jesus wanted His disciples to persist in prayer and not give up while they waited for His return and the culmination of God's kingdom.

A second parable about the Pharisee and the tax collector emphasizes the need for humility in prayer. Both persistence and humility in prayer communicate total dependence on God and a desire to unite with Him through prayer. Prayer is one of the greatest gifts God gives His children, and we should be eternally grateful for it.

The stories that follow in this chapter contrast humble children and a blind beggar with a rich young ruler, further illustrating that salvation comes to those who are humble enough to recognize their need for Jesus and who are willing to follow Him at any cost. Jesus' prediction of His death (see vv. 31-34) reminds readers of the great lengths Jesus went to in order to make salvation possible. The sacrifice God expects from His children pales in comparison to the price Jesus paid to redeem us.

HIGHLIGHT • EXPLAIN • APPLY • RESPOND

19//LUKE 19

MEMORY VERSES

OPTION 1: **Psalm 3:3-4**
OPTION 2: **Proverbs 3:9-10**
OPTION 3: **Matthew 5:7-8**

Luke 19 begins with one of the most well-known accounts in Luke's Gospel—the story of Zacchaeus. Much more than a "wee little man," Zacchaeus gives readers an example of the correct way to respond to Jesus, as compared with the incorrect ways of the tax collector and the rich young ruler in Luke 18. Zacchaeus fits in the category of unlikely people for Jesus to associate with, examples of whom we've seen throughout this Gospel. Yet when he met Jesus, Zacchaeus changed instantaneously. His life became defined by generosity rather than greed, by humility rather than self-gratification. Zacchaeus's salvation prompted Jesus to remind the people of His mission: "to seek and to save the lost" (19:10).

The parable that follows the account of Zacchaeus teaches those whom Jesus has saved how to live while waiting for His return. The answer lies in active faithfulness. This parable draws to a close the section of Luke's Gospel that focuses on Jesus' trek to Jerusalem and the teachings and miracles that took place along the way. In verse 28 the focus shifts to Passion Week and Jesus' final teachings. Both the triumphal entry and the clearing of the temple show the stark contrast between the Messiah people expected and the actual Messiah embodied in Jesus. Although the people expected a strong political leader who would restore Israel to prominence and power, Jesus came in humility to restore all human hearts to God.

HIGHLIGHT · EXPLAIN · APPLY · RESPOND

20//LUKE 20

MEMORY VERSES
OPTION 1: **Psalm 3:3-4**
OPTION 2: **Proverbs 3:9-10**
OPTION 3: **Matthew 5:7-8**

At the close of Luke 19, Luke told readers that the Jewish religious leaders wanted to kill Jesus but couldn't find a way to do it. In Luke 20 Luke revealed that the Pharisees tried to humiliate Jesus over the question of authority. The Pharisees derived their authority from their extensive training. Throughout His entire earthly ministry Jesus had acted and spoken with an authority reserved for God alone. The Jewish leaders wanted to know where this authority came from. Though Jesus didn't directly answer that question, He told a parable that presented Him as the Son of God and the religious leaders as people who rejected and killed the Son.

The religious leaders next questioned Jesus over governmental authority, but again their trap didn't work. Followers of God have an obligation to their governments, which operate within the world He governs.

The religious leaders' third question concerned the resurrection of the dead. Again Jesus answered their question in a way that maintained the truth and authority of God's kingdom without belittling the questioner or succumbing to the trap. Unable to trick Jesus, the religious leaders grew silent, and Jesus took the opportunity to remind listeners of the Messiah's identity as the divine Son of David, God incarnate. Jesus was that promised Messiah, the Son of God, and He was completely in control of the events of Passion Week.

HIGHLIGHT • EXPLAIN • APPLY • RESPOND

21//LUKE 21

MEMORY VERSES

OPTION 1: **Psalm 8:4-5**
OPTION 2: **Proverbs 3:11-12**
OPTION 3: **Matthew 5:9-10**

At the end of Luke 20, Jesus gave warnings to the religious leaders who had questioned him. One criticism He expressed was that they "devour widows' houses" (v. 47), meaning they took advantage of widows in their impoverished state. In chapter 21, in direct contrast to these leaders, Jesus commended the faith of a widow who gave everything she had to the temple offering. Although the offering was small, the faith and obedience behind it were great. Jesus used an unlikely example to highlight how much God values generosity and sacrifice.

The remainder of chapter 21 is devoted to additional teachings about the future, specifically the destruction of the temple in Jerusalem and the importance of being watchful for Jesus' return. Jesus' prophecy about the destruction of the temple was fulfilled in AD 70, when the Roman army burned it to the ground.

Also included in Jesus' teaching about the future was a series of warnings about what His followers could expect in the time between His resurrection and His second coming. Jesus' description included the global threat of false prophets, wars, and natural disasters, as well as the personal threat of persecution and betrayal because of loyalty to Jesus. However, there was hope! Jesus called His followers to persevere in faith because God had sealed them for eternity, and they had the promise of His return to look forward to. Thankfully, we too can cling to the hope of Jesus' return as we live for Him today.

HIGHLIGHT · EXPLAIN · APPLY · RESPOND

22//LUKE 22

In Luke 22 the events of Passion Week quickly escalated as the religious leaders plotted to kill Jesus. Judas gave them their opportunity when he agreed to betray Jesus by helping them arrest Him away from the crowds. That opportunity arose later in the chapter when Jesus was alone with His disciples in the garden of Gethsemane.

Earlier in the evening Jesus had held the Passover dinner with His disciples. The Passover meal had been a part of Jewish tradition since the exodus. God had commanded the Israelite households to sacrifice a lamb and cover their doorposts with its blood so that He would pass over their houses when He struck the firstborn sons of Egypt with a plague (see Ex. 11–12). Jesus' celebration of the Passover brought it new meaning. Jesus was the Passover Lamb, the ultimate sacrifice God sent once and for all to pay the price for people's sins. During this meal with His disciples, Jesus also predicted Judas's betrayal and Peter's denial. Jesus knew His arrest and crucifixion would also bring trials for His followers, but He again called them to humility and self-sacrifice, traits that would be put to the test in the days to come.

The powerful scene in the garden marks the climactic moment of Luke's Gospel. In Luke 9:51 Luke wrote that Jesus "determined to journey to Jerusalem," knowing what awaited Him there. As He prayed in the garden, He fully surrendered to God's plan. Shortly thereafter Jesus was arrested, Peter denied knowing Him, and His trial began. Jesus was the Son of God (see 22:70), and that truth would lead to His death.

HIGHLIGHT • EXPLAIN • APPLY • RESPOND

23//LUKE 23

MEMORY VERSES

OPTION 1: **Psalm 8:4-5**
OPTION 2: **Proverbs 3:11-12**
OPTION 3: **Matthew 5:9-10**

From the beginning of his Gospel, Luke was committed to present evidence that Jesus was the Messiah, the Son of God. The details he included in his record of Jesus' trial and crucifixion further support this focus. Luke described Jesus' trials before Pilate and Herod, two Roman rulers who both struggled to find Jesus guilty. Even though Jesus was innocent, Pilate gave in to the crowd's demands and agreed to have Jesus crucified in exchange for the murderer Barabbas. The inclusion of Barabbas in the crucifixion account provides a dramatic picture of the gospel. Guilty in our sin, we deserve death, but because of the death of Jesus in our place, we've been set free.

The remainder of the chapter describes Jesus' death on the cross and burial in a tomb. Luke recorded three statements by Jesus on the cross, each of which affirmed His identity as the Son of God and united Him with His Heavenly Father (see vv. 34,43,46). One criminal who was crucified on a cross next to Jesus affirmed Jesus' authority and identity. As a result, Jesus acknowledged that his faith had saved him that day. Jesus' prayer in verse 46, "Father, into your hands I entrust my spirit," reveals that Jesus remained in control until the end, further proving He's God the Son. Jesus willingly gave up His own life for the sins of the world. After He died, his body was placed in a tomb, marking what seemed to be the end of His life.

HIGHLIGHT · EXPLAIN · APPLY · RESPOND

24//LUKE 24

MEMORY VERSES

OPTION 1: **Psalm 8:4-5**
OPTION 2: **Proverbs 3:11-12**
OPTION 3: **Matthew 5:9-10**

The Gospel of Luke records the account of Jesus' resurrection and the women's faithful obedience in relaying the angels' message to the rest of the disciples. Luke also included details about Jesus' postresurrection appearances. Jesus' appearances proved His resurrection and provided Him the opportunity to give final orders to His disciples before ascending to heaven.

Jesus appeared to two disciples on the road to Emmaus, when He also confirmed that all of Scripture points to Himself. Jesus later appeared to the apostles and showed them His hands and feet. He encouraged them to believe the resurrection by eating with them and interpreting the Old Testament in light of His sufferings and resurrection. Jesus identified Himself as the Messiah.

Jesus' time on earth ended with a commission to His disciples. He left them with a charge to minister and proclaim the gospel on Jesus' behalf. As Jesus' disciples today, we know Him because others have been faithful to carry His gospel around the world, and we pick up where those disciples left off as Jesus' faithful ambassadors.

HIGHLIGHT · EXPLAIN · APPLY · RESPOND

25//ACTS 1

MEMORY VERSES

OPTION 1: **Psalm 8:4-5**
OPTION 2: **Proverbs 3:11-12**
OPTION 3: **Matthew 5:9-10**

The Book of Acts, which Luke wrote as a second volume to his Gospel, documents the growth of the early church during the first three decades after Jesus' ascension. Throughout those years Christianity, which was first extended to the Jewish people, became predominantly Gentile.

Acts 1 set the stage for the coming of the Holy Spirit, described in Acts 2, by moving readers from Jesus' postresurrection appearances to the disciples prayerfully waiting in the upper room. Luke recorded Jesus' instructions to the disciples for their global mission, a task that would be empowered by the Holy Spirit. Luke also included the account of Jesus' ascension to heaven as the disciples watched. As Jesus prepared to leave, He gave the disciples a new perspective on the kingdom of God by establishing a worldwide scope for this witnessing mission. The church, under the Holy Spirit's guidance and power, was to take the gospel to the ends of the earth, a task that Christ expects us to continue today.

HIGHLIGHT · EXPLAIN · APPLY · RESPOND

26//ACTS 2

Exactly as Jesus had promised, the Father empowered the disciples with the Holy Spirit. Prior to the Pentecost event described in Acts 2, God had given the Spirit's power to certain individuals for particular purposes and periods of time. With Pentecost, however, the Spirit's power became an indwelling part of every Christian. Jesus commissioned His followers to witness about His saving power to the uttermost parts of the earth, and they (and we) would become dependent on the Spirit's power to accomplish this task. The signs that accompanied the coming of the Holy Spirit revealed God's power and presence in His people, as well as the universality of the gospel message.

After this event Peter preached a sermon to the crowd in which he connected the day's events to the message of the gospel. Peter linked the Pentecost event to Old Testament prophecy and gave eyewitness testimony of Jesus' crucifixion and resurrection. Peter's sermon ends with the crowd's response. Having come under conviction by the Holy Spirit, the people asked how they should respond. Peter directed them to confess and repent of their sins, and as many as three thousand did so. Chapter 2 concludes with a picture of the early church in action. Unity, generous giving, sharing with people in need, modeling the gospel in action, worshiping, partaking of the Lord's Supper in fellowship, and serving the Lord through various ministries present a model for ministry the church continues to follow today.

HIGHLIGHT · EXPLAIN · APPLY · RESPOND

27//ACTS 3

MEMORY VERSES

OPTION 1: **Psalm 9:9-10**
OPTION 2: **Proverbs 3:33-34**
OPTION 3: **Matthew 5:11-12**

Many times in the Gospel of Luke, the author noted ways Jesus taught His disciples to follow His example of ministry. In Acts 3 Peter and John did just that as they began the work of growing the church. The disciples met the physical and spiritual needs of people, both inside and outside the body of Christ.

Acts 3 begins with the account of the healing of a lame beggar. From the first healing mentioned in Acts, we learn several important characteristics of the early church's ministry.

1. The disciples healed in the name of Jesus Christ. The primary purpose of their healing was to point people to Jesus and to give the disciples an audience for preaching the gospel.
2. The miraculous healing evoked a response of "awe and astonishment" (v. 10). The miracle earned the disciples the ear of the crowd.
3. The healing was followed with the gospel. Peter's speech to the crowd not only highlighted Jesus' crucifixion and resurrection but also called people to belief and repentance. Just as He did in the first century, God continues to empower His people to meet spiritual and physical needs so that His name will be glorified and people will be drawn to Him.

HIGHLIGHT • EXPLAIN • APPLY • RESPOND

28//ACTS 4

MEMORY VERSES
OPTION 1: **Psalm 9:9-10**
OPTION 2: **Proverbs 3:33-34**
OPTION 3: **Matthew 5:11-12**

People responded to Peter's first sermon on the day of Pentecost by overwhelmingly accepting the gospel message, and that continued to be the case with the second sermon, when another two thousand listeners believed. However, in Acts 4 we see the first evidence of the persecution of Christians, when Peter and John were arrested for teaching people about Jesus. This result shouldn't be surprising; Jesus had prophesied that His followers would be hated because of Him (see Matt. 10:22; 24:9; Mark 13:13; Luke 21:17).

When pressed about the miraculous healing they had done, Peter and John responded by pointing the religious leaders to Jesus and the power of His name. As was often the case with Jesus, the leaders couldn't find significant reason to punish the apostles, so they simply instructed them not to talk about Jesus anymore. Every follower of Jesus today should echo their response: "We are unable to stop speaking about what we have seen and heard" (Acts 4:20). Then they went back to their Christian community and prayed for increased boldness.

Verses 32-37 end this chapter by highlighting the unity of the early church. The believers shared their possessions to meet physical needs. Luke gave special attention to Barnabas, who exemplified this spirit of generosity and would become a key figure in the growth of the early church. Unity, generosity, and boldness are three traits of the early church that the body of Christ does well to imitate today.

HIGHLIGHT · EXPLAIN · APPLY · RESPOND

29//ACTS 5

MEMORY VERSES

OPTION 1: **Psalm 9:9-10**
OPTION 2: **Proverbs 3:33-34**
OPTION 3: **Matthew 5:11-12**

Sadly, not every member of the early church possessed pure motives for sharing with others in need. Ananias and Sapphira were dishonest about their personal contribution and, as a result, experienced the harsh judgment of death. Their story reminds us that the church is made up of imperfect people. For this reason a reliance on the wisdom and guidance of the Holy Spirit in daily life is vitally important. When believers deviate from the leading of the Spirit, we're tempted to imitate the actions of Ananias and Sapphira, who misled the disciples to enhance their own reputations.

Because God is always working to accomplish His good plans in our world, this event served to strengthen the church's public ministry. People sought the church's assistance, which led to gospel conversations about the One who could satisfy every need. As word of their ministry spread, so did the negative response of the Sadducees, who Luke noted "were filled with jealousy" (v. 17). Again Peter, John, and other apostles were jailed for sharing the gospel, but this time their release happened by miraculous means. An angel of the Lord delivered them from prison and instructed them to continue sharing the gospel in the temple courts, where they had been arrested. They obeyed, and the religious leaders who found them were so bewildered that again they didn't know how to handle the situation. The Pharisee Gamaliel stands out as the voice of reason in this encounter, acknowledging that a fight against God isn't a fight anyone can win. God used this Jewish religious leader to protect the lives of His apostles and to continue the advancement of the gospel.

HIGHLIGHT · EXPLAIN · APPLY · RESPOND

30//ACTS 6

As the church continued to grow rapidly, noticeable growing pains began to surface. In chapter 6 Luke recounted that some widows in the Christian community in Jerusalem weren't receiving their daily distributions of food. This incident brought to the church's attention the need for better administration of service so that the apostles could focus on spreading the gospel. The church set apart seven men to carry out this new ministry.

As the gospel went forth, opposition against the church increased. Stephen, one of the seven men appointed to serve the widows, attracted the attention of the corrupt religious leaders because of his fearless proclamation of the word of Christ. His preaching led some unbelieving Grecian Jews to bring him before the Sanhedrin on false charges. When the gospel changes lives through a noticeable impact on a community, opposition will arise. All who desire to live out Jesus' Great Commission in their lives can expect hardship and trouble along the way. God's Spirit will give them, like Stephen, boldness and confidence to stand strong for Him.

HIGHLIGHT · EXPLAIN · APPLY · RESPOND

31//ACTS 7

MEMORY VERSES
OPTION 1: **Psalm 13:5-6**
OPTION 2: **Proverbs 4:23**
OPTION 3: **Matthew 5:13-14**

In Acts 7 Luke recorded Stephen's defense before the Sanhedrin—a powerful testimony of the gospel, traced throughout the Old Testament. Stephen opened with God's call of Abraham in Mesopotamia. He then highlighted Joseph and his brothers' experience in Egypt. Next Stephen recounted the Israelites' slavery in Egypt and their journey to freedom through the desert under Moses' leadership. He reminded the crowd of the Israelites' rebellion and idol worship in the wilderness. After discussing the traveling tabernacle and the temple of Solomon, Stephen emphasized that God doesn't dwell in buildings, emphasizing the change brought about by the arrival of the Holy Spirit at Pentecost.

Stephen boldly warned the religious leaders about "resisting the Holy Spirit" (v. 51). Their ancestors had persecuted and killed the prophets, and now the religious leaders had killed the Righteous One, Jesus, whom the prophets had foretold. Stephen's defense, a powerful witness about Christ, resulted in his death by stoning, making him the first Christian martyr.

HIGHLIGHT · EXPLAIN · APPLY · RESPOND

32//ACTS 8

MEMORY VERSES

OPTION 1: **Psalm 13:5-6**
OPTION 2: **Proverbs 4:23**
OPTION 3: **Matthew 5:13-14**

Stephen's stoning unleashed persecution on the Jerusalem church that forced believers to flee. Saul, later known as the apostle Paul, is introduced at the account of Stephen's death as having an active role in the early church's persecution. However, instead of extinguishing the gospel message, persecution expanded it.

One of the believers who left Jerusalem at that time was Philip, who took the message of the gospel to Samaria. Philip's ministry, like Peter and John's, followed Jesus' example of performing miracles and preaching the Word. Among the people Philip interacted with in Samaria was a former sorcerer who performed miracles like Philip's, except in the power of Satan rather than the Holy Spirit. When Simon witnessed Philip's work among the people, he believed in Jesus and was baptized. However, when Simon witnessed Peter and John's power to perform Spirit baptism, he mistakenly believed he could buy the spiritual power from them. Peter responded by harshly rebuking him. Like Ananias in chapter 5, Simon sought God's gifts and power for personal gain. Peter's response to Simon serves as a good warning for all Christians. God gives His people good gifts, but we're to use them for His purposes and His glory rather than our own.

Chapter 8 ends with Philip's witness to an Ethiopian eunuch. The Ethiopian man, who was curious about spiritual matters, was reading the Book of Isaiah when Philip met him. Philip quoted Isaiah 53:7-8 to illustrate that God's redemptive plan is woven throughout all Scripture. The man responded to Philip's message by believing and being baptized. Despite—or rather because of—the persecution in Jerusalem, the gospel was spreading, and the church was rapidly growing throughout the region.

HIGHLIGHT · EXPLAIN · APPLY · RESPOND

33//ACTS 9

Acts 8 briefly alluded to Saul's acts of persecution against the early church before turning the focus to Philip, but Luke returned to Saul in chapter 9. Saul was on a mission to exterminate all believers in the city of Damascus. On the way Jesus dramatically encountered Saul, causing him to lose his sight. Jesus declared that Saul's acts of persecution against Christians were persecution of Him—God's own Son, the Messiah. By stripping Saul of his sight, Jesus humbled him and left him desperate and dependent on others.

God had big plans for Saul's life, and he sent Ananias to inform Saul of these plans. Saul's reputation was such that even Ananias, a faithful disciple of Jesus, was hesitant to reach out to him, finding it hard to believe he could be God's "chosen instrument to take my name to Gentiles, kings, and Israelites" (v. 15).

After meeting Ananias in Damascus, Saul regained his sight, was filled with the Holy Spirit, and was eventually baptized. Almost immediately Saul began proclaiming the gospel. Few encounters in Scripture provide such a powerful picture of the immediate change Jesus brings to a person's life. If you're a Christian, then like Saul, you have a powerful testimony of being raised from spiritual death to eternal life through the good news of Christ. Don't ever take that story for granted. Acts 9 ends by shifting the focus back to Peter, who continued to perform miracles and preach the gospel in Jesus' name. The church continued to grow as many more people believed.

HIGHLIGHT · EXPLAIN · APPLY · RESPOND

34//ACTS 10

MEMORY VERSES
OPTION 1: **Psalm 13:5-6**
OPTION 2: **Proverbs 4:23**
OPTION 3: **Matthew 5:13-14**

Chapters 2–12 in the Book of Acts primarily focus on Peter's ministry. Through Peter's efforts people understood that the gospel of Jesus Christ applies to the whole world, not just the Jews. In large part this revelation took place as a result of Peter's interactions with Cornelius, a Roman centurion in Caesarea who had a vision in which an angel told him to send men to Joppa to summon Peter. Meanwhile, Peter had a vision in which God commanded him to kill and eat animals that Jews considered unclean. When Cornelius's men arrived, the Holy Spirit instructed Peter to accompany them to Caesarea. When he entered Cornelius's house, Peter stated that God had sent him, and he explained the truth he had learned about not considering anyone common or unclean. As Peter preached the gospel to the people at Cornelius's house, the Spirit descended on the hearers, and they were baptized.

The lesson for Peter and for all Christians today is that in God's kingdom, people are more important than religious regulations or racial differences. All people matter to God, and He desires that all people hear His gospel and experience the salvation He offers through belief in His Son.

HIGHLIGHT • EXPLAIN • APPLY • RESPOND

35//ACTS 11

MEMORY VERSES

OPTION 1: **Psalm 13:5-6**
OPTION 2: **Proverbs 4:23**
OPTION 3: **Matthew 5:13-14**

When Peter shared the gospel with Cornelius's household, he had acted in obedience to the specific calling God had given him, but he had also acted in obedience to the Great Commission that Jesus had issued to His disciples as He ended His earthly ministry (see Matt. 28:18-20). Still it was hard for some of the Christians in Jerusalem to understand that people were being saved by belief in Jesus alone, without observing Jewish practices or customs. The Jews had lived for centuries as God's chosen people, but Jesus made it clear that the gospel was for everyone, not just for the Jews. Peter's explanations of why he had acted as he did at Cornelius's home made it clear that he had acted in obedience to God, and Peter's critics were convinced of the truth.

In Acts 11:19 Luke noted the expansive growth of Christianity among Gentile regions. The church's home base in Jerusalem sent Barnabas to Antioch to validate the ministry efforts taking place there. Barnabas recruited Saul to join him in Antioch, and the two led the discipleship efforts among the new believers there. The church in Antioch would become one of the most influential groups of Christians in the early church, so it's appropriate that they were the first to be called Christians, or Christ followers.

Chapter 11 ends with a brief note about the generosity and love of the Antioch church. Their quick action to send money to other Christians in need shows that the unity of the early church strengthened as Christianity spread.

HIGHLIGHT · EXPLAIN · APPLY · RESPOND

36//ACTS 12

MEMORY VERSES

OPTION 1: **Psalm 16:11**
OPTION 2: **Proverbs 5:20-21**
OPTION 3: **Matthew 5:15-16**

Persecution against the early church continued, even though Paul no longer led the charge. King Herod Agrippa I, the ruler of Judea, beheaded the apostle James, the brother of John, and imprisoned Peter. Acts 12 describes how an angel miraculously freed Peter from prison. When Herod discovered that Peter had escaped, he had Peter's guards executed and traveled to Caesarea, where he suffered a horrible death. In spite of oppression, the gospel continued to flourish. Additionally, Barnabas and Paul completed their relief mission at this time.

It's easy to overlook a small detail in verse 5. While Peter was in prison, the church "was praying fervently to God for him," likely for his safety and strength in the face of persecution. The events that followed reveal the power of their prayers, reminding us that prayer remains our most effective tool against any opposition or temptation we face, both in our personal lives and in the church. Through prayer we commune with God and confess our reliance on Him in every arena of our lives.

HIGHLIGHT · EXPLAIN · APPLY · RESPOND

37//ACTS 13

MEMORY VERSES

OPTION 1: **Psalm 16:11**
OPTION 2: **Proverbs 5:20-21**
OPTION 3: **Matthew 5:15-16**

Acts 13 begins the section of the Book of Acts that describes the first of Paul's three missionary journeys. (Paul was Saul's Greek name, which Luke used for the remainder of Acts.) These journeys make up the rest of Acts, tracking the church's intentional efforts to take the gospel to places it hadn't yet been communicated. Paul's first journey began when the church in Antioch commissioned and dispatched him and Barnabas, a model for missions that the church continues to follow today.

Their first stop was in Cyprus, where they encountered a sorcerer similar to Simon in chapter 8. Luke pointed out that Paul was "filled with the Holy Spirit" (13:9) when he confronted Elymas, a confrontation that led to the faith of Sergius Paulus, the governor of the island. The Spirit's presence with Paul and the Roman leader's response of faith establish the validity and intensity of this first missionary journey. Paul and Barnabas had a clear mission to spread the gospel, and they whole-heartedly focused on that mission.

From Cyprus they traveled to Pisidian Antioch (as opposed to Antioch in Syria, where their journey originated), which was farther north in Galatia, or modern-day Turkey. The scene in Pisidian Antioch was the first of many that would become a pattern of Paul's missionary efforts. On arriving in a community, he first preached to the Jews in the synagogue. When they rejected the gospel, he turned his attention to the Gentiles, many of whom believed. In a scene similar to Jesus' ministry, the Jews grew jealous of the attention Paul and Barnabas received and expelled them from the city. Unfazed, the missionaries followed the Holy Spirit's leading and set their sights on the next town.

HIGHLIGHT · EXPLAIN · APPLY · RESPOND

38//ACTS 14

MEMORY VERSES
OPTION 1: **Psalm 16:11**
OPTION 2: **Proverbs 5:20-21**
OPTION 3: **Matthew 5:15-16**

Paul's missionary endeavors in Acts 14 continued the pattern established in the previous chapter. When they arrived in Iconium, another town in the same region, Paul and Barnabas first went to the Jewish synagogue. They were met with equal parts animosity and acceptance but eventually fled the city when they learned of a plot to have them stoned.

In Lystra Paul's healing of a crippled man led the crowds to assume Paul and Barnabas were gods. The missionaries could have accepted the praise and given in to their pride, but they quickly and adamantly spoke the truth about God and the ways He had revealed Himself in an effort to correct the misguided perception of the crowd. Soon a group of Jews again attacked them and threw them out of the city.

Paul and Barnabas returned to Antioch in Syria by retracing their steps through the various cities they had visited. At each stop they encouraged the new believers in their faith, challenged them to endure any persecution they might face, and appointed elders to lead the churches. When they finally arrived back in Antioch, they gave a full report of God's work through them on their first missionary journey. Paul's example reminds us that serving Christ brings with it both victories and difficulties. Regardless of what we encounter as we live for Christ, God expects us to be faithful in the tasks He has given us.

HIGHLIGHT · EXPLAIN · APPLY · RESPOND

39//JAMES 1

MEMORY VERSES

OPTION 1: **Psalm 16:11**
OPTION 2: **Proverbs 5:20-21**
OPTION 3: **Matthew 5:15-16**

Throughout the Book of Acts we read about several leaders who emerged as influential to the growth of the early church. One of those leaders was James, the brother of Jesus, whom Acts 12:17 identifies as a leader of the local church in Jerusalem. James also authored a book of the New Testament. The Book of James is a practical book that addresses issues Christians deal with both inside and outside the church. Although James's letter was originally written for Christians who had scattered from Jerusalem as a result of the persecution described in Acts, his letter has a much broader appeal that continues to have practical implications for Christians today.

In chapter 1 James reminded his readers that God offers believers wisdom to cope with times of trials and testing. Though temptations are a normal, expected part of life, God never tempts anyone; temptations arise from our sin nature. God, on the other hand, graciously gives only good gifts to those He loves. James also emphasized the importance of preparing our hearts to receive, listen to, and obey the Word of God. By applying God's Word, we give evidence that our religion is genuine. Application of the Word involves controlling speech, caring for needy people, and maintaining purity of life.

HIGHLIGHT · EXPLAIN · APPLY · RESPOND

40//JAMES 2

MEMORY VERSES

OPTION 1: **Psalm 16:11**
OPTION 2: **Proverbs 5:20-21**
OPTION 3: **Matthew 5:15-16**

James began chapter 2 with a more specific example of the genuine religion to which he had called readers at the close of chapter 1. Evidently, a problem among Christians in the early church was a tendency to show favoritism to the rich. Without mincing words, James reminded his readers that Christian love should be blind to the prejudices and judgments of the world. You're to "love your neighbor as yourself" (2:8), no matter who your neighbor is, just as Jesus' parable of the good Samaritan illustrated (see Luke 10:25-37). James went so far as to call favoritism a sin and urged readers to put into practice the mercy and love God showed through the cross.

The second half of James 2 turns from the more narrow issue of favoritism to the broader issue of faith in action. As Christians, we're obligated to love others, and we sin when we fail to do so. Love is one way we put feet to our faith, which, as James pointed out, is dead without actions. To illustrate this point, James gave two Old Testament examples of people whose faith motivated them to act: Abraham and Rahab. Abraham's faith in God was so strong that he willingly placed his son Isaac on the altar of sacrifice (see Gen. 22), an action that showed God how much Abraham trusted Him. Rahab acted against her people when she hid Israelite spies (see Josh. 2) and, like Abraham, showed God that she trusted Him and His purposes. James's point is clear: saving faith in Jesus always leads to good works.

HIGHLIGHT · EXPLAIN · APPLY · RESPOND

41//JAMES 3

MEMORY VERSES

OPTION 1: **Psalm 18:2**
OPTION 2: **Proverbs 6:10-11**
OPTION 3: **Matthew 5:17-18**

A running theme throughout James's letter is faithful Christian behavior. As people transformed by Jesus, Christians are to live and act differently from the rest of the world. In chapter 3 James specifically connected this mandate to speech, using three word pictures to illustrate the power of our words, either for good or for bad: bits that control horses (see v. 3), small rudders that steer massive ships (see v. 4), and single sparks that ignite forest fires (see vv. 5-6). Each illustration makes the point that although the tongue is a small body part, our words have great power, a power we must learn to control and exercise in a God-honoring way.

James warned against the dangers of a Christian with an uncontrolled tongue, but he also challenged believers to be consistent in their speech. With additional illustrations James reminded readers that the words that come from our mouths clearly reflect our true identity. What we say reflects who we are. Words that hurt others hurt God Himself, and they more truly reflect our hearts than we care to believe.

James closed this chapter by reminding Christians to rely on God's wisdom to change their behavior. This reminder is reassuring, especially in light of our universal struggle to control our speech. Only through the work of the Holy Spirit in us can we exhibit the Christlike characteristics James listed at the close of chapter 3.

HIGHLIGHT · EXPLAIN · APPLY · RESPOND

42//JAMES 4

MEMORY VERSES

OPTION 1: **Psalm 18:2**
OPTION 2: **Proverbs 6:10-11**
OPTION 3: **Matthew 5:17-18**

In addition to speech, James also warned against the danger of unaddressed conflict, another practical, universal struggle for Christians then and now. James had already reminded readers of the command to love their neighbors and had warned them against judging others. In chapter 4 he specifically highlighted conflicts between brothers and sisters in Christ. This issue received James's strongest words of warning in his letter, demonstrating the severity of the issue and the danger of this sin.

James highlighted pride and egocentricism as the reasons Christians argue, which he summed up as "friendship with the world" (v. 4) that puts us at war with God. According to James, the only way to overcome this type of behavior is through humble submission to God. James called on readers to submit and draw near to God through repentance and humility. When we do, God is ready and willing to give us the grace needed to correct our selfish attitudes that lead to conflicts.

Verses 13-17 provide a specific example of a person whose life decisions are self-centered. James used the example of a person who makes business decisions and plans without any regard for God's will. At issue here is the mindset behind the decision making. Are our decisions rooted first in obedience to God and our role as His servant, or are they rooted first in self-interests and personal pursuits? The latter, James pointed out, is a sinful way to live life, one we all should try to avoid.

HIGHLIGHT · EXPLAIN · APPLY · RESPOND

43//JAMES 5

MEMORY VERSES
OPTION 1: **Psalm 18:2**
OPTION 2: **Proverbs 6:10-11**
OPTION 3: **Matthew 5:17-18**

Before bringing his letter to a close, James addressed one more practical problem the early church faced. This problem again centered on money and wealth but this time on the person who pursues worldly wealth at the oppression or expense of others. James reminded readers that earthly treasures have no lasting value in the kingdom of God, so to pursue and hoard them, especially at the expense of loving God and others well, is a worthless endeavor. Often throughout Scripture we're reminded that money in and of itself isn't evil, but the way we approach money can be. As Jesus taught in the Sermon on the Mount, God's kingdom people seek heavenly treasures rather than earthly ones (see Matt. 6).

James 5:7-20 ends the letter by calling for believers to be patient through suffering as they await Jesus' return and to endure on the basis of God's nature. James mentioned the Old Testament prophets and Job as examples of people who lived with patient endurance. For each of those individuals, God was faithful to His promises, so we can trust that He will be faithful to His promise to send Jesus back as well. In the meantime we're to maintain our faith in God and utilize the power of prayer He has given us, as the prophet Elijah modeled for us.

HIGHLIGHT · EXPLAIN · APPLY · RESPOND

44//ACTS 15

MEMORY VERSES
OPTION 1: **Psalm 18:2**
OPTION 2: **Proverbs 6:10-11**
OPTION 3: **Matthew 5:17-18**

As the church continued to grow, so did the need for clarity between Jewish and Christian beliefs and practices. Paul and Barnabas met with the council in Jerusalem to clarify the role of circumcision and the Old Testament law in the life of new-covenant believers. Some Jewish Christians argued that Gentile believers should adhere to these practices and customs of the Jewish faith. However, Peter told the council that God had sent him to proclaim the gospel to Gentiles and had shown him that the traditional Jewish practices had been fulfilled in Jesus and were no longer necessary for faith. Peter declared that Jews were saved by grace and faith in Jesus through the Holy Spirit, just as Gentiles were.

Paul, Barnabas, and James (the brother of Jesus, the leader of the Jerusalem church, and the writer of the Book of James, not to be confused with the apostle James, whom Herod had executed in Acts 12) also affirmed God's intention for Gentiles to be included in His chosen family. James concluded that believers shouldn't demand that Gentiles become Jewish converts in order to become Christians. To do so would add an unnecessary burden to their salvation. In a response of affirmation, the council sent an official letter to the Gentile believers in Antioch, making them aware of the council's decision.

Christians today should exemplify this council's debate and resolution. The message of the gospel and the unity of the church remained at the forefront throughout the meeting, despite the differing opinions and passionate feelings involved.

HIGHLIGHT · EXPLAIN · APPLY · RESPOND

45//ACTS 16

MEMORY VERSES

OPTION 1: **Psalm 18:2**

OPTION 2: **Proverbs 6:10-11**

OPTION 3: **Matthew 5:17-18**

Following the Jerusalem council, Paul set out on his second missionary journey, and at this point Barnabas and Paul parted ways because of a disagreement over John Mark. In response to a vision, Paul traveled to Philippi with Silas, where Lydia and her household became believers.

While in Philippi, Paul and Silas encountered a slave girl possessed by a fortune-telling spirit. After days of being ridiculed by the spirit, Paul exorcised the demon in the name of Jesus. However, for the girl's owners, this exorcism meant a loss of income from the money they made from her demonic gift, and they had the missionaries thrown into prison. An earthquake opened the jail's doors, but the prisoners refused to escape. Paul and Silas shared Christ with the jailer, and he and his household became believers. Because of Paul's Roman citizenship the missionaries were freed and resumed their journey. Throughout this chapter we see a continued emphasis on belief in Jesus' saving grace, both as the basis for faith and as the source of strength in adversity.

HIGHLIGHT · EXPLAIN · APPLY · RESPOND

46//GALATIANS 1

MEMORY VERSES
OPTION 1: **Psalm 19:14**
OPTION 2: **Proverbs 9:9-10**
OPTION 3: **Matthew 5:19-20**

The apostle Paul, whose conversion and ministry are recorded in the Book of Acts, wrote thirteen books of the New Testament. Many of these books were written to churches he had ministered to or helped establish on his missionary journeys. He wrote the Letter to the Galatians to churches in the region of Galatia, which included the cities of Iconium, Lystra, and Derbe, where Paul had ministered on his first trip (see Acts 14). As with many of his New Testament letters, Paul wrote this letter with a specific purpose and audience in mind, in this case to correct the Galatians' faulty understanding of gospel faith and practice.

Like the men disputing with the apostles at the Jerusalem council (see Acts 15), many in Galatia were Judaizers, falsely believing Gentiles had to be converted to Judaism in order to be Christians. However, as Paul argued in this letter, that belief opposes the freedom from bondage to the law that's at the heart of Jesus' gospel. Paul began his letter to the Galatian Christians with a common greeting of "grace … and peace" (1:3) but quickly moved to a stern rebuke because of their abandonment of the basic gospel message that salvation is by faith in Jesus alone. Paul reminded his readers that the only true gospel is the one preached by Jesus, no matter how convincing others may sound.

HIGHLIGHT · EXPLAIN · APPLY · RESPOND

47//GALATIANS 2

MEMORY VERSES

OPTION 1: **Psalm 19:14**

OPTION 2: **Proverbs 9:9-10**

OPTION 3: **Matthew 5:19-20**

At the close of Galatians 1 and the beginning of chapter 2, Paul used his own story and experiences to build the case that Jewish religious customs no longer bound Christian practice. Among the details Paul highlighted were his time in ministry with Barnabas and Titus, God's specific calling for Paul to preach to the Gentiles, and the affirmation he received from key apostles. Each instance supported Paul's authority as a teacher of the gospel and therefore of the gospel message he preached: salvation by grace and faith alone.

Paul also referred to his confrontation with Peter (Cephas) when Peter confused some of the young Christians in Antioch by trying to please both the Gentiles and the Judaizers. Peter was a Jew acting like a Gentile by choosing not to follow Jewish customs, yet for a time he argued that Gentiles needed to be circumcised. This mixed message was confusing at the least, if not dangerous, for the Gentiles to whom Peter ministered. Paul, on the other hand, argued that the law, apart from Jesus, can't save anyone. That's why Jesus had to come in the first place. The law had been intended to be a set of rules that highlighted humanity's brokenness and need of a Savior. To say that grace and faith in Jesus alone aren't sufficient for salvation is to say that "Christ died for nothing" (v. 21).

HIGHLIGHT · EXPLAIN · APPLY · RESPOND

48//GALATIANS 3

Having established his credibility and provided the background for his argument, Paul spent the next two chapters of Galatians giving his defense of the gospel as being rooted in salvation by grace and faith in Jesus alone. Paul wanted his readers to clearly understand that the law and grace are both important to Christianity, but only one has the power to save: the grace extended to us through the death of Jesus. Paul emphasized that justification—being made right before God—comes by grace through faith in Christ, not by keeping the law.

Paul contrasted living under the law with living by faith. The law fulfilled its purpose by acting as a guardian for God's people, protecting them as a foreshadowing or representation of the blood of Christ that was to come. The law was also a guide that pointed to the coming Messiah. When Christ came, He fulfilled the law; therefore, faith in Him is the only requirement to experience His saving grace. In verses 26-29 Paul reminded readers that salvation in Jesus unites all people—regardless of race, social status, or gender—as sons and daughters of God and inheritors of His promises. Sons and daughters of God live out their faith in Him by obeying His law.

HIGHLIGHT · EXPLAIN · APPLY · RESPOND

49//GALATIANS 4

MEMORY VERSES
OPTION 1: **Psalm 19:14**
OPTION 2: **Proverbs 9:9-10**
OPTION 3: **Matthew 5:19-20**

Galatians 4 begins by continuing Paul's description of children of God. Paul's images of a child, symbolizing people under the law but apart from Christ, and a slave help readers understand that until Jesus came with the gift of salvation, it was impossible to receive the full benefits of being a child of God.

The most important of those benefits is the indwelling presence of the Holy Spirit, which comes at the moment of salvation. God has adopted believers as His children and has given them the Holy Spirit. We're no longer slaves but heirs of God, so we offend God when we obey the law in an attempt to earn His love and grace. Another benefit, which the Spirit enables, is the personal access that believers in Jesus gain to God the Father, something the law always prohibited. Rather than being separated from God by rules, we're reunited with God by grace.

Verses 8-20 contain Paul's personal plea for the Galatians not to turn back to the law as the basis of their relationship with God. These verses reflect how deeply Paul cared for these brothers and sisters and how grave their mistake was. One obvious change Paul noticed in them was a loss of joy they once had as a result of their freedom in Christ.

Paul closed this section of his letter with an illustration from the life of Abraham, which he hoped would motivate his readers to choose the truth of the gospel over the false teachings to which they were being exposed. It's clear from this section of Paul's letter that both salvation and justification come through faith in Jesus alone.

HIGHLIGHT • EXPLAIN • APPLY • RESPOND

50//GALATIANS 5

Throughout his letter to the Galatians, Paul emphasized that God's call to salvation in Christ is a call to freedom. The remainder of the letter helps Christians understand how choosing the freedom of the gospel influences the way we live. This freedom isn't license to sin but liberation to serve others.

Paul summarized the impact of the gospel when he wrote, "What matters is faith working through love" (v. 6). Loving others fulfills the law. Infighting among Christians, however, is destructive, as is any item on the list of "the works of the flesh" mentioned in verses 19-21. The freedom we receive in Christ can make it tempting to abuse the grace of Jesus, but the heart truly changed by Jesus will reject such temptations.

In contrast to sinful acts, the Holy Spirit's activity in Christians produces a cluster of virtues—the fruit of the Spirit—which provides evidence that a person belongs to Christ. These virtues include "love, joy, peace, patience, kindness, goodness, faithfulness, gentleness, and self-control" (vv. 22-23). Each virtue enriches our relationships with God and others, and to live it out the way Jesus modeled requires dependence on the Spirit at work in us. The point Paul repeatedly made in Galatians was that true spiritual transformation comes only through the gospel.

HIGHLIGHT · EXPLAIN · APPLY · RESPOND

51//GALATIANS 6

MEMORY VERSES

OPTION 1: **Psalm 23:1-2**
OPTION 2: **Proverbs 10:9**
OPTION 3: **Matthew 5:21-22**

Paul ended Galatians 5 with a reminder that believers in Jesus live by the Holy Spirit. The fruit of the Spirit is a present reality in every Christian's life. What follows in chapter 6 is one practical example of what the outworking of the Spirit looks like in a person's life. Christians are to hold one another spiritually accountable in the face of sin. They're expected to walk through the struggles and burdens of sin with one another, supporting and encouraging one another to withstand temptation and endure in the fight against the enemy.

Furthermore, when we're tempted to think we've conquered sin and won the battle, the Spirit's continual work of conviction reminds us of our need for Jesus and the truth that He alone has won that battle for us. The humility that conviction brings enables us to sympathize with our brothers and sisters in Christ even more.

In verses 6-9 Paul specifically challenged the Galatian Christians to financially support their spiritual teachers as a way of bearing their burdens. This was a tangible way they could invest in the Spirit and eternity, and it's a challenge the church has continually risen to since. In verse 10 the call to "work for the good of all" extends from meeting the needs of teachers to positively influencing the lives of everyone we come in contact with. Paul closed his letter by reminding the Galatians that the crucifixion of Jesus alone has the power to change a person's life.

HIGHLIGHT · EXPLAIN · APPLY · RESPOND

52//ACTS 17

MEMORY VERSES

OPTION 1: **Psalm 23:1-2**
OPTION 2: **Proverbs 10:9**
OPTION 3: **Matthew 5:21-22**

Following their miraculous release from prison, Paul and Silas continued on their journey, traveling next to Thessalonica, Berea, and Athens. On arrival in Thessalonica, Paul shared the gospel in the synagogue, focusing on the cross and Jesus' resurrection. In Thessalonica both Jews and Gentiles were receptive to the gospel. Not surprisingly, however, jealous Jews gathered a group of dissenters ("wicked men," v. 5), who started a riot in response. Unable to find Paul and Silas, the mob turned on the people who had welcomed the missionaries into the city. This reaction forced Paul and Silas to move on to Berea, where many more people accepted their message of Christ. Again Jews from Thessalonica caused trouble, so Paul left for Athens.

The account of Paul in Athens gives readers insight into the way Paul changed his approach to sharing the gospel based on his environment and audience. The message never changed, but Paul understood that the way he told Jews in the synagogue about Jesus had to differ from the way he told Greeks in the marketplace, who lacked the Old Testament foundation the Jews had. Observing the people in the marketplace, Paul used their curiosity about spiritual matters to begin a conversation about the one true God. The gospel message we share with others can't change, but like Paul, we must be able to meet people with that message, no matter what their circumstances are in life.

HIGHLIGHT · EXPLAIN · APPLY · RESPOND

53//ACTS 18

MEMORY VERSES

OPTION 1: **Psalm 23:1-2**
OPTION 2: **Proverbs 10:9**
OPTION 3: **Matthew 5:21-22**

From Athens Paul traveled to Corinth, where he befriended Priscilla and Aquila, who made a living as tentmakers. When Jews in the synagogue rejected Paul, he took the message to the Gentiles, and for eighteen months he taught the word of God in a house. Antagonistic Jews accused Paul of breaking the law, but Gallio, the proconsul, dismissed the charges. As his ministry continued, Paul's steadfast commitment to the gospel evidenced that God's hand was on him.

Verse 23 marks the beginning of Paul's third missionary journey, the last one recorded in Acts. Again Paul set out from Antioch, where he had returned after his time in Corinth. Acts briefly breaks from Paul's travels to tell readers about a man named Apollos. Apollos was preaching about Jesus in Ephesus, where Priscilla and Aquila had stayed after Paul left. Apollos was well intentioned in his preaching, but his knowledge of Jesus' life and ministry was incomplete. He "knew only John's baptism" (v. 25), which means he understood John the Baptist's teaching about the coming Messiah but didn't yet have a full understanding of the person and work of Jesus Christ. When Priscilla and Aquila heard his message, they took the opportunity to tell him the rest of the story: not only was Jesus the Messiah, but He had also died on the cross, risen from the dead, and brought the gift of the Holy Spirit for all who believed in Him. With a complete understanding of the gospel, Apollos continued to preach and teach.

Apollos responded to correction with openness and humility. Sometimes we'll receive correction in our walk with the Lord. As long as that correction aligns with Scripture, we should humbly embrace it as Apollos did.

HIGHLIGHT · EXPLAIN · APPLY · RESPOND

54//1 THESSALONIANS 1

MEMORY VERSES

OPTION 1: **Psalm 23:1-2**
OPTION 2: **Proverbs 10:9**
OPTION 3: **Matthew 5:21-22**

During his time in Thessalonica, briefly mentioned in Acts 17, Paul formed a strong bond with the Christians there. The new believers had enthusiastically embraced the gospel and formed a church, but because of Paul's abrupt departure the believers were immature in the faith. For that reason, just a couple of years after helping form the church there, Paul wrote this letter to the young believers in Thessalonica.

After beginning with his standard greeting of "grace … and peace" (1 Thess. 1:1), Paul thanked God for the transformation he witnessed in their lives as a result of embracing the gospel. Paul also reminded the Thessalonians of key events in their lives as believers, beginning with their salvation, which, Paul emphasized, was a work of the Holy Spirit in their lives.

The Thessalonians' newfound faith was so strong that word of it had spread throughout the region and had become an example to others of turning from a life of sin and idolatry to a life of faith in Jesus. They were outstanding examples for other Christians, both near and far, specifically in their faith, love, and hope (see v. 3). Even in the face of "severe persecution" (v. 6), these people chose to believe the gospel message Paul preached. Like them, we should be people about whom it can be said that we "serve the living and true God and … wait for his Son" (vv. 9-10).

HIGHLIGHT · EXPLAIN · APPLY · RESPOND

55//1 THESSALONIANS 2

MEMORY VERSES

OPTION 1: **Psalm 23:1-2**
OPTION 2: **Proverbs 10:9**
OPTION 3: **Matthew 5:21-22**

In chapter 2 Paul reminded the believers in Thessalonica about the purpose of his ministry while he lived among them. Verses 1-12 focus on the time he and his missionary team spent with the Thessalonians and the degree to which they loved these new believers.

The apostle Paul is our foremost example of what Christians are to believe and how we're to behave as we seek to grow in Christlikeness. Throughout his life and ministry, Paul emphasized loving others and boldly sharing the gospel. As he demonstrated, we're to live in such a way that both our words and our actions draw people to the saving grace and transforming love of God. We do this, like Paul, by being as gentle as a mother and as encouraging as a father. The root of both of these relationships is love. This passage provides one of the clearest examples of discipleship in all Scripture as Paul models for us how to nurture new believers in Christ.

Verses 13-16 highlight the Thessalonians' response to the gospel. Paul's reminders of their shared history encouraged them to stand strong in their faith and not to abandon it or grow frustrated as they waited for Jesus' return. Verses 17-20 show us Paul's love for these believers and his intense desire to return to them.

HIGHLIGHT · EXPLAIN · APPLY · RESPOND

56//1 THESSALONIANS 3

MEMORY VERSES
OPTION 1: **Psalm 23:3-4**
OPTION 2: **Proverbs 10:27-28**
OPTION 3: **Matthew 5:23-24**

Paul devoted the first part of his letter to complimenting the Thessalonian Christians on their actions and to reminding them of his expectations for them. In chapter 3 he transitioned to the practical application of the gospel. Paul was concerned for the Thessalonians' present and future sanctification, a concern highlighted by his urgency to hear how they were doing when he couldn't be with them. For that reason he sent Timothy to check on the young church and report back to him about the strength of their faith and their commitment to the gospel.

Timothy's report to Paul about the church's faith and love was overwhelmingly positive, and it became a source of hope for Paul and his missionary companions, who were in the midst of intense persecution for their faith. To hear that the church was continuing to grow and mature meant God was continuing to bless the missionaries' efforts, so their suffering wasn't in vain.

The prayer in verses 11-13 provides a glimpse into Paul's heart for this church. Paul specifically asked God to "cause you to increase and overflow with love for one another and for everyone" (v. 12) and to "make your hearts blameless in holiness" (v. 13) before God. Love for and service to God and others remain the most important ways we live out our faith as believers in Christ today. We should lift up these same prayers to God for ourselves and our church on a daily basis. Only through the power of the Holy Spirit will we grow in love for God and others.

HIGHLIGHT · EXPLAIN · APPLY · RESPOND

57//1 THESSALONIANS 4

MEMORY VERSES

OPTION 1: **Psalm 23:3-4**
OPTION 2: **Proverbs 10:27-28**
OPTION 3: **Matthew 5:23-24**

Because persecution prevented Paul from returning to Thessalonica to further minister to the young church, he took some time to teach and encourage them in this letter. Paul was encouraged by their faith and love, and he began this section by urging them to continue in their devotion to the Lord. Everything they did was to be driven by the overarching goal of pleasing God in daily living.

Specifically, Paul urged the Thessalonians to work on their sanctification in two key areas: sexual purity (see vv. 3-8) and brotherly love (see vv. 9-12). Much like Christians today, the Thessalonians lived in a world where immorality was the norm and sexual purity was countercultural. Being set apart as God's children meant pursuing holiness in this area of life, no matter what the world said differently.

Brotherly love, or love for others, is another important way God's people live lives of holiness. Evidently, the Thessalonians thrived in this area, but Paul reminded them there's always room to grow in love for others. The twofold goal of each of these challenges was personal sanctification (growing in Christlikeness) and evangelism.

Paul's instructions at the close of chapter 4 and the beginning of chapter 5 also included teaching about Jesus' second coming. The Thessalonians had clung to Paul's promise of Jesus' return, but assuming He was coming back soon, they were growing impatient. Understandably in the face of persecution, they wanted to be reunited with Jesus sooner rather than later. Paul encouraged them to believe Jesus was coming back because He promised He would.

HIGHLIGHT · EXPLAIN · APPLY · RESPOND

58//1 THESSALONIANS 5

MEMORY VERSES

OPTION 1: **Psalm 23:3-4**
OPTION 2: **Proverbs 10:27-28**
OPTION 3: **Matthew 5:23-24**

First Thessalonians 5 begins where chapter 4 left off, with the promise of Jesus' second coming. We all have questions about Jesus' return, as the Thessalonians did, but it's important to remember that Jesus' return is to be a source of hope, comfort, and motivation for our present walk with Christ. While we wait for Jesus to return, we're to be united with other believers in the church who are striving for Christlikeness along with us. For believers, faith in God and love for one another are nothing new. These attitudes are to characterize the Christian life from the beginning. An ongoing challenge for twenty-first-century believers is to show that we're living in anticipation of Jesus' return through behavior distinguished by love, faith, and hope (see 1 Thess. 5:8).

Paul closed chapter 5 with a series of instructions that alternated between corporate challenges (church life) and personal ones. Among the instructions for church life, Paul encouraged the believers to respect their teachers and leaders, pursue peace in the body of Christ, practice accountability and patience, and serve people in need. The reminders for personal life included practicing joy and gratitude, as well as praying continually.

Paul's letter ends with another brief prayer for the Thessalonians' continued spiritual growth and a plea for prayer on the missionary team's behalf. Overall, the letter of 1 Thessalonians is one of Paul's more practical letters. It leaves readers with hope in the return of Jesus and a clear challenge to live for Him in the meantime.

HIGHLIGHT · EXPLAIN · APPLY · RESPOND

59//2 THESSALONIANS 1

MEMORY VERSES

OPTION 1: **Psalm 23:3-4**

OPTION 2: **Proverbs 10:27-28**

OPTION 3: **Matthew 5:23-24**

Shortly after Paul had written and sent his first letter to the group of new believers in Thessalonica, he received a report about specific issues confronting them, prompting him to send them a follow-up letter. Their questions concerned Jesus' second coming, an event Paul had briefly addressed in his first letter.

Before correcting the false teaching these believers were being exposed to, Paul affirmed their strong faith and continued spiritual growth, as he typically encouraged other churches where he ministered. Because of the strength of their faith, Paul knew the Thessalonians would be able to endure the persecution they faced. During His time on earth, Jesus often linked earthly suffering for God with heavenly reward, because enduring suffering shows the strength of a person's faith. Paul encouraged these suffering Christians to persevere, being confident in Jesus' return and their future with Him in eternity. He prayed that God would make them "worthy of his calling" (v. 11) and would continue to use them, even in their suffering, to draw more people to Himself.

Suffering is all but guaranteed for believers who live out their faith in our broken, sinful world, but Paul's words to this young church remind us that the God-honoring way to respond to suffering is with our eyes fixed on eternity. When we live in anticipation of Jesus' return, the temporary trials of this world are easier to endure, and our faith points people to Jesus.

HIGHLIGHT • EXPLAIN • APPLY • RESPOND

60//2 THESSALONIANS 2

MEMORY VERSES

OPTION 1: **Psalm 23:3-4**
OPTION 2: **Proverbs 10:27-28**
OPTION 3: **Matthew 5:23-24**

Second Thessalonians 2 contains Paul's direct argument against a false teaching that had made its way into the Thessalonian church. Paul had taught this church about Jesus' promise to return one day, but after Paul left, someone had led them to believe that God's great day of judgment had already happened; therefore, Jesus was coming back any day. As a result, some people quit working and became lazy as they waited for Jesus. Jesus never specified when He would return, so Paul didn't either. Instead, the clear command of Jesus was to live diligently for Him in the meantime, taking advantage of the time to tell people about Him and build His kingdom (see Matt. 25; Mark 13).

The teaching in the Thessalonian church stood in direct contrast to the teachings of Jesus and Paul. To help correct this false teaching, Paul identified three key events that hadn't yet happened but that would happen before the Day of the Lord: the apostasy, the man of lawlessness, and the removal of his restraints (see 2 Thess. 2:3-8). Interpreters differ on what these events specifically refer to, but Paul adamantly insisted that these events hadn't yet happened.

In verses 13-17 Paul offered encouragement to the Thessalonians on how they were to live as they waited for Jesus' return—not idly but firmly rooted in the truths of the gospel and actively engaged in the work of ministry to which Jesus had called them. While we continue to wait for Jesus' return, we must remember that God is sovereignly in control of the world's events, including the end times, and He continues to delay His coming in order to draw as many people as possible to Him. Our mission is to help in that effort while we wait.

HIGHLIGHT • EXPLAIN • APPLY • RESPOND

61//2 THESSALONIANS 3

MEMORY VERSES

OPTION 1: **Psalm 23:5-6**
OPTION 2: **Proverbs 11:24-25**
OPTION 3: **Matthew 5:25-26**

Each chapter of 2 Thessalonians emphasizes God's sovereignty in a variety of situations. In chapter 3 Paul asked for prayer for his ministry efforts, specifically for the rapid spread of the gospel. In light of his previous teachings, this was a good reminder to the church of the important work all believers are called to. Paul also asked them to pray for his deliverance from persecution, and he prayed the same for them. He pointed to God's justice, both now and in the future, which enables believers to feel safe despite troubling circumstances.

Paul encouraged the Thessalonians to hold one another accountable and to encourage one another in their pursuit of Jesus. Specifically, he called them to avoid people who believed false teachers and chose idleness rather than living in obedience to God. Nevertheless, members were also to point out their sin and lead them back to Christ. Paul pointed to his own time of ministry among the Thessalonians as the example they were to follow, an example of hard work and self-sufficiency.

Paul brought 2 Thessalonians to a close in the same way it began, with reminders of the peace and grace of God made available through Jesus. This letter reminds us that we can endure together because God has proved His faithfulness to us through the life, death, and resurrection of Jesus. Through Jesus we can lay hold of the promise God has given us of eternal life with Him.

HIGHLIGHT • EXPLAIN • APPLY • RESPOND

62//ACTS 19

After Paul's time in Thessalonica and Athens, he traveled to Corinth and then later to Ephesus. Acts 19:4-7 gives readers one of the most complete accounts of Paul's church-planting efforts. He recruited disciples of Apollos who, like Apollos, had a solid foundation in the teachings of John the Baptist but lacked some of the details about the gospel and the presence and work of the Holy Spirit. Paul taught these men what they lacked, baptized them into the faith, and then used them to form the foundation of the church in Ephesus.

This chapter also tells us that Paul encountered serious opposition in Ephesus from the silversmiths of the city. Seeing Paul as a threat to their business, which largely focused on making idols, they instigated a riot in which they portrayed Paul as the archenemy of their city and the temple of Artemis. Paul could have been killed if not for the intervention of others.

To remain true to the gospel, Paul witnessed of the only true God by revealing the foolishness of worshiping idols. Likewise, we should stand against the values of our communities whenever its values run contrary to the truth of the Scriptures. When we speak out, we may become a disrupting presence and may expect conflict and criticism. Only when we're willing to risk our pride and reputations will we be able to influence our world with the truth of the gospel.

HIGHLIGHT • EXPLAIN • APPLY • RESPOND

63//1 CORINTHIANS 1

MEMORY VERSES

OPTION 1: **Psalm 23:5-6**

OPTION 2: **Proverbs 11:24-25**

OPTION 3: **Matthew 5:25-26**

During Paul's time in Ephesus, he received a troubling report about the state of the church in Corinth, so he wrote a letter to the congregation that's included in our canon of Scripture. After a brief introduction that expressed Paul's gratitude for the believers in Corinth and for God's work in their lives, Paul jumped right to the point. One of the main issues facing this church was a lack of unity. Many teachers, some of whom presented different messages, visited the churches in the New Testament. As a result, various factions that favored one Christian leader over another threatened the unity of the church and undermined its effectiveness.

Paul's solution was the gospel. He reminded the Corinthians that the church is a community that should be centered on Jesus and His message. The power in the message of the cross is that God sent His one and only Son, Jesus, to save the world from sin and death. Those who preach and teach this gospel are preaching and teaching the message of Christ, not their own messages. Division, no matter the cause, is destructive to the body of Christ because it distracts people from the gospel, the singular truth that should draw people in and motivate them toward spiritual growth. Paul also reminded the Corinthian believers that God had chosen them to love and serve Him; therefore, they should boast in Him alone.

HIGHLIGHT · EXPLAIN · APPLY · RESPOND

64//1 CORINTHIANS 2

MEMORY VERSES
OPTION 1: **Psalm 23:5-6**
OPTION 2: **Proverbs 11:24-25**
OPTION 3: **Matthew 5:25-26**

The Corinthian church was fractured by loyalties to different teachers who had risen among the congregation. To restore the church's unity, Paul pointed them back to the message of Christ, which includes the gift of the Holy Spirit and the wisdom He brings. The Corinthians were elevating the ministries of their leaders over the ministry of God, so Paul's emphasis on the Spirit was an attempt to bring them back into unity around the source of all wisdom and the only One whose ministry changes lives.

When the gospel is preached, the Holy Spirit is the One whose words are brought forth. His wisdom reveals the truths of God. People without Christ don't have the Spirit to aid them in comprehending God's revealed truth; therefore, they don't receive what comes from God's Spirit. However, those indwelled by the Spirit of the Lord have the mind of Christ. Although no human being can know everything about God, our understanding of Him and His purposes always has room to expand. God will give us the needed spiritual insight to understand more about Him through the Holy Spirit's activity in our lives. And God will give us the words to share the gospel with others through the Holy Spirit's power.

HIGHLIGHT • EXPLAIN • APPLY • RESPOND

65//1 CORINTHIANS 3

MEMORY VERSES

OPTION 1: **Psalm 23:5-6**

OPTION 2: **Proverbs 11:24-25**

OPTION 3: **Matthew 5:25-26**

In chapter 3 Paul returned to the issue that prompted his letter: divisions in the Corinthian church. The lack of unity in the church proved to Paul that these Christians were still infants in their spiritual maturity. This is why he focused much of his letter on instructing and reminding them how to live and mature as followers of Christ in the church.

The Corinthians' weakness highlighted the need for spiritual leaders in the church. Paul used the example of his own ministry to give these believers a clear picture of what godly leadership looks like. Paul taught that church leaders serve God and, as a result, are accountable first and foremost to Him. He referred to himself and his fellow ministers as servants, and he used several word pictures to illustrate this concept. Paul compared himself to a worker who plants and waters the seed of the gospel but depends on God to make it grow. He also compared himself to a builder who's building on the foundation Jesus laid and whose work Jesus will test. Paul's teaching here emphasizes the important role of church leaders in pointing people to Jesus and His gospel. These verses also remind us of the enduring significance and relevance of God's church in the world and of the importance of treating it with the respect and honor it deserves.

HIGHLIGHT · EXPLAIN · APPLY · RESPOND

66//1 CORINTHIANS 4

MEMORY VERSES

OPTION 1: **Psalm 24:3-4**
OPTION 2: **Proverbs 12:2-3**
OPTION 3: **Matthew 5:27-28**

Because the Corinthians were divided by loyalties to different spiritual leaders in their church, Paul reminded them that Christian leaders are first and foremost servants of Christ. He insisted that being an effective Christian leader includes humbly enduring suffering for the faith, whether physically or through criticism.

Paul sought to present the Corinthians with a servant image of leadership, one that followed Jesus' example. Viewing spiritual leaders as servants of Christ removes the potential for division, because the gospel brings unity. Leadership is a call to serve humbly, not to strut proudly. Above all, spiritual leaders must prove faithful. Paul claimed that all leaders should be evaluated only by the standard of fidelity to Christ, not by eloquence and pretentious human wisdom.

As he did with the Thessalonians, Paul sent Timothy to check on this young church and to help them understand Paul's letter and put it into practice. Paul's teaching in 1 Corinthians 4 reminds us that all believers, not just leaders, are servants of Christ and should give our entire lives to serving Him. When we recognize our accountability to God and pursue His agenda rather than our own, the result will be unity in the church.

HIGHLIGHT · EXPLAIN · APPLY · RESPOND

67//1 CORINTHIANS 5

MEMORY VERSES
OPTION 1: **Psalm 24:3-4**
OPTION 2: **Proverbs 12:2-3**
OPTION 3: **Matthew 5:27-28**

Because of the lack of solid leadership in the Corinthian church, the church faced a number of issues that weren't being properly dealt with. The body of believers desperately needed spiritual growth and godly leadership. Paul focused on three specific issues in chapters 5–6: incest, lawsuits among believers, and prostitution.

Paul said he was stunned by an incident of immorality in the church involving a man's inappropriate sexual misconduct with his stepmother. Apparently, the church turned a blind eye toward this behavior, to the point that Paul even called them arrogant about the situation (see 5:2). The appropriate response, according to Paul, should have been one of deep grief. Paul severely rebuked both the man and the church. The church's role in the matter was not only to express displeasure with the man's behavior but also to actively seek to change his behavior. As a means of discipline, Paul encouraged the believers in Corinth to expel the man in question from its fellowship in the hopes that he would see the error of his ways, repent of his sins, and be restored to Christian community.

Paul used the illustration of yeast in bread to describe the danger of allowing immoral behavior to continue in the church. If left unaddressed, sin spreads throughout the entire Christian community, just as yeast spreads throughout an entire batch of dough. This image reminds readers of the severity of sin and the great lengths to which we should go in order to hold one another accountable.

HIGHLIGHT • EXPLAIN • APPLY • RESPOND

68//1 CORINTHIANS 6

MEMORY VERSES

OPTION 1: **Psalm 24:3-4**
OPTION 2: **Proverbs 12:2-3**
OPTION 3: **Matthew 5:27-28**

In 1 Corinthians 6:1-11 Paul further emphasized the church's responsibility to live morally by addressing the matter of lawsuits among believers. The Corinthian church members needed to embrace Christian ethics completely and to reject any immoral conduct in their fellowship. At issue was one believer suing another believer in a secular court. Paul argued that the matter should be dealt with internally in the church. Taking an issue to court showed that the goal of the dispute was rooted in malicious greed rather than a desire for righteous justice or the edification of the parties. Paul feared that involving secular courts in such arguments distracted people from the gospel message and portrayed the church as a divisive group of people instead of the unified body of Christ.

Verses 9-11 remind readers that in Christ everything about a person's identity changes, and we become people set apart from the rest of the world. Our relationships and behaviors should look distinctly different because of Jesus. Paul closed this chapter with a reminder that Christian freedom isn't a license to do anything we want but rather the ability to embrace Christian morality as God intended. With salvation a person's body becomes a temple of the Holy Spirit. On both personal and corporate levels, reflecting on Christ's work of forgiveness and reconciliation in our lives reminds us of our need to repent of sins and rely on His grace.

HIGHLIGHT • EXPLAIN • APPLY • RESPOND

69//1 CORINTHIANS 7

MEMORY VERSES

OPTION 1: **Psalm 24:3-4**
OPTION 2: **Proverbs 12:2-3**
OPTION 3: **Matthew 5:27-28**

Generally speaking, the first six chapters of 1 Corinthians are Paul's response to a report he had received with some alarming revelations about the conduct of some church members in Corinth. After dealing with these matters, Paul began to address questions the Corinthians had raised in a letter to him. The following chapters contain teachings on church life and Christian practice.

The Corinthians' first question concerned marriage and sexuality. Having addressed sexual immorality in chapters 5–6, Paul addressed in chapter 7 a related question about whether it was good for a Christian to be married. He first stated the importance of sex within marriage, as God ordained it, and the danger of temptation when spouses aren't united sexually. In verses 8-9 Paul spoke to unmarried people like him, reminding them of God's call to abstinence. Verses 10-16 highlight the importance of avoiding divorce when no justifiable reason exists.

The remainder of chapter 7 supports Paul's belief that every person should faithfully live for God, regardless of the relational status He has given him or her for each given season. Paul used the image of slavery to remind readers that they're first and foremost slaves of Christ. This fact means regardless of relational circumstances, we're to fully give ourselves to Jesus and the advancement of His gospel.

HIGHLIGHT · EXPLAIN · APPLY · RESPOND

70//1 CORINTHIANS 8

MEMORY VERSES

OPTION 1: **Psalm 24:3-4**
OPTION 2: **Proverbs 12:2-3**
OPTION 3: **Matthew 5:27-28**

In 1 Corinthians 7 Paul used the image of slavery to talk about a person's relationship with Christ. Paul often described himself as a slave of Christ because he understood that he was to give his whole life in service to Jesus and His mission to spread the gospel. However, one of the great paradoxes in the Christian faith is that only through slavery or submission to Christ do we find true freedom. This is a recurring theme in Paul's letters. Living for God is more important than everything else in life.

Chapters 8–10 give insight into what Christian freedom is and what it looks like in practice. Paul's instructions answer the second question raised by the Corinthians: whether they could eat food that came from animals previously sacrificed to idols. The Corinthians wanted to know whether they would practice idolatry by eating that food. Paul first reminded the Corinthians that because of their love for God, they knew the world's idols were worthless. This meant in theory, eating the meat from sacrifices wouldn't harm them or constitute a sin.

The greater issue Paul wanted them to consider, however, was the way that action would look to new or immature Christians who had previously practiced idol worship. When exercising Christian freedom, we must take into account the faith of the people around us. If our actions could potentially cause other believers to question their faith or revert to habitual sins, exercising our freedom isn't worth the cost. Christians show maturity when they avoid behavior that isn't inherently sinful but might hinder another believer's spiritual growth.

HIGHLIGHT · EXPLAIN · APPLY · RESPOND

71//1 CORINTHIANS 9

MEMORY VERSES

OPTION 1: **Psalm 25:4-5**

OPTION 2: **Proverbs 13:2-3**

OPTION 3: **Matthew 5:29-30**

The city of Corinth was known for its immorality and perversion, which created a challenging atmosphere for new Christians to live out their faith and its counter-cultural practices. To compound the problems, many of the Corinthian Christians were impressed with their own knowledge and spirituality. This pride led to insensitivity in their relationships with other Christians and inappropriate conduct.

In chapter 9 Paul used himself as an example of the principle he taught in chapter 8: mature believers should avoid behavior that can cause less mature believers to sin. Throughout this passage Paul talked about his rights as an apostle, such as the right to eat certain foods or accept financial support. However, Paul didn't take advantage of rights like these for fear they would draw people away from Christ. He didn't want any of his actions to hinder his sharing the gospel. Instead, everything he did was intentionally designed to point people to Christ and receive the heavenly reward that awaited him.

Paul regularly emphasized his goal of reaching people for Christ and leading them to more focused discipleship. For him, that mission outweighed every other consideration. Paul's deep passion for sharing the gospel at all costs is evident in this passage.

HIGHLIGHT • EXPLAIN • APPLY • RESPOND

72//1 CORINTHIANS 10

MEMORY VERSES

OPTION 1: **Psalm 25:4-5**
OPTION 2: **Proverbs 13:2-3**
OPTION 3: **Matthew 5:29-30**

To help his readers better understand Christian freedom, Paul returned in 1 Corinthians 10 to the issue of food that had been offered to idols. As Christians, his readers had an obligation to resist all forms of temptation. Paul urged mature Christians to embrace the responsibility of seeking what was good for other believers over exercising their freedom in Christ to engage in certain activities. Paul used the example of the Israelites in the wilderness to warn the Corinthian Christians that their faith may not be as strong as they thought it was and that they may not be able to withstand temptations to sin, such as going to the idol temples.

Paul recounted several occasions when groups of Israelites faced God's judgment because they gave in to sin by practicing idolatry, committing sexual immorality, testing the Lord, and grumbling against Him. Each of those sins led to grave consequences that should warn the Corinthians and us not to abuse Christian freedom. Paul reminded his readers that although temptation is an unavoidable aspect of the Christian life in this broken world, God will be faithful to help His children withstand temptation if they look to Him.

With freedom in Christ comes great responsibility. As new creations in Christ, we need to choose actions that further God's kingdom and mission. When we abandon our will and control, we allow someone else to rule and lead our lives. Following Christ gives us a desire to change our ways and a desire for the gospel to be known. As Paul wrote, the driving force behind everything a Christian does should be living "for the glory of God" (v. 31).

H I G H L I G H T · E X P L A I N · A P P L Y · R E S P O N D

73//1 CORINTHIANS 11

In this chapter Paul turned to the matter of proper conduct in worship. Specific questions concerned head coverings, fellowship meals, and the Lord's Supper. Paul began with the participation of Christian women in worship. The issue of head coverings pointed to the disunity between Jewish and Greek customs, both of which were coming together in the church. These instructions were Paul's attempt to unify the church so that such matters didn't distract from worship or cause further conflict. He reminded the Corinthians that every Christian is primarily subject to the authority of Christ, the Head of the church.

Paul also provided instructions on the Lord's Supper, highlighting the irreverent approach some Corinthians took toward that practice. The result was sin against one another by neglecting the poor among them and, more gravely, sin against God for the "unworthy manner" (v. 27) in which they were taking the supper. The Lord's Supper wasn't to be a time to indulge or feast but a time to reflect on and rejoice together over Jesus' sacrifice for sin. The key problem at the root of the worship-related issues addressed in this chapter was selfish behavior that was inconsistent with the holy lives Christians are called to lead.

HIGHLIGHT · EXPLAIN · APPLY · RESPOND

74//1 CORINTHIANS 12

Among the many problems the Corinthian church faced, one thorny issue centered on the nature and purpose of spiritual gifts. Some church members viewed the type of gift a believer possessed as a measuring stick for that believer's level of spirituality. They considered some gifts to be more important than others.

In response to this misconception, Paul set out a basic rule for considering all spiritual gifts: all Christians share the common confession of faith that Jesus is Lord. On this foundation Paul affirmed the value of all spiritual gifts and declared that each gift comes from one and the same source—the Holy Spirit. God gives every believer his or her gifts and determines the way they're to be used for His purposes.

Starting in verse 12, Paul used the analogy of a body to highlight the importance of every spiritual gift. When you think about the physical body, you think about the importance of every part, no matter how small. The eye, the ear, the hand—each part has a unique, important function that no other part can perform. Furthermore, if you remove any one of those parts, the body functions at a weakened level. The same is true in the church. Whether someone has the gift of teaching, hospitality, service, and so on, each gift, like each Christian, is vitally important to the healthy functioning of the church.

HIGHLIGHT · EXPLAIN · APPLY · RESPOND

75//1 CORINTHIANS 13

MEMORY VERSES
OPTION 1: **Psalm 25:4-5**
OPTION 2: **Proverbs 13:2-3**
OPTION 3: **Matthew 5:29-30**

In the previous chapter Paul argued that every spiritual gift is necessary for the health of the church. In chapter 13 he revealed the "even better way" (12:31) spiritual gifts should be put into practice.

All gifts, no matter what purpose they serve in the church, must be governed by Christlike love. Without love as their motive, spiritual gifts are empty shells. In his letter to the Galatians, Paul listed love as the first fruit of the Spirit (5:22). The love Paul had in mind, therefore, isn't something believers must produce on their own but a gift God gives to them through His indwelling Holy Spirit.

First Corinthians 13:4-7 lists the qualities or characteristics of this Spirit-given love with both positive (what it is) and negative (what it isn't) examples. Love is patient, kind, joyful, bearing, believing, hoping, and enduring in all things. Love isn't envious, boastful, arrogant, rude, self-seeking, irritable, or record keeping. Church members are to demonstrate that we're the body of Christ on earth by loving one another in this manner.

In verses 8-13 Paul went on to highlight the permanent nature of the Holy Spirit's love. All spiritual gifts will eventually fade because the day will come when Jesus returns and those gifts are no longer needed to further His kingdom on earth. When that day comes, love alone will remain. For this reason love is the most important attribute Christians can possess and express.

HIGHLIGHT · EXPLAIN · APPLY · RESPOND

76//1 CORINTHIANS 14

MEMORY VERSES

OPTION 1: **Psalm 26:2-3**
OPTION 2: **Proverbs 13:13-14**
OPTION 3: **Matthew 5:31-32**

First Corinthians 14 brings Paul's instructions on corporate worship to a close by warning against the abuse of certain spiritual gifts, specifically prophecy and speaking in tongues. Although commentators debate whether these gifts remain today, that issue isn't a primary concern for understanding this passage.

The gift of tongues was a spiritual gift the Corinthians considered to be better than others, a false belief that Paul had already corrected. Here Paul argued that more important than exercising spiritual gifts in corporate worship was the clear communication of the gospel. This is why Paul called attention to the gift of prophecy, which communicated about God and the gospel in a way everyone could understand, with or without an interpreter. While spiritual gifts are given first and foremost to serve the church, it's always important to keep in mind ways those gifts can be used to encourage unbelievers and point them to Jesus. Every gift can fulfill this purpose when practiced the way it's meant to be practiced.

Verses 26-40 reveal that among the issues in the Corinthian church was the overall disorderly conduct of their corporate worship services. The practice of speaking in tongues without interpretation was just one example of the way their services had become disruptive. When the church gathers for worship, the purpose should always be to exalt God and strengthen all who are present. Orderly worship creates an environment in which these goals are most likely to be fulfilled.

HIGHLIGHT • EXPLAIN • APPLY • RESPOND

77//1 CORINTHIANS 15

MEMORY VERSES

OPTION 1: **Psalm 26:2-3**

OPTION 2: **Proverbs 13:13-14**

OPTION 3: **Matthew 5:31-32**

A chief purpose of 1 Corinthians was to answer questions and challenges from the Corinthian church, none of which were more pivotal than their questions about the resurrection. Some church members were questioning the resurrection, not because they doubted Jesus' resurrection but because they failed to understand how Jesus' resurrection guaranteed that God would raise all believers.

Paul asserted that the resurrection of Jesus Christ was a historical reality. The resurrected Jesus appeared in flesh and blood to many witnesses. This fact is important because the resurrection is the centerpiece of Christian doctrine and human history. Without it our beliefs have no merit. Getting the resurrection right means getting Christianity right.

Additionally, Jesus' resurrection and the believer's resurrection are connected because of our union with Christ, a major theme throughout Paul's correspondence with the Corinthians. First Corinthians 15 describes the grand sweep of human history, from the fall of Adam to the consummation of God's kingdom. Every Christ follower's story ends with bodily resurrection and eternal communion with Christ, and our glorious future reminds us that we're not to live only for the present day. Because our actions have eternal consequences, each day's choices are important. The future hope of being with Christ and being made new shapes every aspect of our Christian life. We live for His purposes in the present because everything we do for Christ matters eternally.

HIGHLIGHT · EXPLAIN · APPLY · RESPOND

78//1 CORINTHIANS 16

Paul had ended 1 Corinthians 15 with the reminder that while the Corinthians waited for Jesus to return, they should be "always excelling in the Lord's work" (v. 58). Chapter 16 begins with a tangible, specific way they could do that: through the financial support of the Christians in Jerusalem who were facing a famine. Paul encouraged the Corinthians to set aside money from their earnings to give as a gift to their suffering brothers and sisters. Paul would encourage this act of giving again in his second letter to this church, and in Acts 24:17 we see that Paul was eventually able to deliver the financial gift to the Jerusalem church. Practicing generosity is a clear way the church continues to excel in the Lord's work and to ensure that our labor isn't in vain.

This letter closes, as many of Paul's letters do, with a series of personal requests. Paul intended to return to Corinth and spend time with the believers there. He asked that in the meantime they accept Timothy on Paul's behalf and welcome him into their community.

Along with the final greetings, Paul left the Corinthians with a clear set of marching orders to carry out until his return. This instruction, summarizing everything Paul wrote in the letter, is a worthy goal for disciples of Christ today: "Be alert, stand firm in the faith, be courageous, be strong. Do everything in love" (1 Cor. 16:13-14).

HIGHLIGHT · EXPLAIN · APPLY · RESPOND

79//2 CORINTHIANS 1

MEMORY VERSES

OPTION 1: **Psalm 26:2-3**

OPTION 2: **Proverbs 13:13-14**

OPTION 3: **Matthew 5:31-32**

Paul wrote a handful of letters to the church in Corinth, but only two made their way into Scripture. The purposes of 2 Corinthians were to express Paul's joy in the good report he had received about the church, to strengthen his ties with individual church members, to confront outsiders who were trying to undermine Paul's ministry in the church, and to encourage the Corinthian believers to participate in a relief offering for the church in Jerusalem.

In chapter 1 we witness the vital connection between Paul's commitment to Christ and his commitment to Christ's church. Paul reminded the Corinthians that God is a God of comfort. The apostle described the suffering he had experienced and sought to comfort them in their suffering for the gospel as well. Although God has warned that serving God brings suffering, He also equips His servants to comfort one another through suffering with the promises that they don't suffer in vain and that eternal peace awaits.

One truth about God we can't miss in this letter is that we serve a God who keeps His promises, as shown throughout the entirety of Scripture. Paul described God's promises as being yes in Christ. We know God will keep His promises to us because He has proved Himself trustworthy through the life, death, and resurrection of Jesus Christ, who's the same yesterday, today, and for eternity (see Heb. 13:8). Because God keeps His promises, we can confidently wait for Him to fulfill them all. With this confidence in God's promises, we can follow in Paul's footsteps of unrelenting commitment to the gospel.

HIGHLIGHT · EXPLAIN · APPLY · RESPOND

80//2 CORINTHIANS 2

MEMORY VERSES
OPTION 1: **Psalm 26:2-3**
OPTION 2: **Proverbs 13:13-14**
OPTION 3: **Matthew 5:31-32**

The end of 2 Corinthians 1 and the beginning of chapter 2 record Paul's explanation for not coming to visit the Corinthians as he had planned. Although not a lot of clarity is given, it's evident that the Corinthians had failed to follow some of the instructions Paul had given them, either in 1 Corinthians or in another letter that's now missing. Paul had visited the church in an effort to provide the church with spiritual guidance, but the trip was so painful that Paul said he wasn't going to make another one. Instead, he wrote 2 Corinthians to defend his ministry, which false teachers were calling into question, and to provide further spiritual guidance for the young church.

That guidance begins in verses 5-11 with a call for the church to extend forgiveness to someone among them who had sinned but later repented. Paul said it was time for the church to forgive him and put the incident behind them so that Satan wouldn't gain leverage over the congregation.

The remainder of chapter 2 begins Paul's defense of his ministry decisions that were being questioned. He described the reason for an unplanned trip to Macedonia, reminding his readers that God was the One who charted the course of His missionary journeys. Paul understood that God was at work spreading His gospel message, and sometimes that reality meant Paul's plans had to change.

HIGHLIGHT • EXPLAIN • APPLY • RESPOND

81//2 CORINTHIANS 3

MEMORY VERSES

OPTION 1: **Psalm 27:10**
OPTION 2: **Proverbs 14:2-3**
OPTION 3: **Matthew 5:33-35**

Second Corinthians 3 continues Paul's description of gospel ministry, which spoke both to his ministry to this congregation and their ministry to the world. While false teachers among the Corinthians wrote their own letters of recommendation to try to validate their authority as ministers, Paul reminded the Corinthians that *they* were his letter; their changed lives and commitment to the gospel validated Paul's ministry efforts.

Paul's method of discipleship mirrors the way Jesus designed gospel ministry to work and the way He modeled it for us. Discipleship is a process of replication. Disciples go out and make disciple makers, who make more disciple makers, and that process continues. When replication occurs, disciples' ministries are validated, and disciples can be confident in the work God is doing through them.

Paul took a few moments at this point to talk about the superiority of the gospel to the Old Testament law. He wanted the Corinthian believers to understand that the ministry he did, the same ministry to which they were called, was guided by the work of the Holy Spirit in their lives. As Moses reflected God's glory when he came down from the mountain, a believer's life is to reflect God's glory, made possible by the Spirit who lives in each of us. Paul wanted his readers to be confident in the work to which God called them and to remember that they didn't labor alone.

HIGHLIGHT · EXPLAIN · APPLY · RESPOND

82//2 CORINTHIANS 4

MEMORY VERSES

OPTION 1: **Psalm 27:10**
OPTION 2: **Proverbs 14:2-3**
OPTION 3: **Matthew 5:33-35**

Although things were going well in the Corinthian church, Paul had opponents there who were raising doubts about his message and motives. He responded to those opponents by reminding the Corinthians of his qualifications and his work among them. To prove his case, Paul highlighted all the suffering he had endured, contending that his suffering proved that ministry success rested in God's power, not in human accomplishments.

To help his readers understand, Paul used the image of jars of clay, in which people in his day stored their most valuable possessions. In the gospel of Jesus Christ, God has given His people the greatest treasure in the universe. But believing in this treasure doesn't make us impervious to pain. Instead, we hold this treasure in claylike lives. Just as people of the time had to shatter the clay jar to reveal the treasure, God at times must break His people for the gospel to shine forth. When a person is broken, Jesus shines through. God uses our experiences of brokenness to bring glory to Himself and to mold us into His image.

HIGHLIGHT • EXPLAIN • APPLY • RESPOND

83//2 CORINTHIANS 5

MEMORY VERSES

OPTION 1: **Psalm 27:10**
OPTION 2: **Proverbs 14:2-3**
OPTION 3: **Matthew 5:33-35**

Because of the hardships Christians endure in living for the gospel, as Paul described in chapter 4, it's important that we learn to set our eyes on eternity. Suffering because of Christ prepares us for eternity because it challenges us to faithfully serve God and to live each day for our future with Him.

Although eternity holds the promise of hope for Christians, it brings the promise of judgment and condemnation for those who don't know Jesus. For this reason Paul also emphasized the importance of the ministry of reconciliation, both with God and with others. Paul's motivation for seeking reconciliation with others was God's love. Christ's love compelled him to continue loving and reaching out to the Corinthians, even when they wronged him. He couldn't accept reconciliation from God and then refuse to pursue reconciliation with other believers.

As we recognize the true price Jesus paid for our sin, we should be more and more grateful for His willing sacrifice on our behalf. As we grow to understand our identity in Christ, we'll embrace the great task with which God has blessed us in Christ: to be His ambassadors of Christ's message of reconciliation.

HIGHLIGHT • EXPLAIN • APPLY • RESPOND

84//2 CORINTHIANS 6

At the close of 2 Corinthians 5, Paul urged unbelievers who might hear his letter read aloud to "be reconciled to God" (v. 20). He reminded listeners that Jesus died for that very goal: to reconcile unbelievers to God. Chapter 6 picks up with that point, urging people to immediately respond to God's offer of grace. The quotation in verse 2, from Isaiah 49, encourages people not to waste any time before responding to God's offer of salvation.

The next section of 2 Corinthians 6 supports Paul's testimony about the validity of his ministry, which he began in chapter 1 as a response to false teachers who were questioning his authority as an apostle of Christ. Paul reminded people that he worked hard not to do anything that would cause others to stumble into sin. What follows is a catalog of experiences he faced through which he was able to remain a faithfully committed servant of God. The list includes everything from general hardship, beatings, hunger, and dishonor to purity, kindness, and great rejoicing. No matter the situation, Paul served Jesus by guiding people to Him and helping them grow in their faith. He challenged the Corinthian believers to do the same, beginning with their love for and affirmation of Paul.

Paul followed this encouragement with a word of caution against becoming "partners with those who do not believe" (v. 14). Paul didn't mean that they shouldn't associate with unbelievers (he often encouraged just the opposite) but that a Christian's loyalty should always be first and foremost to Jesus. Secondary relations that hinder our primary relationship with Jesus are to be avoided.

H I G H L I G H T · E X P L A I N · A P P L Y · R E S P O N D

85//2 CORINTHIANS 7

MEMORY VERSES
OPTION 1: **Psalm 27:10**
OPTION 2: **Proverbs 14:2-3**
OPTION 3: **Matthew 5:33-35**

Second Corinthians 7 provides additional insight into Paul's interaction with the church in Corinth. Having received a report from Titus about the church, Paul rejoiced that their once-strained relationship was improving. His goal throughout his long-distance relationship with Corinth was to maintain love and intimacy.

This affirmation gave Paul the opportunity to talk about godly sorrow versus worldly sorrow. He knew the criticism included in his previous letter had caused the Corinthians sorrow, but he noted that it was necessary in order to move them to a point of repentance. Not until sin is exposed and grieved over can a person truly turn away from it and turn back to God, which is the meaning of repentance.

Paul described godly sorrow as a type of sorrow that leads to repentance and salvation. This understanding of sorrow makes it a necessary, albeit unpleasant, part of spiritual growth. In contrast, worldly sorrow refers to something like the grief that comes from being caught in sin, not grief over the sin itself. This type of sorrow doesn't generate a repentant heart and can lead to eternal death if never corrected (see v. 10). Though coming face-to-face with one's sins is never pleasant, God offers great hope and restoration to those who turn to Him in repentance. This is the example the Corinthians set for us, and Paul rejoiced when he heard about it.

HIGHLIGHT · EXPLAIN · APPLY · RESPOND

86//2 CORINTHIANS 8

Moving to more practical matters, Paul addressed the need for a relief offering for needy Christians in Jerusalem, a topic he had briefly mentioned in 1 Corinthians 16. The church began practicing sacrificial generosity from its very conception (see Acts 2:44-45); therefore, Paul reminded the church that generosity should be a fundamental part of their ministry to one another. He told the Corinthians about the generosity of the Macedonian churches, who, despite their own poverty, had raised money for the poor Christians in Jerusalem. Even though they were poor, they gave generously because the Christian community was in need. Paul further affirmed the faith, speech, spiritual wisdom, and love the Corinthians modeled, and he challenged them to excel the same way in practicing generosity.

Second Corinthians 8:9 reveals the motivation for all believers to willingly sacrifice of themselves for the sake of others in the community: Jesus' sacrifice for us. Jesus practiced and taught sacrificial giving. Gratitude for what Jesus has done for us motivates us to demonstrate responsible stewardship of our lives and our possessions. In verses 14-15 Paul reminded the Corinthians that because of their generosity to the Jerusalem Christians, other churches would be generous to them in their own time of need.

HIGHLIGHT · EXPLAIN · APPLY · RESPOND

87//2 CORINTHIANS 9

MEMORY VERSES

OPTION 1: **Psalm 30:5**

OPTION 2: **Proverbs 14:12**

OPTION 3: **Matthew 5:36-37**

Continuing the topic of giving from chapter 8, Paul wrote about his intent to return and collect the Corinthians' offering. He had spoken highly to the Macedonians about the Corinthians' generosity, but Paul's words in this letter suggest that their enthusiasm for giving may have waned since he first mentioned the offering. Therefore, he would bring a small contingent with him to motivate the Corinthians to collect the financial gift and have it ready to be delivered when he arrived.

Paul's words in chapter 9 focus on the attitude behind generosity rather than the act of giving itself. He challenged the Corinthians to give freely and cheerfully, not by compulsion, so that their gift would be a blessing, not only to the recipients but to the givers as well. As with all the other outworkings of a person's faith in God, generosity begins in the heart of the giver. A generous heart reflects God's love and generosity to the world, and it has the power to point people to Christ.

HIGHLIGHT · EXPLAIN · APPLY · RESPOND

88//2 CORINTHIANS 10

MEMORY VERSES

OPTION 1: **Psalm 30:5**
OPTION 2: **Proverbs 14:12**
OPTION 3: **Matthew 5:36-37**

After reminding the Corinthians that giving would be a witness for the gospel to others, Paul changed his topic and tone. He aimed to directly confront "certain people" (v. 2) in the church who were undermining him and his ministry coworkers. Readers can infer their specific criticism from Paul's defense. Critics questioned his authority as an apostle and accused him of lacking the boldness in person that he expressed in his letters (see vv. 1-2). They tried to convince the Corinthians that Paul wasn't as powerful as he claimed to be in Christ, and they criticized his speaking abilities (see vv. 7-10).

In response to these accusations, Paul argued that he belonged to God and that his motives for serving God were pure. In defending himself and his teaching, Paul reminded his readers then and now that we're in the midst of a very real spiritual battle, one that takes place largely in our minds (see vv. 3-5). In the battlefield of the mind, we must be on guard for and actively battle against wrong ways of thinking that can interfere with our personal growth in Christ and our witness to the world. By calling us to take our thoughts captive, Paul reminds us that we must actively align our thoughts with the mind of Christ.

HIGHLIGHT · EXPLAIN · APPLY · RESPOND

89//2 CORINTHIANS 11

MEMORY VERSES
OPTION 1: **Psalm 30:5**
OPTION 2: **Proverbs 14:12**
OPTION 3: **Matthew 5:36-37**

Paul spent much of 2 Corinthians proving his authority as an apostle of Jesus, a defense that mattered because he wanted to make sure the Corinthian believers trusted his teachings about the gospel. This defense continued in chapter 11. He began by referring to his "foolishness" (v. 1). Paul was the most famous missionary of their time, and his influence was well known throughout the region. To think he had to go to such great lengths to remind them of his authority and his calling from God undoubtedly felt foolish to him. But he offered a defense because he cared so much for the Corinthians, and he feared that false teachers were leading them astray by planting doubts about Paul in their minds and leading them into false teaching.

Paul reminded the Corinthians of his résumé, an impressive one by Jewish standards. He was a Hebrew, an Israelite, a descendant of Abraham, and a servant of Christ. But rather than focus on his knowledge, experience, and abilities, Paul cited his suffering as the clearest evidence of his integrity and devotion to Christ. The list of trials he endured to preach Christ is long, including everything from imprisonments to beatings, from shipwrecks to homelessness. Paul also endured the emotional struggles of the weight of his ministry, namely the burden of love and concern he felt for the young churches he had planted. All of this hardship increased Paul's personal feelings of weakness and his temptation to fall into sin. Through all of these difficulties, Paul learned the life-changing truth that God's power is demonstrated in the midst of human weakness.

HIGHLIGHT · EXPLAIN · APPLY · RESPOND

90//2 CORINTHIANS 12

MEMORY VERSES

OPTION 1: **Psalm 30:5**
OPTION 2: **Proverbs 14:12**
OPTION 3: **Matthew 5:36-37**

Chapter 12 continues Paul's defense of his apostolic ministry that he began in chapter 11. In addition to his weaknesses, Paul highlighted a special vision and several "extraordinary revelations" (12:7) as evidence that his ministry efforts were rooted in God-given authority. These personal visions and revelations from God could have made it easy for Paul to become prideful in his ministry, but that was never the case, thanks in large part to the "thorn in the flesh" (v. 7) God gave him.

Much debate has been given to the identity of Paul's thorn, but the specifics don't matter for his argument. What matters is that this thorn constantly reminded Paul of his weakness and humility, compared with God's power and majesty. The thorn helped Paul remain dependent on God, whether or not his ministry thrived. Paul was honest with the Corinthians in admitting that he "pleaded with the Lord" (v. 8) to remove this thorn. Rather than removing Paul's suffering, however, God gave him something better: sufficient grace for Paul to rise above it by depending on God's power. Like Paul, we have weaknesses that can open the door for God's power to flow through us, changing not only our lives but also the lives of the people with whom we come into contact.

The remainder of chapter 12, beginning in verse 11, records Paul's concern for the Corinthians. He strongly believed they shouldn't have required this exhaustive defense in order to trust him, but they did, and it both frustrated Paul and moved him to write to them and then visit them again. No one can question Paul's love for this church and his desire to see it grow in Christ.

HIGHLIGHT · EXPLAIN · APPLY · RESPOND

91//2 CORINTHIANS 13

Paul closed his second letter to the Corinthians with a series of warnings. He would come to visit them for the third time, and he wanted to see true repentance of sin. Paul had invested much instruction, encouragement, and accountability in them, and he wanted to see spiritual growth in this area. He challenged the Corinthians to test themselves, meaning he wanted them to take a serious look at the validity and strength of their faith. Were they Christians? If the answer was yes, were they living like it, or were they living in unrepentant sin? Everything Paul had written was to build up their faith (see v. 10), in hopes that they would be convicted of their sin, repent of it, and grow in their faith.

Although we can't know for sure what the outcome of Paul's visit was, we know the church faithfully and generously gave the collection of money to the Jerusalem Christians (see Rom. 15:26-27), and nothing in his other letters in Scripture points to the Corinthians' continued unfaithfulness.

Paul's letter is a great reminder for believers today of the love we're to have for our brothers and sisters in Christ, the seriousness with which we're to take Scripture and its teaching, and the importance of personal spiritual growth.

HIGHLIGHT · EXPLAIN · APPLY · RESPOND

92//MARK 1

MEMORY VERSES

OPTION 1: **Psalm 32:1**
OPTION 2: **Proverbs 14:26-27**
OPTION 3: **Matthew 5:38-39**

Each of the Gospel writers chose to begin his Gospel in a unique way. While Luke began with the birth stories of John the Baptist and Jesus, Mark began when Jesus' earthly ministry launched thirty years after His birth. Much of Mark's Gospel focuses on the actions of Jesus and ways people responded to Him.

Chapter 1 begins with the preparations made for Jesus' ministry. John the Baptist called for repentance from sin and proclaimed the One (Jesus) to follow him. Though Jesus had no sins for which He needed forgiveness, He presented Himself for baptism to identify with His people. Mark next introduced Jesus as a proclaimer of the message of good news with a call to repentance. Jesus formally invited four fishermen to follow Him.

Jesus further demonstrated His oneness with God by displaying authority over unclean spirits and healing many physical illnesses. Although many people sought Him because of His healing power, Jesus shied away from the crowds and devoted most of His time to training the twelve disciples. A final healing, however, showed Jesus' ministry to be marked by compassion for people in need. From the beginning of Mark's Gospel, we see that in Jesus' ministry, meeting people's spiritual and physical needs went hand in hand. This is the model He demonstrated for us.

HIGHLIGHT · EXPLAIN · APPLY · RESPOND

93//MARK 2

MEMORY VERSES
OPTION 1: **Psalm 32:1**
OPTION 2: **Proverbs 14:26-27**
OPTION 3: **Matthew 5:38-39**

The events in Mark 2 share the common theme of the religious leaders' opposition to Jesus. The healing of the paralyzed man is one of Jesus' most well-known miracles. When Jesus saw the faith of the man's friends, He was moved to extend spiritual healing to the man, the most important healing Jesus offers. Jesus' words "Your sins are forgiven" (v. 5) raised an issue with the teachers of the law who were present, because they knew God alone has the authority to forgive sins. Jesus, being God, knew their thoughts, so to validate His authority, He healed the man's paralysis as well.

The second account describes Jesus' encounter with the tax collector Levi (Matthew), who would become one of Jesus' disciples and would write the Gospel of Matthew. We see in this passage that Jesus' association with tax collectors and known sinners upset the religious leaders. Jesus took this opportunity to clearly articulate His mission: "It is not those who are well who need a doctor, but those who are sick. I didn't come to call the righteous, but sinners" (v. 17). Every person is born sick, born into sin. Jesus came to earth in order to heal humanity's brokenness and restore our relationship with God. The religious leaders couldn't see that they needed this healing just like the "sinners" (v. 16) with whom they refused to associate.

The two accounts that end this chapter record additional instances when the actions of Jesus and His disciples frustrated the Pharisees. Both encounters gave Jesus the opportunity to teach that the Pharisees were so focused on following their own rules that they failed to see that Jesus, the author of the law Himself, was in their midst. It's easy for us, like the Pharisees, to become so blinded by our efforts to follow God's rules or to think we follow them so well that we fail to recognize our daily need for Jesus' forgiveness and grace.

HIGHLIGHT · EXPLAIN · APPLY · RESPOND

94//MARK 3

MEMORY VERSES
OPTION 1: **Psalm 32:1**
OPTION 2: **Proverbs 14:26-27**
OPTION 3: **Matthew 5:38-39**

Mark 3 begins, as chapter 2 ended, with another account of Jesus' controversial action on the Sabbath. When He healed a man's shriveled hand, the Pharisees considered His act to be disobedience to the law. However, Jesus stated that caring for others is obedience to God's law.

As Jesus traveled throughout Galilee teaching and performing miracles, large crowds began to follow Him. Mark pointed out that the evil spirits Jesus exorcised as part of His healings knew He was the Son of God, but Jesus wanted them to remain quiet until He was ready for His identity to be revealed.

While Jesus silenced the demons, the religious leaders accused Him of being one Himself. They knew His power was greater than anything they had witnessed before, but they couldn't bring themselves to believe He had authority from God, because His identity and actions didn't fit with the Messiah they anticipated. In response Jesus reminded them that His power was greater than Satan's, because He had the power to cast out spirits and forgive sin, both of which eliminate Satan's control over a person's life. Jesus argued that Satan wouldn't cast out his own demons, so Jesus' power must be greater. The only One with greater power than Satan is God.

Jesus' statement about family that Mark included at the close of chapter 3 is an important word for readers then and now about the nature of a relationship with Jesus. Jesus considers anyone who follows Him a part of His family. This means no matter what your relationship with your earthly family is like or what a relationship with Jesus may cost you, you're a part of God's family forever.

HIGHLIGHT · EXPLAIN · APPLY · RESPOND

95//MARK 4

MEMORY VERSES
OPTION 1: **Psalm 32:1**
OPTION 2: **Proverbs 14:26-27**
OPTION 3: **Matthew 5:38-39**

Mark 4 records three parables and one miracle by Jesus. Each parable teaches key characteristics of the kingdom of God. The first one, also included in Luke's Gospel, is the parable of the four soils. Seeds were scattered on four different types of soil, only one of which was capable of yielding a healthy plant. Because this teaching was in the form of a parable, the disciples who heard it asked Jesus for an explanation. Before giving them one, He reminded them that because of their relationship with Him, they would be able to understand His parables, unlike people apart from Him. Jesus explained that the seed in the parable is the Word of God, taught by the sower. The different ways people hear and respond to the gospel indicate the types of soil in the parable. People who respond positively to God's Word are those who accept it and put its truths into action.

In the second parable the lamp represents the truths Jesus' disciples would be responsible for telling the world, a responsibility Jesus wanted them to take seriously. The parable of the growing seed continued the image He used in the first parable, this time teaching that God would make sure His kingdom grew and spread. Even though His kingdom came from humble beginnings, God would cause it to grow. It would continue to do so as the gospel spread throughout the world and across generations.

In verse 35 Mark shifted from a series of teachings to a series of miracles. Jesus' calming of the storm showed His power over creation, a power only God could possess. The same voice that spoke creation into being calmed it with just a word, leaving the disciples in a state of fear and awe as their understanding of Jesus continued to grow.

HIGHLIGHT · EXPLAIN · APPLY · RESPOND

96//MARK 5

MEMORY VERSES

OPTION 1: **Psalm 33:4-5**
OPTION 2: **Proverbs 14:34**
OPTION 3: **Matthew 5:40-42**

Mark 5 continues with three more miracles, each unique in demonstrating the type of work Jesus did and what the miracle revealed about Him. The first story recounts a time when Jesus exorcised a group of demons from a man powerless to resist them. Verses 1-5 paint a graphic picture of the effect Satan's demons had on this man, who lived in isolation and torment. When they saw Jesus, the demons immediately recognized Him as the Son of God and knew the power He had over them. Casting the demons out of the man, Jesus allowed them to enter a herd of pigs.

What follows is one of the most vivid New Testament descriptions of Jesus' saving work in a person's life. Verse 15 stands in direct contrast to verses 1-5. Rather than naked, the man was clothed. Rather than mentally insane from the demonic possession, he was now "in his right mind." Rather than being isolated from everyone, he was with Jesus. What an incredible picture of the saving grace of Jesus.

The next two miracles in Mark 5 also reveal Jesus' power to heal and restore, but they're unique in their focus. When Jesus healed the bleeding woman in response to her faith in His power, He brought physical restoration to her body. Not only did her healing bring freedom from disease, but it also brought her emotional and spiritual peace and restored her to her community. Jesus went on to raise Jairus's daughter from the dead, the ultimate display of His power as the Son of God—power to give the gift of life itself. Each miracle in Mark 5 is different, but the running thread is Jesus' compassion and love for all people.

HIGHLIGHT · EXPLAIN · APPLY · RESPOND

97//MARK 6

MEMORY VERSES

OPTION 1: **Psalm 33:4-5**
OPTION 2: **Proverbs 14:34**
OPTION 3: **Matthew 5:40-42**

One characteristic that sets the Gospel of Mark apart from the other three Gospels is its nonstop action. Nowhere is that seen more clearly than in Mark 6. Mark darted from event to event in Jesus' ministry, beginning with Jesus' reception in His hometown and ending with His miraculous walking on water.

Evidently, Jesus' growing fame didn't impress the people in His hometown, and they refused to believe He was the Messiah. Their rejection didn't surprise Jesus, but it meant His ministry in Nazareth was limited. Instead, He and His disciples focused their efforts elsewhere, and He sent them out in pairs to call people to repentance. To validate their ministry, He gave them the authority to cast out demons and heal the sick. This marked the beginning of the disciples' ministry, which was modeled on that of Jesus.

Mark briefly broke from the accounts of Jesus' work to describe how King Herod had John the Baptist killed. This incident served as a warning for Jesus' disciples about what they could expect when they joined Him on mission. Although all believers won't face death for their relationship with Jesus, opposition is guaranteed. Jesus never hid the fact that living for Him comes at great personal cost.

The two miracles that close chapter 6 show that one reason Jesus performed miracles was to help His disciples understand who He was and realize the power He had. This purpose was the driving force behind both His feeding of the five thousand and His walking on water. Only when His disciples truly understood Jesus to be the Son of God could they wholeheartedly commit to joining Him in His work of redemption.

HIGHLIGHT · EXPLAIN · APPLY · RESPOND

98//MARK 7

MEMORY VERSES
OPTION 1: **Psalm 33:4-5**
OPTION 2: **Proverbs 14:34**
OPTION 3: **Matthew 5:40-42**

As word about Jesus continued to spread, religious leaders came from Jerusalem to investigate him. Among the things they didn't like about Him was His seeming disregard for their religious rules and rituals. Jesus didn't follow all their rules, and He didn't instruct His disciples to do so either. He used their questions and criticism as opportunities to correct their hypocritical nature.

The Pharisees had misplaced motives for obeying God and His law. Their appearance on the outside mattered more to them than the state of their hearts. In other words, they cared more about looking religious than loving God. Furthermore, they made up their own religious rules and placed them at a level of greater importance than God's law. This practice is seen most clearly in the ways they used obedience to their laws as an excuse to avoid helping people.

Verses 24-37 describe Jesus' ministry among people with whom the religious leaders would never have associated, including Gentiles (Greeks) and the demon-possessed. Mark repeatedly emphasized Jesus' compassionate heart, here showing how different it was from the hearts of the religious leaders. At this point in Jesus' ministry, His popularity had reached new heights, as had the religious leaders' hatred for Him.

HIGHLIGHT · EXPLAIN · APPLY · RESPOND

99//MARK 8

MEMORY VERSES

OPTION 1: **Psalm 33:4-5**

OPTION 2: **Proverbs 14:34**

OPTION 3: **Matthew 5:40-42**

One important lesson in Mark's Gospel is Jesus' investment in His disciples. Jesus wanted to teach His disciples as much as He could while on earth so that they were equipped to continue His ministry after He left. Occasionally, this meant they needed to hear the same lesson more than once, as in the case of the feeding of the multitudes. Like the miracle in Mark 6, this feeding showed Jesus' power to provide. It also showed that the disciples were slow to learn. Even though they had witnessed many of Jesus' miracles, they still doubted His power, and they still had difficulty understanding His teaching (see 8:14-21).

The healing of the blind man in the miracle that followed provided an instructive visual image for the disciples. The man was completely blind, but through a series of actions, Jesus restored his sight to the point that he could clearly see. Similarly, the disciples started out blind to Jesus' identity as the Messiah, the Son of God. But gradually, as they followed Him and learned from Him, they began to see Him for who He truly was. Their level of understanding reached a pinnacle in verses 27-30. When Jesus asked them who they thought He was, Peter correctly answered, "You are the Messiah" (v. 29). Slowly but surely their eyes were being opened to who Jesus was and the hope He brought to the world.

HIGHLIGHT · EXPLAIN · APPLY · RESPOND

100//MARK 9

Mark 8 ends on a somber note, with Jesus rebuking Peter and describing the cost of following Him. Because of the great level of sacrifice required, it's important that we understand who Jesus is, and that was the point of His transfiguration in chapter 9. On a high mountain Jesus was transformed before Peter, James, and John. Elijah and Moses joined Him. Jesus used this event to further inform the disciples about His coming death and victorious resurrection.

As soon as they came down from the mountain, the disciples were reminded of the importance of faith in God as the foundation for ministry. A desperate father asked the disciples to cast a demon out of his deaf, mute son. They tried and failed. When Jesus discovered their inability to cast out the demon, He attributed it to a lack of faith on their part. In contrast, the father displayed faith by trusting Jesus to heal the boy. No matter what Jesus calls you to do and what sacrifice is required as His disciple, it's vitally important to put your faith and trust in Him as you carry out that call.

HIGHLIGHT · EXPLAIN · APPLY · RESPOND

101//MARK 10

MEMORY VERSES

OPTION 1: **Psalm 34:8**
OPTION 2: **Proverbs 15:1-2**
OPTION 3: **Matthew 5:43-44**

Many times during His earthly ministry, Jesus predicted His death and the suffering His disciples would endure. He wanted those who followed Him to have a clear picture of the cost. Connecting with the mission of Jesus requires sacrifice. Contrary to the way the disciples viewed it, Jesus defined effective discipleship as humble service to other people and downplayed success as an attainment of position and power (see vv. 42-45). Real effectiveness in ministry comes through serving, not through being served.

This mindset was countercultural in Jesus' day, and it remains countercultural in ours. Serving others requires an active attentiveness to people's needs and genuine compassion for people's souls. When we struggle to show this kind of humility and compassion to others, it's important to remember that this is how God loves us. Recognizing the love, compassion, and grace of God in our own lives enables us to love others from an overflow of His love for us.

HIGHLIGHT · EXPLAIN · APPLY · RESPOND

102//MARK 11

MEMORY VERSES

OPTION 1: **Psalm 34:8**
OPTION 2: **Proverbs 15:1-2**
OPTION 3: **Matthew 5:43-44**

Prior to this point in his Gospel, Mark had given an account of Jesus' ministry in Galilee and then in surrounding regions. Mark 11 marks the shift to Jesus' ministry in Jerusalem, which would culminate at the cross. Like all of the Gospel writers, Mark included the account of Jesus' entry into the city, which was the epicenter of Judaism in Jesus' day. This similarity with the other writers indicates how important and symbolic this event was for Jesus' time on earth. Most notably for Mark, the triumphal entry demonstrated Jesus' humble nature and divine mission. Riding on a donkey rather than a war horse highlighted that Jesus was a humble servant, while the acclamation of the people proclaimed His identity as the Messiah and King.

Once Jesus was in Jerusalem, his first act was cleansing the temple, which was bookended by the symbolic withering of the fig tree. What Jesus found when He went into the temple was heart-wrenching; the center of Jewish worship had been overrun by greed and materialism. By quoting Isaiah, Jesus referred to the temple as "My house" (Mark 11:17), again declaring His authority and unity with God. This event marked a deepening divide between Jesus and the religious leaders, who were now determined to kill Him.

Jesus used the symbolism of the withered fig tree to teach His disciples that the nation of Israel had become as spiritually fruitless as the tree Jesus cursed. The same lesson is important for today's followers of Jesus to understand as well. A person can look spiritually healthy on the outside, but the best indicators of spiritual health are a person's faith in God and love for others (see vv. 22-25). Faith that moves mountains is faith that believes Jesus is who He says He is and acts on that truth.

HIGHLIGHT · EXPLAIN · APPLY · RESPOND

103//MARK 12

MEMORY VERSES
OPTION 1: **Psalm 34:8**
OPTION 2: **Proverbs 15:1-2**
OPTION 3: **Matthew 5:43-44**

A lot happens in Mark 12, but the running theme throughout the chapter is Jesus' growing tensions with the religious leaders and their repeated questions about His authority, picking up where Mark concluded chapter 11. Chapter 12 begins and ends with accounts that illustrate God's generous love, in contrast with the self-gratifying nature of the religious leaders. The religious authorities knew they were the wicked tenants in the parable, and Jesus knew they would succeed in having Him killed. However, they didn't know they were acting in accordance with God's gracious plan to redeem His people and break down barriers that stood in the way of a relationship with Him.

Verses 13-34 document three specific conversations Jesus had with the religious leaders, each of which was an attempt to catch Him speaking out against God or the ruling authorities in a way that would give them grounds to arrest or even kill Him. They asked Jesus questions about paying taxes, the resurrection of the dead, and the greatest commandment. Jesus answered each question in a way that displayed His superior understanding of God's law and His divine authority to speak on these matters.

The chapter ends with a warning against the hypocritical ways of these leaders and a contrasting illustration of a person who was faithfully and humbly committed to God. The religious leaders did everything, even the most important aspects of religious life, for their own honor and glory. Jesus warned that their judgment was imminent. The poor widow, however, humbly and sacrificially gave to God above her means. When we truly understand the sacrifice Jesus, the Son of God, made on our behalf, we can't help but give all of ourselves to Him in gratitude and service.

HIGHLIGHT · EXPLAIN · APPLY · RESPOND

104//MARK 13

MEMORY VERSES

OPTION 1: **Psalm 34:8**
OPTION 2: **Proverbs 15:1-2**
OPTION 3: **Matthew 5:43-44**

This section of Mark's Gospel closely aligns with Luke's, which also follows the account of the generous widow with a teaching on the future and Jesus' imminent return. One clear point Jesus wanted to make is that all people who faithfully love and serve God like that widow can hope in Jesus' promised return. However, this promise doesn't hold true for people like the religious authorities who pursued Jesus.

Jesus foretold the destruction of the temple in Jerusalem and the wrath of God's judgment on those who refuse to believe in Him. When pressed on the timing of these events, Jesus responded with signs of the end times and instructions on the way His followers should live in the meantime. Jesus encouraged them to stand firm in His teachings and not to be led astray by false teachers. He told them not to be alarmed by wars and natural disasters but instead to anticipate them as necessary events before He returns. He also prepared them to stand firm, through the power of the Holy Spirit, in the face of intense persecution that He knew would follow His death and resurrection.

The hope in the midst of all this hardship is the promise of Mark 13:24-31: Jesus will return, and when He does, He will gather His children into His presence. We can't know when this day will come, but like the servants described in verses 34-37, we're to continually anticipate Jesus' return while we live for Him today.

HIGHLIGHT · EXPLAIN · APPLY · RESPOND

105//MARK 14

MEMORY VERSES

OPTION 1: **Psalm 34:8**

OPTION 2: **Proverbs 15:1-2**

OPTION 3: **Matthew 5:43-44**

Mark began his Gospel by referring to it as "the gospel of Jesus Christ, the Son of God" (1:1). From chapter 14 to the end of the book, we clearly see Jesus' purpose in leaving His place with the Father in heaven and coming to earth. Mark helps us understand that Jesus came as a humble servant whose singular focus was to pay the sacrifice for humanity's sin and restore their relationship with God. To do this, He had to face the suffering awaiting Him at Calvary.

As the cross drew closer, Jesus had a few teachable moments left with His disciples, giving Him opportunities to prepare them for what was about to unfold. The first came when a woman interrupted dinner to anoint Jesus with expensive perfume. The disciples were shocked by the waste of expensive oil, but Jesus praised her action as a sacrifice for God and as preparation for His coming burial. The following verses contrast this woman's generosity with Judas's selfishness and greed.

The second teaching opportunity came during the celebration of the Passover meal, when Jesus gave new meaning to this significant moment in Jewish history. Through His description of the bread and the cup as his body and blood, respectively, Jesus helped His disciples see that He was the ultimate Passover Lamb who would be sacrificed for their sins once and for all. Jesus' sacrifice wouldn't come without great personal agony, as His prayer in the garden of Gethsemane revealed. The humanity and vulnerability Jesus showed in the garden give even greater weight to the cross, further revealing the depths of Jesus' love for us.

HIGHLIGHT · EXPLAIN · APPLY · RESPOND

106//MARK 15

MEMORY VERSES
OPTION 1: **Psalm 37:4-5**
OPTION 2: **Proverbs 15:16-17**
OPTION 3: **Matthew 5:45-46**

Jesus' trial began in Mark 14 in front of the Sanhedrin and the Jewish religious authorities, including Caiaphas, the high priest. Caiaphas accused Jesus of blasphemy and in chapter 15 sent Him to the Roman authorities, who had the power to have Him crucified. Jesus stood trial before Pilate, the Roman governor. For Pilate, the greater issue than blasphemy against God was Jesus' claim to be the King of the Jews, an assertion that encroached on Pilate's authority and sense of power. At the urging of the crowd, Pilate released a different prisoner, the murderer Barabbas, and sentenced Jesus to be crucified. In a sense every one of us is Barabbas. We were sentenced to death because of our sin, but Jesus took our place and died the death we deserved, even though He had never sinned.

As Mark described the crucifixion, he payed special attention to individual people involved in or present for this event, including Simon, who carried Jesus' cross; the soldiers who cast lots for his clothes; people who walked by the cross and insulted Jesus; and Jesus' friends who were present for His death. Each face represented a person for whom Jesus made the ultimate sacrifice, whether or not they loved Him.

Mark also highlighted some of the most significant events that accompanied Jesus' crucifixion, including two miraculous ones: the darkness that overtook the land and the tearing of the temple veil from top to bottom, symbolizing the union between God and humanity made possible through Jesus' death. To confirm that Jesus actually died, Mark included a description of Jesus' burial. The Son of God had accomplished His mission by giving up His life as the payment for our sin.

HIGHLIGHT · EXPLAIN · APPLY · RESPOND

107//MARK 16

MEMORY VERSES

OPTION 1: **Psalm 37:4-5**

OPTION 2: **Proverbs 15:16-17**

OPTION 3: **Matthew 5:45-46**

All of Scripture points to the work and mission of Jesus, which seemed to have ended the day He hung on the cross at Calvary. At least that's how things appeared to His disciples, who watched the promised Messiah die. Little did they know the cross was only the first scene of Jesus' redemptive act. With His death on the cross, Jesus paid God's penalty for the sins of the world, sins that required a blood sacrifice to purify sinners. However, Jesus didn't remain in the grave. On the third day He rose from the dead and defeated death—the ultimate consequence of sin.

Mark's Gospel documents the moment when three of Jesus' faithful followers, all women, showed up at the tomb to anoint His body. There they encountered an angel, who told them the news of Jesus' resurrection. The angel also told them to take the news to the disciples and Peter, the same disciples who had deserted Jesus at the cross. God wanted this great news to be conveyed as an offer of restoration and forgiveness. Through the cross and resurrection of Jesus, God made a way for you—a sinful, broken son or daughter—to receive His forgiveness and grace and to be reunited with Him.

The Gospel of Mark ends with Jesus' appearances to the other disciples; His Great Commission to spread the gospel, the good news about Him, around the world; and His ascension to heaven. Throughout this book readers see a clear picture of Jesus, the Servant-King. He calls His followers to the same life of service and sacrifice, with the goal of drawing as many people as possible into a life-saving relationship with Him.

HIGHLIGHT · EXPLAIN · APPLY · RESPOND

108//ROMANS 1

During his third missionary journey Paul spent time in Greece, during which he wrote his letter to the Romans. Paul's plan was to visit Rome, so he wrote this letter to the Christians there in order to communicate his life calling and the message he longed to tell others. Paul was writing to proclaim the gospel, a message built on the foundation of the Old Testament and fulfilled in Jesus Christ. With this goal in mind, Paul's letter delays the customary greeting of his other letters and proceeds with a detailed description of Jesus (see Rom. 1:3-6) and a note about his desire to reach Rome and share the gospel there in person.

The Book of Acts shows how important it was for Paul to reach Rome, and he expressed that longing at the start of this letter. To establish the universal need for the gospel, Paul pointed to the undeniable presence of sin in our world and our lives. At its core, sin is idolatry, the worship of the creation instead of the Creator. God made Himself known to people through creation, but people quickly turned to His creation to fulfill their needs. That exchange negatively affects everything in our lives, from relationships to worship. As a result, God allowed people to live in their sin, and Paul described the destruction that followed. In the closing verses of Romans 1, Paul painted a terrifying but realistic picture of who we are apart from Christ—people given over to sin and the destruction it creates.

HIGHLIGHT · EXPLAIN · APPLY · RESPOND

109//ROMANS 2

Paul's description of sin continued in chapter 2, but he moved from what we might consider worldly sins to a word about God's judgment of people who judge the sins of others. Paul wanted to make one point clear: the depravity of sin affects every person who walks on the earth. Everyone is born a sinner; therefore, everyone deserves God's wrath and eternal judgment. Paul declared that God will judge those whose hearts are unrepentant. On the other hand, He will give eternal life to those who show by their actions that His law is written on their hearts.

Paul placed an emphasis on obedience, both of heart and of action. Simply listening to and knowing God's truths aren't enough; the person who obeys the law will receive God's favor because obedience is the fruit of a heart changed by God. However, obedience alone won't save us. Paul's main point was that until we realize we're sinners by nature, we won't recognize our desperate need for salvation and appreciate God's grace. Once we come to that life-altering realization, He will change our hearts, and we'll desire to walk in obedience.

The last half of this chapter continues Paul's warning but focuses exclusively on the Jews. Many Jews in Jesus' day believed their religious heritage was enough to make them right with God, but Paul argued that the same obedience was expected of them as it was of Gentile believers. A life of faith in Jesus is a life of obedience to His call to discipleship.

HIGHLIGHT · EXPLAIN · APPLY · RESPOND

110//ROMANS 3

MEMORY VERSES
OPTION 1: **Psalm 37:4-5**
OPTION 2: **Proverbs 15:16-17**
OPTION 3: **Matthew 5:45-46**

Paul spent a significant portion of Romans helping the Jews understand that they needed God's grace as much as Gentiles (non-Jews) did. The truth that all people stand condemned for sin meant that Jews and Gentiles were equally guilty before God. Verses 9-18 culminate Paul's teaching that everyone is unrighteous; everyone is sinful to very core of their being. Because no one can be justified by the works of the law, everyone needs Jesus.

With the words "But now" in verse 21, Paul's letter turned from the negative reality of sinful humanity to the positive picture of God's saving work. God knew everyone deserved His wrath, yet He set into motion a plan to rescue His people from the consequences of sin. God wanted to restore His people to the relationship He had with them in the garden, before sin broke the fellowship He had with His creation. With that desire in mind, God made a way for unrighteous people to become righteous. Paul noted that all of Scripture, from the Law to the Prophets, points to God's gracious act of redemption through Jesus Christ. God made salvation available by grace through faith in His Son, Jesus. When people believe in Jesus for salvation, they're justified—declared righteous before God.

Paul's warning against boasting reminds us that we can't boast in our own righteousness, because our righteousness falls short of God's glory. If we could achieve righteousness—right standing before God—on our own, we wouldn't need Jesus' sacrifice. For this reason a Christian's life displays God's mercy and grace.

HIGHLIGHT · EXPLAIN · APPLY · RESPOND

111//ROMANS 4

One goal of Paul's letter was for his readers to clearly understand God's saving work, which includes justification from sin. Paul had described justification in chapter 3: God making unrighteous, sinful people righteous by taking away their sin through Jesus. Because a large number of Paul's audience were Jewish, he wanted them to understand that they were saved through this same process of justification, not through their adherence to the law.

Paul reminded his Jewish readers that the covenant promises God made to Abraham and his descendants were assured by faith, not by the law. He pointed to Genesis 15:6 to prove his point: "Abram believed the LORD, and he credited it to him as righteousness." God's promises displayed grace to Abraham and to all who respond to God with faith like Abraham's, faith that trusts "the God who gives life to the dead and calls things into existence that do not exist" (Rom. 4:17). For Paul, Abraham's example proved that the gospel of Jesus Christ continued and fulfilled what had always been God's plan of salvation. People who come to God by placing their faith in Jesus are forgiven of sins and are made right with God.

HIGHLIGHT · EXPLAIN · APPLY · RESPOND

112//ROMANS 5

MEMORY VERSES
OPTION 1: **Psalm 37:23-24**
OPTION 2: **Proverbs 15:22-23**
OPTION 3: **Matthew 5:47-48**

Paul began Romans 5 by focusing on the benefits that come from justification, namely, peace, hope, and love from God. A believer can count on these benefits every day. The peace Paul had in mind is eternal peace with God that comes when He removes our condemnation for sin. In Christ we live in a state of peace that transcends our earthly circumstances, no matter how chaotic and disruptive they may feel.

Similarly, the hope Paul spoke of is hope in God's promises of eternity. Throughout Scripture God promises to give an eternal home to His children so that they can live in His presence forever. He also promises that Jesus will return to call people to Himself. When Christians place their hope in these promises, they can face the sufferings and sorrows of life in a broken world.

God doesn't save us by grace only to make us try to live for Him in our own power. He gives us His grace to help us stand today, tomorrow, and on that future day when we'll appear before His throne. Paul also emphasized that God redeemed us when we were at our worst, demonstrating how great His grace is.

Both peace and hope are the result of God's love being poured into us. Jesus' death on the cross is the ultimate demonstration of that love. Starting in verse 12, Paul taught that just as everyone is born into sin through Adam, salvation is available to everyone through Jesus.

HIGHLIGHT · EXPLAIN · APPLY · RESPOND

113//ROMANS 6

MEMORY VERSES
OPTION 1: **Psalm 37:23-24**
OPTION 2: **Proverbs 15:22-23**
OPTION 3: **Matthew 5:47-48**

In Romans 6 Paul discussed reasons Christians can no longer think and live in the old ways of sin. Believers have died to the old life by being baptized into Jesus' death and raised into new life through His resurrection. We serve a new Master who liberated us from bondage to sin and empowers us to grow in faith, thus producing the spiritual fruit that shows we have eternal life. Through our obedience we display Christ and His character to the world. Only by allowing Christ to live in us can we truly have an impact for the kingdom of God.

Paul went on to contrast living as a slave to sin with living as a slave to Christ. He used the slavery analogy to help his readers understand what it meant to surrender their lives to following Christ. Paul argued that everyone is a slave to something, either to sin or to God. Christians aren't freed from sin to live as they please but rather to live in daily service to God and His will. This slavery to righteousness brings with it the benefits of holiness and eternal life, neither of which is possible apart from Jesus.

Paul often talked about freedom in his New Testament letters, so the slavery analogy may sound strange to some readers, but the good news Paul wanted to communicate is that because of Jesus' work, people no longer have to live as slaves to sin. Giving our lives to God is the most liberating choice we can make.

HIGHLIGHT · EXPLAIN · APPLY · RESPOND

114//ROMANS 7

MEMORY VERSES
OPTION 1: **Psalm 37:23-24**
OPTION 2: **Proverbs 15:22-23**
OPTION 3: **Matthew 5:47-48**

Paul opened chapter 7 by using marriage to illustrate the meaning of being dead to sin and free from the law's condemning power. When a person's spouse dies, he or she is released from the covenant of marriage. When a person dies with Christ, as Paul had described in chapter 6, he or she is released from the covenant of the law. This freedom doesn't mean that a person doesn't obey the law but rather that Jesus' authority has superseded the law's authority. A Christian now has a new heart and the indwelling presence of the Holy Spirit, meaning failure to obey the law to the fullest no longer brings condemnation for sin. Although we're set free from the power of the law and can freely serve God by His Spirit, the law still has good purposes in making us aware of our sinfulness and in guiding us to Christ.

Paul concluded chapter 7 by focusing on Jesus' power and presence in his life, in contrast with his struggle with sin. Verses 14-25 give readers an inside look at Paul's struggle with sin, one that should sound familiar to all of us. Paul hated sin, but no amount of hate was enough for him to completely avoid it. As long as we live in this broken world, we'll continue to struggle with sin. The good news for Christians is that Jesus gives us the power to withstand temptation and to choose not to sin, a power we lacked apart from Him. While this war wages within us, we can rest in the comfort that Jesus has won the battle for us and that someday our struggle with sin will be gone forever.

HIGHLIGHT • EXPLAIN • APPLY • RESPOND

115//ROMANS 8

MEMORY VERSES
OPTION 1: **Psalm 37:23-24**
OPTION 2: **Proverbs 15:22-23**
OPTION 3: **Matthew 5:47-48**

Romans 8 is one of the most hopeful, encouraging chapters in Paul's letter, if not in all of the New Testament. In his battle against sin, Paul found help. Through Christ the Holy Spirit's power resides in us, enabling us to live in ways that honor God. Paul painted a detailed picture of a life given over to the sinful nature, in contrast with a life controlled by the Spirit. The former is identified by death, hostility to God, and enslavement to fear, while the latter is identified by life, peace, and sonship.

Specifically, Paul drew attention to the Spirit's help in resisting sin and making decisions. Furthermore, the Spirit confirms that we're God's children, adopted into His family, and we can address Him as Father. Therefore, nothing we face on earth can be compared to the glory that awaits us. Paul stated that creation groans in anticipation of God's completed redemption, the day when sin is eradicated forever and all creation is restored to its former glory. In the meantime we rely on the power of the Spirit to help us in our weakness and to intercede for us in prayer.

Paul emphasized that our hope in Christ is certain. Though we often feel discouraged, we have a limitless source of hope. Our challenge is to patiently persevere in the face of any difficulty in the present.

Paul closed Romans 8 by affirming that God is at work in all things. Whenever we feel crushed under the brokenness of this world, we must remember that even then God is working out His good plans and that nothing we face surprises Him or interferes with His work. God and His love will win in the end.

HIGHLIGHT · EXPLAIN · APPLY · RESPOND

116//ROMANS 9

MEMORY VERSES

OPTION 1: **Psalm 40:1-2**
OPTION 2: **Proverbs 16:9**
OPTION 3: **Matthew 6:1-2**

In Romans 1–8 Paul had developed the doctrine of salvation by faith alone, concluding that God's purposes for His people can never fail. However, it seemed that His purposes for the Israelites had indeed failed because most of them had rejected Jesus as their Messiah.

Paul addressed this issue in chapter 9, emphasizing that God is sovereign in all matters, including salvation. Next, to explain that God wasn't being unjust toward those He didn't choose, Paul focused on God's mercy, which is utterly undeserved and can never be earned. Paul used Pharaoh as an illustration of someone who didn't receive God's mercy. Then Paul emphasized God's patience to Jews and Gentiles alike. The result is that members of both ethnic groups have access to His mercy and can be saved. For the most part, the Israelites had tried to obtain salvation by obeying God's law, but no humans can ever save themselves, regardless of their zeal. No one can do enough good works to earn or receive salvation. Faith—simply believing—and the grace that comes by it are the only ways to a right relationship with God.

Paul ended chapter 9 by noting where the nation of Israel stood in its relationship with God at the time of his writing. Paul referred to Jesus as the Jews' "stumbling stone" (v. 32) because they refused to believe in Jesus as their promised Messiah and instead had Him killed, causing them to remain in a state of unbelief and unrighteousness. Israel's unbelief and its consequences are the focus of chapter 10.

HIGHLIGHT · EXPLAIN · APPLY · RESPOND

117//ROMANS 10

MEMORY VERSES

OPTION 1: **Psalm 40:1-2**
OPTION 2: **Proverbs 16:9**
OPTION 3: **Matthew 6:1-2**

Paul dedicated Romans 9–11 to teachings about the nation of Israel's relationship with God. In the Old Testament, Israel was God's chosen people, but when the time came for God to set them free from the law and redeem them through Jesus, they failed to believe in Him. Romans 10 begins with Paul's heartfelt plea for the Jews to come to know Jesus. Belief in the God of the Old Testament wasn't enough to save them if they rejected Jesus and His atoning work on the cross. According to Paul, the Jews had elevated the law to such a place of importance in their faith that it blinded them to the fulfillment of the law—Jesus—when He came to them.

Verses 8-13 provide one of the most succinct explanations of salvation in all of Scripture. Salvation comes not through obedience to the law but through the belief and profession that Jesus is Lord and that He died and rose again. Paul described this as a heart transformation, stating that salvation is possible for anyone who calls on the name of the Lord.

Finally, Paul noted how the gospel message spreads to both Jews and Gentiles. To believe in this message of salvation, people must hear its message, so someone has to share it. This process of evangelism brought Paul great joy, and it was the mission of his life. Unfortunately, not everyone who hears the gospel will believe it, but that fact doesn't diminish its impact or the need for people to share it.

HIGHLIGHT · EXPLAIN · APPLY · RESPOND

118//ROMANS 11

MEMORY VERSES

OPTION 1: **Psalm 40:1-2**
OPTION 2: **Proverbs 16:9**
OPTION 3: **Matthew 6:1-2**

Chapter 11 concludes Paul's teaching about Israel's relationship with God. Chapter 9 described their relationship in the past, chapter 10 taught about the current state of their relationship, and chapter 11 sets forth hope for Israel's future. God has a great plan for history that includes saving many people, both Jews and Gentiles. At the time when Paul wrote, God's saving purposes centered on bringing many Gentiles to faith in God, but he wanted to make sure readers understood that God had never rejected Israel. God had broadened His offer of salvation, but it always remained available for the Israelites.

This fact is evident when we consider the remnant of Jews in the New Testament who believed in Jesus. Though the nation as a whole rejected Christ, heavily influenced by the religious leadership, many individual Jews who met Jesus or heard the gospel after His resurrection chose to believe in Him. Paul referred to them as "a remnant chosen by grace" (v. 5) and "the elect" (v. 7). Through the image of grafted branches, Paul reminded readers that God had made a covenant with the nation of Israel and that He's always faithful to His covenant promises. The Gentiles were grafted into God's covenant with Abraham through their belief in Jesus. The day will come when God's saving plan will be accomplished as both Jews and Gentiles acknowledge Him as Lord and Savior. Our response should be praise for the wonder of His saving plan.

HIGHLIGHT · EXPLAIN · APPLY · RESPOND

119//ROMANS 12

MEMORY VERSES

OPTION 1: **Psalm 40:1-2**

OPTION 2: **Proverbs 16:9**

OPTION 3: **Matthew 6:1-2**

Romans 12 marks the most important transition in Romans as Paul began to answer the "So what?" question. What difference should salvation make in a believer's life? In this chapter Paul focused on two specific impacts: the way we live and the way we love.

The first effect of salvation is that we offer our lives to God in sacrifice and worship by committing to live for Him. Paul used the phrase "a living sacrifice" (v. 1) to speak to the church body as a whole. In other letters he used the image of slavery to communicate the same concept: Christ followers give their entire lives to serving God. His will and His purpose become their will and their purpose. To be the type of sacrifice God requires, we must let the Word of God transform our thinking, which will result in knowing and experiencing the will of God, as well as in worshiping God.

Our salvation also affects the church body as we wisely use our spiritual gifts to serve others. Paul was aware that it's possible to exercise the gifts of the Spirit without displaying the fruit of the Spirit—specifically, love. For that reason he reminded his readers that Christian love is genuine, opposed to evil, and committed to what's good. Verses 9-21 include one practical example after another of how Christ followers live set apart from "this age" (v. 2). Love modeled after the example of Jesus is at the heart of every example Paul provided.

HIGHLIGHT · EXPLAIN · APPLY · RESPOND

120//ROMANS 13

MEMORY VERSES

OPTION 1: **Psalm 40:1-2**
OPTION 2: **Proverbs 16:9**
OPTION 3: **Matthew 6:1-2**

In Romans 12 Paul dealt with ways a follower of Christ should relate to God and to the church. In chapter 13 he provided instruction on the effects of salvation in a person's relationship with government and neighbors.

We obey God by obeying the rules and rulers of our world. Christians are expected to show respect for leaders and to pay taxes. Paul reminded his readers that part of God's sovereign rule over the world means He rules over all earthly institutions as well. God appoints or, at a minimum, allows all earthly rulers to rise to power, so to obey authority is to submit to the order of our world as God has orchestrated it. Paul's teaching on paying taxes is consistent with the teaching Jesus gave during His earthly ministry.

Paul again returned to the overarching theme of love when he reminded readers that the Ten Commandments teach us how to love our neighbors. Jesus' disciples are also expected to maintain high moral standards in daily relationships—specifically, in sexual behavior, sobriety, and integrity of speech. What's the motivation for following this Christian code of ethics? The answer, for Paul, is the imminent return of Jesus. Every day Jesus' return draws closer, so every day we must live ready to see Him face-to-face.

HIGHLIGHT • EXPLAIN • APPLY • RESPOND

121//ROMANS 14

Paul's words in Romans 14 continue the focus on relationships with others by encouraging us to maintain unity by not judging others for their convictions and by not causing others to stumble into sin. The specific example Paul used is one addressed in many New Testament letters: eating meat previously sacrificed to idols. Paul took the stance that doing so wasn't a sin, but it might tempt and cause Christians who converted from paganism to sin.

Although the issue of sacrificed food isn't relevant today, we can think of many examples of not-necessarily-sinful choices that could cause a brother or a sister to sin. Whatever the specific issue, Paul encouraged readers to live in a way that brings love and encouragement to other people's lives. Everything we do, Paul reminded, is to be done for God's glory and purpose, as He had established in chapter 12 with the language of living sacrifices.

The heart of Paul's teaching in Romans 14 is found in verses 16-18: God's kingdom is more important than our rights, so we must always let love, the chief characteristic of kingdom people, determine the way we act toward one another. When love, rather than judgment, is the undercurrent in our relationships, the result is Spirit-filled peace and joy.

HIGHLIGHT · EXPLAIN · APPLY · RESPOND

122//ROMANS 15

In chapter 15 Paul offered two examples that help us understand the actions and attitudes our salvation should produce: the examples of Jesus and Paul himself. Verses 1-13 highlight the example of Christ. First and foremost, Jesus lived self-lessly. Everything He did from the time He left heaven was for the benefit of others and at great cost to Himself. Christ became a servant of the world in order to save the world from sin and self. We glorify God by living in harmony with one another and by remembering the life of the Lord Jesus. Christians ought to treat others the same way Jesus treats His people—with compassion, sacrifice, and grace. Paul also encouraged the Romans to be filled with abundant hope through the Holy Spirit.

Verses 14-33 shift the focus to Paul's personal ministry and his relationship with the Christians in Rome. Like Jesus, Paul devoted his life to the glory of God. For Paul, this meant being wholeheartedly and selflessly committed to spreading the gospel wherever he could. This gospel message was the heart of his letter to the Romans, and he reminded them of its importance as he drew his letter to a close. Nothing was more important to Paul than introducing people to Jesus and His gospel of grace, and the same should be true of everyone who's a disciple of Jesus today.

HIGHLIGHT · EXPLAIN · APPLY · RESPOND

123//ROMANS 16

MEMORY VERSES
OPTION 1: **Psalm 42:1-2**
OPTION 2: **Proverbs 17:27-28**
OPTION 3: **Matthew 6:3-4**

Paul concluded his letter to the Romans with personal information about his plans to visit Rome and to spread the gospel even farther. He also sent personal greetings to many people he knew in the Roman church, people whom he had met on his missionary journeys through that part of the world. A few names on this list are people we also read about in the Book of Acts, including Priscilla, Aquila, and Timothy.

Paul's personal greetings are noteworthy in that they include men and women and in that they reveal the rapid, dedicated growth of the early church. Paul hadn't yet made it to Rome, but many people he knew had, and they were planting churches, meeting in homes, and going to prison for their faith. These people followed the example of Paul and, more important, the example of Jesus as they dedicated their lives to growing the church.

As he brought his letter to a close, Paul issued a brief warning against those who would disrupt the unity of the church, then complimented the Romans once more for their reputation. Fittingly, the final words of his letter are a doxology of praise to God for His greatness and glory. God's victory was coming (see Rom. 16:20) and with it the advancement of "the obedience of faith among all the Gentiles" (v. 26). The only question that remains is what part we'll play in its advancement.

HIGHLIGHT · EXPLAIN · APPLY · RESPOND

124//ACTS 20

Paul was finishing his third period of missionary activity. Having spent three years in Ephesus, he departed, evidently shortly after the episode with the silversmiths (see Acts 19). Paul traveled through Macedonia, revisiting the churches there, then went on to Corinth in Greece, where he stayed for three months.

Acts 20 catalogs several stops on this missionary journey, but two warrant special attention. While in Troas, Paul spent several hours one evening teaching in the upstairs room of a home. A man named Eutychus fell asleep and tumbled out of the window, instantly dying. However, Paul was able to raise him from the dead. Luke's account of this event is subtle; it mentions only that Paul put his arms around the man and proclaimed him to be alive. This event highlighted the power of God at work through Paul.

The second emphasis in this chapter was on Paul's words of encouragement to the leaders of the church in Ephesus and his anticipation of the dangers that awaited him in Jerusalem because of his faith. Several phrases in Paul's farewell speech highlight his overwhelming commitment to God's call and the great physical and emotional toll it took on him. Jesus said serving Him would come with a cost, and Paul's life exemplified that reality. But Paul's depth of love for these brothers in Christ and his laserlike focus on spreading the gospel show that living for Jesus makes it worth the cross He asks us to bear.

HIGHLIGHT • EXPLAIN • APPLY • RESPOND

125//ACTS 21

MEMORY VERSES

OPTION 1: **Psalm 42:1-2**
OPTION 2: **Proverbs 17:27-28**
OPTION 3: **Matthew 6:3-4**

Despite several warnings and a good understanding of the suffering that awaited him, Paul continued to Jerusalem. Along the journey many people who dearly loved him (including Luke, the writer of Acts) begged him not to go, but he was determined. Even the prophet Agabus, who told Paul he would be arrested, couldn't dissuade him from his mission. In his own words, he was "ready not only to be bound but also to die in Jerusalem for the name of the Lord Jesus" (v. 13).

When Paul and his companions arrived in Jerusalem. Paul immediately went to meet with the leaders of the Jerusalem church, including James, the brother of Jesus. He shared with them the amazing work God was doing among churches all across the region. He also encouraged the believers in Jerusalem and cleared up lingering questions about Jewish customs in the Christian faith.

At the temple a mob of Jews attacked Paul, accusing Him of teaching against Jewish laws, similar to the accusations leveled against Jesus prior to His crucifixion. He likely would have been killed if the Romans hadn't taken him into custody. Acts 20–21 reveals Paul's undivided focus on the advancement of the gospel. Like Paul, when we're fully convinced of who Jesus is and what He has done, we'll be obedient to His call and passionate about His priorities in spite of the cost.

HIGHLIGHT · EXPLAIN · APPLY · RESPOND

126//ACTS 22

Acts 22 describes Paul's imprisonment in Jerusalem. After he was arrested, Paul addressed the Jewish mob in the temple courtyard—the same mob that moments before had sought to kill him. Paul's speech included proof of his Roman citizenship and of his Jewish identity. He also described Jesus' call on his life—a call he was being obedient to follow, even in chains. Paul described his life before he met Jesus and then detailed his encounter with the resurrected Jesus on the road to Damascus. Paul also included his interaction with Ananias, a devout, respected Jew. This detail, along with Paul's personal history, helped him communicate his connection to the Jews rather than his opposition to them.

However, Paul's mention of God's command to take the gospel to the Gentiles ignited the fury of the crowd. When the angry crowd abruptly ended Paul's speech, he was taken into the Roman barracks. A Roman centurion was ordered to flog and interrogate Paul to determine the true nature of the Jews' grievances against him. Paul revealed his Roman citizenship to the centurion, who quickly informed his commanding officer. From that point on, the Romans treated Paul much differently.

Seeing Jewish men and women reject the mission of God deeply grieved Paul. In the midst of these circumstances, God reminded Paul that He's always at work and would empower him to preach the gospel in Rome. God's Word and God's work in our lives strengthen us to continue living for Him in spite of all obstacles.

HIGHLIGHT · EXPLAIN · APPLY · RESPOND

127//ACTS 23

MEMORY VERSES
OPTION 1: **Psalm 46:10**
OPTION 2: **Proverbs 18:10**
OPTION 3: **Matthew 6:5-6**

The Roman commander who had put Paul in prison wanted to learn more about why people so vehemently opposed him, so he took Paul to a meeting of the Sanhedrin, the Jewish ruling council. Unfortunately for Paul, the meeting didn't start out well. He immediately offended Ananias, the high priest, by claiming to have lived a righteous, holy life. He offended him a second time by accusing Ananias of hypocrisy. In verse 6 we see that Paul then took a different approach, calling attention to his belief in the resurrection as the reason he was hated. This claim was true, since belief in Jesus' resurrection, which proved He's the Messiah, sets Christianity apart from Judaism, but it also distracted the Sanhedrin. The members of the council held two opposing views on this topic, so Paul's statement launched a debate. It also united half of the group, the Pharisees, with Paul.

When the meeting grew violent, the commander, fearing for Paul's life, ordered his troops to remove him from the Sanhedrin. Verse 11 gives insight into Paul's relationship with God, who told him to "have courage" and promised that he would share the gospel in Rome. The rest of the chapter describes the plot to kill Paul, which has many similarities to the plot to kill Jesus, and the divine intervention of Paul's nephew and the Roman commander who had already spared Paul's life twice. God's sovereign control over Paul's life and protection of Paul's gospel ministry is a thread that runs throughout all of Acts, but it's seen even more clearly in these final chapters. Nothing was going to stop the gospel from reaching Rome.

HIGHLIGHT · EXPLAIN · APPLY · RESPOND

128//ACTS 24

Because of Paul's Roman citizenship, the commander sent Paul to Caesarea to appear before Felix, the Roman governor of Judea, who called for a formal hearing of Paul's case. Verses 5-6 record the official accusations against Paul: he was a trouble-maker who upended the peace of the Jews wherever he traveled. The "sect of the Nazarenes" (v. 5), a term the Jewish leaders used to refer to the early Christians, pointed to Paul's leadership in the church as another of his offenses.

In his defense Paul argued that although he was a leader in the early church, he always acted peacefully and never stirred up trouble. Sometimes trouble followed him, but others always initiated it. Paul reminded his audience that when he entered the temple, he still adhered to the Jewish rituals and always acted with the best interests of others in mind. He ended his defense by asking his accusers to name a crime he had committed, which they were obviously unable to do. Although Paul's accusers brought serious charges against him, they were unable to prove his guilt, leading Felix to postpone the trial until a later date. Although Felix never reconvened Paul's trial, he kept Paul in confinement throughout the remaining two years of his term as governor.

HIGHLIGHT · EXPLAIN · APPLY · RESPOND

129//ACTS 25

MEMORY VERSES

OPTION 1: **Psalm 46:10**
OPTION 2: **Proverbs 18:10**
OPTION 3: **Matthew 6:5-6**

When Felix's replacement, Festus, came into office, the Jewish leaders requested that Paul be brought from Caesarea to Jerusalem for trial. They were persistent in their efforts against Paul, waiting for more than two years to try having him condemned. They still lacked any real crime with which to charge Paul, and he defended himself against any violations of Jewish or Roman law. Festus also struggled to handle Paul's case since he could find no clear source of guilt, but he wanted to give the Jews a favor. This and many other details in Paul's trial bear a striking resemblance to Jesus' trial.

Realizing the danger to his life in traveling to Jerusalem, Paul exercised his right as a Roman citizen to appeal to Caesar. Festus accepted the appeal, thus setting Paul's course for Rome. Not long after Paul made his appeal to Caesar, the Jewish king, Agrippa, arrived in Caesarea. Festus hoped Agrippa would counsel him in what to do with this man who seemed to have broken no Roman laws.

Throughout his ministry Paul seized every opportunity to share the gospel, and God continually opened doors for that purpose. Similarly, when we truly grasp the love God demonstrated for us through the death and resurrection of His Son, we're compelled to live for Him and to share that good news with others.

HIGHLIGHT · EXPLAIN · APPLY · RESPOND

130//ACTS 26

Because King Agrippa expressed interest in hearing from Paul, the apostle had the opportunity to defend himself and his gospel ministry before the king. Paul's testimony became the basis for his appeal. As he had done several times in Acts, Paul reminded Agrippa and the others listening that he had been raised a devout Jew and had lived as an obedient, faithful Pharisee. Like all Jews, Paul had been waiting for the Messiah to come, and because at first he hadn't believed Jesus was that Messiah, he had led the way in persecuting Christians.

Paul again recounted his Damascus-road encounter with Jesus, the defining moment in his life. On that road he realized that the Messiah had come and had been killed by the Jews but resurrected from the dead. After Paul met Jesus, everything changed for him. Verses 16-18 clearly articulate the mission Jesus gave him, a mission to which Paul was being faithful even in this moment before Agrippa. Jesus sent Paul to turn people from darkness to light and to rescue them from sin and Satan.

As Paul demonstrated, our personal stories of God's work are often the best way to share Jesus with others. Paul knew his obedience to Jesus was the cause of his imprisonment. Still he pressed the king to acknowledge Christ as the Savior foretold by the prophets. The king rose to his feet and ended the hearing, clearly moved by Paul's words but unable to believe them yet. As he and Festus departed, the two agreed on Paul's innocence. Paul was then sent to Rome to appear before Caesar.

HIGHLIGHT · EXPLAIN · APPLY · RESPOND

131//ACTS 27

The journey to Rome ordinarily took a couple of months at most, but Paul's party encountered bad weather, delaying the trip six additional months. Because of the weather, the ship sailed off course from its normal route. However, the delay to reach Rome didn't hinder Paul's evangelistic efforts. God gave Paul insight into the troubles that lay ahead, and Paul tried to warn the crew. When the crew failed to heed Paul's advice, disaster resulted in the form of a massive storm.

In the midst of the crew and passengers' despair, Paul predicted they would all be delivered, and the events unfolded just as he said. God was establishing Paul as a trustworthy leader in order to gain the listening ears of the crew. Because of Paul's leadership and the accuracy of his predictions, his life was spared once again. When the soldiers wanted to kill the prisoners, the centurion, their leader, came to Paul's defense, and neither he nor any other prisoners were killed.

Paul's life proves time and again that when we're faithful to God's direction, He protects and empowers us to carry out His will. God gives us innumerable promises in His Word to help us endure our storms and point others to Christ.

HIGHLIGHT · EXPLAIN · APPLY · RESPOND

132//ACTS 28

The ship on which Paul was traveling wrecked on the island of Malta, south of Sicily. Paul immediately impressed the island's inhabitants when God delivered him unharmed from a viper's bite. As a result, Paul was able to carry out a ministry of healing among the islanders. After the winter had passed and the seas were again safe for travel, Paul's party secured passage to Italy. As they completed their journey to Rome on foot, two groups of Roman Christians came out to greet Paul.

Once in the city, Paul was allowed to live in an apartment rented at his own expense as long as he remained imprisoned under military guard. Luke's account ends with Paul's living under house arrest in Rome for two years as he awaited his hearing before Caesar. During that time he freely witnessed to all who came to hear him share the gospel. Paul could have easily allowed his circumstances to override his passion for sharing the gospel, but instead, he continued to proclaim God's love to all who would listen. We must do the same. Christ calls us to make the most of every opportunity to share the gospel with others.

HIGHLIGHT · EXPLAIN · APPLY · RESPOND

133//COLOSSIANS 1

MEMORY VERSES

OPTION 1: **Psalm 51:10-11**

OPTION 2: **Proverbs 18:21**

OPTION 3: **Matthew 6:7-8**

Paul wrote his letter to the Colossians during his first imprisonment in Rome. The letter primarily served to correct misunderstandings in the church body that had been advanced by false teachers who were urging believers to blend other religious ideas with Christianity. The theme that dominates the letter is the centrality and superiority of Christ.

Though Paul didn't personally know many of these believers, he was concerned for their spiritual welfare. He began his letter to them by affirming and encouraging them in their faith and by sharing specific prayers for them. Paul prayed for their lives to bear the fruit of the gospel; an increased knowledge of God; and God-given endurance, patience, and joy.

Paul's teaching about Christ in verses 15-20 is one of the greatest affirmations of the person and work of Christ found in the New Testament. Paul affirmed Christ's deity as well as His lordship over all creation, maintaining that Jesus is not only the Creator but also the Sustainer of all things. As such, He was able to bring about our reconciliation to God through His cross.

Paul closed chapter 1 with a note about his commitment to spreading the gospel. Making Jesus' name known was Paul's chief aim in life, and no amount of suffering would stop him from doing that, as the Book of Acts documents. That clear communication of gospel truth was the goal of his letter to the Colossians as well.

HIGHLIGHT • EXPLAIN • APPLY • RESPOND

134//COLOSSIANS 2

MEMORY VERSES
OPTION 1: **Psalm 51:10-11**
OPTION 2: **Proverbs 18:21**
OPTION 3: **Matthew 6:7-8**

After establishing the supremacy of Christ over all things in Colossians 1, Paul transitioned to the main point of his letter in chapter 2 by attacking a false doctrinal teaching that had become a problem for the Christians in Colossae. From Paul's letter we can get a sense of what this heretical teaching involved. Paul made several references to the mystery of God, now revealed in Jesus, which combated the heretical teaching that God reserved special or secret wisdom about His salvation for a limited number of people.

Paul also argued against the teaching that "human tradition, based on the elements of the world" (v. 8) carried as much weight as or more weight than the teachings of Jesus. Paul also reminded the Colossians that the rituals and traditions of the Jewish faith, though important, were never meant to be a means of salvation. Jewish religious traditions were meant to point people to Jesus.

Paul challenged the believers to continue demonstrating commitment to Christ and gratitude for the privileges that belonged to them in Him. Our lives should be grounded in the supreme foundation of Jesus, and our faith should be fixed on Him as a result. When we see Jesus like this and lose sight of our own lives in His greatness, we understand who we truly are and what we were created for.

HIGHLIGHT · EXPLAIN · APPLY · RESPOND

135//COLOSSIANS 3

MEMORY VERSES

OPTION 1: **Psalm 51:10-11**
OPTION 2: **Proverbs 18:21**
OPTION 3: **Matthew 6:7-8**

Chapters 1–2 form the theological or doctrinal section of Colossians, while chapters 3–4 compose the practical part of Paul's letter. After the apostle Paul had discussed theological issues facing the Colossians, he turned to practical concerns for their daily lives and for their call to pursue holy living. Paul reminded them that through their conversion experiences they had died to their old way of life and had risen with Christ to walk in newness of life, as symbolized by baptism.

Paul then addressed some of the most prevalent sins in the first-century Greco-Roman world, listing attitudes and behaviors the Colossians were to "put to death" (3:5) in their lives. In contrast, he also provided a list of virtues these believers were to "put on" (v. 12). If the Colossians were to genuinely serve Christ, they had to conduct their lives in a manner worthy of Him. Even today such qualities should be evident in our lives as a result of a right relationship with Christ. We're responsible for reflecting Christ to the world, which means pursuing His holiness in all we say and do.

HIGHLIGHT · EXPLAIN · APPLY · RESPOND

136//COLOSSIANS 4

MEMORY VERSES
OPTION 1: **Psalm 51:12-13**
OPTION 2: **Proverbs 18:22**
OPTION 3: **Matthew 6:9-11**

The close of Paul's letter to the Colossians bookends with the way it began. Paul had opened the letter with an elaborate prayer for the Colossians, and in chapter 4 he asked them for prayer in return. Specifically, Paul challenged them to be people of prayer who lived in expectation of and gratitude for all the ways God answered their prayers. Paul also asked for prayer for himself and his missionary team: that God would open doors for them to share the gospel and that they would clearly and boldly communicate it.

Paul then gave a final reminder to the Colossian believers to live in a way that points other people to Jesus. Like Paul, they were responsible for sharing the gospel with others, so Paul challenged them to do so in a way that was encouraging and hopeful. Both the words we say and the way we say them matter greatly when we tell others about Jesus.

Paul's letter to the Colossians reminds readers that Jesus, the Son of God, is the foundation for all of spiritual life. No secret wisdom or set of rules can save a person; only belief in Jesus and His gospel message has the power to do that, and this message is available to everyone.

HIGHLIGHT · EXPLAIN · APPLY · RESPOND

137//EPHESIANS 1

MEMORY VERSES
OPTION 1: **Psalm 51:12-13**
OPTION 2: **Proverbs 18:22**
OPTION 3: **Matthew 6:9-11**

Paul took advantage of his imprisonment in Rome to write letters to many different people and churches, among them Colossians and Ephesians. His purpose in the letter to the Ephesians was to communicate God's redemptive plan and power and to challenge his readers to become everything God wanted them to be as His people.

At the start of his letter, Paul described at length the wonder of God's redemptive purpose in salvation. He revealed that God's plan is much more extensive than simply saving individual people in isolation. God gives believers His power to enable them to live for Him and to carry out His gospel mission in the world. Paul began by listing a series of spiritual riches bestowed on Christians as children of God. Included among these riches are redemption from sin; the holiness and righteousness that are ours because of Jesus; our identity as adopted children of God; and the indwelling presence of the Holy Spirit, who also secures our place with God in eternity.

As he did in the letter to the Colossians, Paul also included a prayer for the Ephesian Christians, thanking God for their faith and praying for their increased knowledge of God. Then he reminded them of Jesus' supremacy and lordship over everything, including His church. The remainder of Paul's letter would instruct the Ephesians in how to live in unity with Christ and in unity with His body, the church.

HIGHLIGHT · EXPLAIN · APPLY · RESPOND

138//EPHESIANS 2

MEMORY VERSES

OPTION 1: **Psalm 51:12-13**

OPTION 2: **Proverbs 18:22**

OPTION 3: **Matthew 6:9-11**

In chapter 2 Paul reminded his readers of who they were before they came to know Jesus and who they were in Christ. He began by describing the desperation and depravity of their condition before they responded to the gospel (see vv. 1-3). The "But God …" statement in verse 4 is one of a handful of similar statements in Paul's New Testament letters, and it marks one of the most important contrasts in all of Scripture. Apart from Christ a person is dead. But in Christ—because of God's great love and mercy—a person is alive. The heart of the gospel is that God brings life to the dead and light to the darkness.

Verses 5-10 address the results of salvation. Because we've received grace, we're to reflect God's love and grace to others. The good works a believer does are the result of salvation, with the purpose of giving glory to God so that others can know Him. What matters most about us isn't what the world tells us, the way people around us see us, or even the way we see ourselves. Our identity is determined by what God says about us. Apart from Christ we were dead and hopeless. But in Christ we're alive and will live forever with Him. When we believe what God says about us, we find the freedom to walk in the good works He has planned for us.

In verses 11-22 Paul emphasized the corporate or relational dimension of salvation. Belief in Jesus brings a unifying power; both believing Gentiles and Jews become one in the body of Christ.

HIGHLIGHT · EXPLAIN · APPLY · RESPOND

139//EPHESIANS 3

In Ephesians 2 Paul had developed his understanding of God's salvation. Now in chapter 3 he pointedly reminded the readers of his personal role in spreading the good news. Again the language of mystery surfaced as Paul described the revelation God gave him about the good news of Jesus and his personal call to open others' eyes to this mystery.

In this context Paul elaborated on the mystery as being God's offer of salvation beyond the Jews to all people everywhere. Paul's ministry was a gift of grace—an example of accepting opportunities to serve God. He viewed his time in chains, which gave him the opportunity to write these letters, as a divine appointment as well.

As Paul concluded this part of the letter, he was compelled to pray for his readers yet again. This prayer highlights God's power, Christ's love, and believers' experience of God's power. His prayer closes with a statement of praise to God for His immeasurable greatness and glory.

As we experience God's strength, we too will be equipped to fulfill all God calls us to. That's the theme Paul focused on in the second half of his epistle. Right thinking about God and salvation will have a practical effect on the way a believer lives today.

HIGHLIGHT · EXPLAIN · APPLY · RESPOND

140//EPHESIANS 4

As Paul moved into the more practical portion of his letter, he reminded his readers to live lives worthy of their calling as disciples of Jesus. Though believers can do this in many ways, Paul gave a few specific examples: be humble, gentle, patient, and loving while living in oneness and peace. These are all Spirit-given traits that deeply affect our relationships with other believers.

With the role of the Holy Spirit in mind, Paul reviewed the matter of spiritual gifts. While Christians are united as one body in Christ, each individual believer possesses a unique set of gifts to strengthen the body as a whole. Paul's list of gifts in verse 11 is by no means exhaustive but focuses on gifts the church can use to teach and train people in the gospel and gospel ministry. The Spirit gives these ministry gifts to the church for the specific purpose of "equipping the saints for the work of ministry, to build up the body of Christ" (v. 12).

Paul next urged the Ephesian believers to work together for their collective good, using the analogy of a physical body that grows to maturity. He also contrasted the moral behavior of Christians with the behavior of non-Christians. He gave an additional list of virtues that characterize the Christian life, comparable to those at the beginning of the chapter. This list includes honesty, kindness, compassion, gentleness, and edifying speech.

Simply put, believers are to live differently from the world. We're to be different in our moral behavior, our desires, our speech, our relationships, our priorities, and our identities. We're to be like Christ to people who don't know Him.

141//EPHESIANS 5

MEMORY VERSES

OPTION 1: **Psalm 51:16-17**
OPTION 2: **Proverbs 18:24**
OPTION 3: **Matthew 6:12-13**

In Ephesians 4 Paul had described how Christians can live uniquely and distinctly set apart to Christ. In chapter 5 he emphasized that ultimately, we're called to imitate Christ. Because God is love, we're to extend His love to others. Because God is pure in speech and behavior, we're to behave with purity. Because God is light, we're to live as children of the light. Paul communicated a clear sense of urgency in living like Christ. We must make the most of every opportunity to reflect Jesus' love to others, because our days are numbered and eternity is at stake.

As Paul continued to address the way God expects His people to behave, he next considered family relationships. If our faith doesn't make our marriages measurably stronger or cultivate better relationships between parents and children, we'll find it difficult to disciple others in these areas. Submission to others is at the heart of each of these relationships, and it's rooted in mutual submission to Christ. This means yielding to the best interests of the other person, just as we're to yield our entire lives to the will of Jesus. A married person's relationship with Christ should form the foundation of an enduring, joyful relationship with the person's spouse.

HIGHLIGHT · EXPLAIN · APPLY · RESPOND

142//EPHESIANS 6

MEMORY VERSES
OPTION 1: **Psalm 51:16-17**
OPTION 2: **Proverbs 18:24**
OPTION 3: **Matthew 6:12-13**

From marriage the apostle Paul went on to consider the impact knowing Jesus has on other relationships. Those relationships include the parent-child relationship and the employer-employee relationship. Roman slavery was quite different from American chattel slavery. Slaves in the first century were bond servants with rights. The relationship between slave and master would be analogous to the employer-employee relationship today. A healthy parent-child relationship should be characterized by obedience and honor. Similarly, a healthy employer-employee relationship emphasizes respect, service, and obedience.

Paul closed his letter with a call to be prepared for the spiritual battle the Christian life inevitably demands. Paul's letters frequently encouraged his readers to be strong, withstand persecution, and endure in their faith. Here Paul explained why. The church is engaged in a very real spiritual battle with the enemy, Satan. This spiritual warfare is evident all around us every day, just as it confronted the believers in Ephesus. The only hope we have against this enemy is to stand strong, depending on God, fully dressed in the spiritual armor He has given us to engage in this battle.

This armor is both offensive and defensive in nature. God gives us specific weapons that help us withstand attack from our enemy and others that help us actively fight against him. We must wear each piece of armor at all times so that we're always ready to do battle against evil and are never taken by surprise. No matter what attacks we face, we must rely on God's immovable strength and protection.

HIGHLIGHT · EXPLAIN · APPLY · RESPOND

143//PHILIPPIANS 1

MEMORY VERSES

OPTION 1: **Psalm 51:16-17**

OPTION 2: **Proverbs 18:24**

OPTION 3: **Matthew 6:12-13**

Paul also wrote his letter to the Philippians while he was imprisoned in Rome. This letter was deeply personal because he considered the Christians in Philippi to be gospel partners. They had helped him in the past, and during his imprisonment they again had come to his aid. He wrote this letter as both a note of gratitude and a challenge for the Philippian believers to choose joy in Christ in every circumstance.

Paul began his letter by assuring the Philippians of his thankfulness for their partnership with him. He prayed that their love would continue to grow as they discerned the most important things in life and prepared themselves to face God's judgment with confidence.

The apostle also wrote that he was convinced his imprisonment was causing the gospel to advance. He viewed his circumstances as a part of God's greater plan for the spread of the gospel; nevertheless, these verses reflect the tension he felt within himself. Paul wasn't afraid of death, but he felt torn between the desire to depart and be with Christ and the desire to remain in the flesh and help the Philippians and others grow in the faith. Paul also faced unimaginable suffering but expressed his ability to continue rejoicing. Whatever the outcome, Paul had assurance that Christ would be glorified and that the gospel wouldn't be defeated.

HIGHLIGHT · EXPLAIN · APPLY · RESPOND

144//PHILIPPIANS 2

MEMORY VERSES
OPTION 1: **Psalm 51:16-17**
OPTION 2: **Proverbs 18:24**
OPTION 3: **Matthew 6:12-13**

A key theme of Paul's New Testament letters is unity. Paul challenged Christians to be united with Jesus in His will and purpose for their lives. Then unity with one another would be a natural by-product of their faith. As Paul encouraged his friends to greater unity, he cited Christ's example to inspire them.

Specifically, Paul pointed to Jesus as the ultimate example of humility. To truly live in unity with God and others, we must tap into Spirit-given humility that empowers us to put the needs and interests of others ahead of our own. Jesus modeled humility when He gave up all the benefits of heaven to come to earth, live as a man in our broken world, and die on the cross to redeem our world from sin. Jesus knew the trajectory of His life on earth before He left heaven, yet He yielded to His Father's redemptive plan. This is humility and servanthood in its purest form, and Paul calls us to follow this example. When we imitate Christ, we shine as His light in the world, displaying to others the good news of the gospel.

Paul again called the Philippians to rejoice, even when their faith brought great suffering and sacrifice. Those are expected consequences for anyone who follows Jesus' example, as the ministries of Timothy and Epaphroditus demonstrate.

HIGHLIGHT · EXPLAIN · APPLY · RESPOND

145//PHILIPPIANS 3

MEMORY VERSES

OPTION 1: **Psalm 51:16-17**

OPTION 2: **Proverbs 18:24**

OPTION 3: **Matthew 6:12-13**

Paul had already used Jesus, Timothy, and Epaphroditus as examples of how to serve God in joy and humility. In Philippians 3 Paul used his own experience in Christ to provide another example, contrasting his background in Judaism with his present life in Christ.

Though Paul experienced every privilege Judaism offered, he didn't regret his decision to follow Christ. He described his life in Christ as continually striving to reach the goal of spiritual maturity. The prize he would earn when he reached this goal referred to eternity in Jesus' presence. This single-minded focus on growing in Christlikeness motivated Paul in his missionary endeavors and in his writing. His constant focus on eternity also enabled Paul to choose joy in all things.

In following Jesus' example, Paul made great sacrifices for the sake of discipleship. He gave up power and prestige as a Pharisee, relationships like marriage and family, and countless physical comforts. Like Paul, we're citizens of heaven, and he challenges us in this letter to follow his example. The sacrifices that discipleship requires of us may be different, but we'll undoubtedly experience consequences of following Christ. The goal of our lives should be unity with Jesus. Although we won't fully attain this goal until eternity, we can strive for it every day.

HIGHLIGHT · EXPLAIN · APPLY · RESPOND

146//PHILIPPIANS 4

MEMORY VERSES
OPTION 1: **Psalm 55:22**
OPTION 2: **Proverbs 19:17**
OPTION 3: **Matthew 6:14-15**

In Philippians 4 Paul concluded his message to his friends by challenging, instructing, and thanking them. Throughout this letter Paul had challenged the Philippians to seek unity in Christ. In this chapter he mentioned a specific relationship that needed unity and healing. Euodia and Syntyche were two women who had partnered with Paul in gospel ministry but found themselves in a contentious relationship. Paul encouraged them to work toward unity and encouraged the other believers to assist them. The work of Christ is too important to be sidetracked by relational discord.

Verses 4-9 issued final challenges for the Philippian believers to live in Christ. They were to rejoice in the Lord; be steadfast in prayer, which leads to peace from God; and meditate on attitudes consistent with the faith they professed to believe. Though the Philippians had struggles, Paul still loved them and encouraged them to grow in their relationship with Christ and to focus on eternity at all times. Finally, Paul encouraged these believers to be content in any and every circumstance, trusting in God's provision.

HIGHLIGHT · EXPLAIN · APPLY · RESPOND

147//PHILEMON

MEMORY VERSES
OPTION 1: **Psalm 55:22**
OPTION 2: **Proverbs 19:17**
OPTION 3: **Matthew 6:14-15**

Unlike Colossians, Philippians, and other letters Paul wrote to churches and groups of believers, the letter of Philemon was written to an individual who's believed to have been a wealthy member of the church in Colossae. Although Paul's letter began as most of his letters do, with a greeting and a prayer for the recipient, it had a very narrow focus: to restore the relationship between Philemon and Onesimus, one of Philemon's slaves who had run away.

When Onesimus escaped to Rome, he met Paul, heard his teaching, and became a Christian. Paul felt that the two needed to restore their relationship now that they were brothers in Christ (see v. 16). Specifically, Paul challenged Philemon to welcome Onesimus home in the same manner he would welcome Paul. Onesimus and Paul had grown close during their time together, and Paul would have even preferred for Onesimus to stay with him in Rome.

The call to forgiveness and restoration that Paul directed to Philemon is pertinent in all of our relationships. Jesus modeled forgiveness for us when He died on the cross to forgive us of our sins. Many times in His teachings He also urged His followers to forgive (see Matt. 5:23-24; 6:14-15; 18:21-22; Luke 17:3-4). Forgiveness isn't optional for followers of Christ. We must do everything we can to make sure our relationships with others are healthy, reflecting the love, grace, and mercy God has shown us.

HIGHLIGHT · EXPLAIN · APPLY · RESPOND

148//HEBREWS 1

Although the writer of the Book of Hebrews is unknown, his purpose was clear. He wrote to Hebrew (Jewish) Christians who needed encouragement to grow into mature followers of Christ rather than revert to the comfort of their Jewish heritage. One running theme throughout Hebrews is Jesus' superiority to everything the Jews' religious system offered. This emphasis was intended to encourage readers to persevere in the faith.

The writer began by declaring that in the past God had spoken through the prophets, but now God spoke through His Son, Jesus. He went on to list five descriptions of Jesus that highlighted His deity, redemptive death, and exaltation: the heir of all things, the radiance of God's glory, the sustainer of all creation, the purification for sins, and his superiority to the angels.

A series of quotations from the Old Testament follow that support Jesus' deity and superiority to every created being, even the angels. The seven quotations in verses 5-13 come from Psalm 2:7; 2 Samuel 7:14; Deuteronomy 32:43; Psalm 104:4; Psalm 45:6-7; Psalm 102:25-27; and Psalm 110:1. Together these Scriptures highlight the relationship between God the Father and God the Son. They also give clarity to Jesus' role as Creator and Sustainer of the universe.

From the beginning of the book, readers learn that Jesus is the Son of God, the Creator and Sustainer of the universe, and the eternal Ruler of God's kingdom. He's worthy of our worship and the perseverance a life of discipleship requires.

HIGHLIGHT • EXPLAIN • APPLY • RESPOND

149//HEBREWS 2

MEMORY VERSES

OPTION 1: **Psalm 55:22**
OPTION 2: **Proverbs 19:17**
OPTION 3: **Matthew 6:14-15**

In light of Jesus' superiority, which was established in chapter 1, the writer of Hebrews warned believers against neglecting the salvation God provided through His Son. This is the first of four warnings that appear in this book.

First-century Hebrew Christians converted from Judaism, a religion steeped in tradition, rituals, and family heritage. It would have been easy for them to drift back into Judaism in the face of persecution or hardship. The writer urged readers to listen to the truths of salvation and the movement of the Holy Spirit in their lives. Actively listening to God and reminding ourselves of the gospel keep us firmly rooted in our faith.

The writer then explained why God's Son had come to earth in the form of a man. God had originally given humans the assignment of managing His creation, but they hadn't done so. Genesis 3 makes clear that sin had prevented people from fulfilling God's purpose for them. Hebrews 2 shows that Jesus became human to provide a solution for humankind's sin problem, doing for people what they couldn't do for themselves. Through His death He made salvation available. In this way Jesus is the High Priest who sacrificed Himself for human sin so that people could be forgiven. Only through faith in Christ can people fulfill all God created them to be.

HIGHLIGHT · EXPLAIN · APPLY · RESPOND

150//HEBREWS 3

In chapter 3 the writer offered Jesus and Moses as examples or models of faithfulness. These Jewish converts would have looked to Moses as the model of faith. In the same way the writer established Jesus' superiority to the angels, he pointed to Jesus' superiority to Moses as well. The image of the builder and the house portrayed Jesus as "the one who built everything" (v. 4). While Moses was a faithful servant *among* God's people, Jesus was the faithful Son *over* God's people.

Verses 7-19 present readers with the second of the writer's warnings, this time against slipping into unbelief, or turning away from God. The writer quoted Psalm 95:7-11 to warn readers not to be unfaithful to God and rebel against Him. He pointed to the Israelites who wandered in the desert as an example of the danger of unbelief. Although they had witnessed some of God's greatest miracles and faithfulness—from the parting of the Red Sea to the provision of quail and manna—they repeatedly turned from God toward idolatry, discontentment, and faithlessness. The readers of Hebrews were warned not to harden their hearts against God's will or to allow unbelief to turn them away from Him. Rather, they were to encourage one another daily and to be true to their professions of faith in Christ.

HIGHLIGHT · EXPLAIN · APPLY · RESPOND

151//HEBREWS 4

In chapter 4 the writer of Hebrews expressed his desire for his readers to obey God and enter His rest, a spiritual reality symbolized by the promised land. For the Israelites who wandered in the desert, the promised land was a place that offered physical rest from the exhaustion of wandering and homelessness. At the same time, it offered spiritual rest by fulfilling God's promise to His people.

The Sabbath rest encouraged in Hebrews 4 signifies the rest that comes from a relationship with Jesus. While this rest has a physical aspect—the practice of the Sabbath, a day set aside for rest and worship—the other aspect is spiritual, referring to the rest for weary souls that can be found only in a relationship with Jesus. Jesus alone brings peace to the turmoil and restlessness caused by sin, and a relationship with Him brings the promise of eternal rest in God's presence. The writer stressed that genuine believers have entered God's rest through faith and obedience. Because God sees us as we are, we must confess and repent of our sins so that we can be forgiven. Then we'll find true, unshakable rest that transcends the circumstances of life.

HIGHLIGHT · EXPLAIN · APPLY · RESPOND

152//HEBREWS 5

Previously, the writer of Hebrews had made a case for Jesus' greatness in comparison to the angels and Moses. At the close of chapter 4 and the beginning of chapter 5, he also established Jesus' greatness compared to the high priests of Judaism.

The Old Testament described the high priest as the person God chose to represent the people before Him. The high priest served in the temple, and once a year on the Day of Atonement, he entered the inner sanctuary of the temple and offered a sacrifice on behalf of everyone's sins. This practice foreshadowed Jesus' role as our great High Priest who became the once-for-all atoning sacrifice for the sins of the world. Just as God called the Israelites' high priests to their roles, He also called Jesus to be the ultimate High Priest. Unlike human high priests, however, Jesus was sinless; He didn't need to offer sacrifices for Himself. Jesus is qualified, as God's Son who died for our sins, to be the Savior and High Priest for everyone who trusts Him.

Verses 7-10 remind readers of Jesus' humanity. Inasmuch as He was God incarnate (in the flesh), He was also fully human, and His sacrifice on humanity's behalf cost Him greatly. His example of selfless obedience to God the Father is a model for every Christian to follow.

The writer then turned to the problem of his readers' spiritual immaturity, lamenting the fact that they should have been spiritually mature but weren't due to their laziness.

HIGHLIGHT • EXPLAIN • APPLY • RESPOND

153//HEBREWS 6

MEMORY VERSES

OPTION 1: **Psalm 63:1**
OPTION 2: **Proverbs 19:21**
OPTION 3: **Matthew 6:16-18**

Hebrews 5:11–6:12 presents the writer's third warning to his readers. Lamenting the fact that his readers should have been more spiritually mature, he warned them not to fall into a permanent state of spiritual immaturity and lack of growth. Though no true follower of Christ can lose his or her salvation, faith must be fed to grow.

Using the image of an infant who survives on the nourishment of milk alone, versus an adult who needs the benefits of solid food, the writer told his readers they needed someone to teach them basic Christian doctrines. Because they were still spiritual infants, he advised them to take deliberate action to grow in their faith, love, and hope. Rather than becoming lazy, they should imitate worthy examples of faith and perseverance.

The writer's warning against falling away was direct and harsh. Anyone who turned away from Jesus could expect judgment from God. His gift of salvation was too costly to be taken lightly.

Hebrews 6:3-20 reminds us that God's faithfulness to His promises should encourage believers to maintain our hope in Him and in eternity. Jesus' high priest-hood gives us solid hope anchored in what He has done on our behalf.

HIGHLIGHT • EXPLAIN • APPLY • RESPOND

154//HEBREWS 7

MEMORY VERSES

OPTION 1: **Psalm 63:1**
OPTION 2: **Proverbs 19:21**
OPTION 3: **Matthew 6:16-18**

The writer of Hebrews had concluded chapter 6 by stating that because of Jesus' high priesthood, believers' hope is anchored in what Jesus has done on our behalf. In chapter 7 the writer explained how the priesthood of Melchizedek was far superior to Abraham and Aaron's priesthood.

Melchizedek is mentioned in only three places in Scripture: Genesis 14; Psalm 110; and Hebrews 5–7. In Genesis 14:17-20 we learn that Melchizedek was a priest and a king who blessed Abraham and to whom Abraham paid a tithe. In both the Psalms and Hebrews passages, he's mentioned as a foreshadowing of Jesus, the great High Priest and King of kings. The writer of Hebrews argued that if the sacrificial system under Aaron's priestly line could have redeemed people, a high priest in Melchizedek's order wouldn't have needed to come. Because the sacrificial system couldn't save, however, Jesus came as a High Priest in that order.

The writer of Hebrews pointed to five attributes of Christ that qualified Him to serve in this priestly role: holy, innocent, undefiled, separated from sinners, and exalted above the heavens. Jesus is the Son of God and eternal with God Himself, so the hope provided through Jesus' work as High Priest is guaranteed. Because His priesthood is forever, Jesus' work on the cross to save sinners is permanent, and believers' hope is secure.

HIGHLIGHT · EXPLAIN · APPLY · RESPOND

155//HEBREWS 8

MEMORY VERSES

OPTION 1: **Psalm 63:1**
OPTION 2: **Proverbs 19:21**
OPTION 3: **Matthew 6:16-18**

In Hebrews 8 the writer continued his emphasis on Jesus as the High Priest believers need by bringing attention to God's Old Testament covenant and the tabernacle under Moses. In chapter 7 the writer had presented the need for a high priest who was greater than Aaron, and in chapter 8 he explained the need for a new covenant that was greater than the old.

The old covenant refers to the law God gave to Moses, beginning with the Ten Commandments (see Ex. 20:1-17), and expanded on throughout Deuteronomy and Leviticus. God established this law not only as a standard of living for His people but also as a means of highlighting their sin and their need for Him. It's impossible for anyone to live up to the standards of the old covenant on their own. This reality highlights humanity's need for a Savior and gives insight into the new covenant.

In Hebrews 8:8-12 the writer of Hebrews quoted the prophet Jeremiah (see 31:31-34), who had foretold this new covenant. The covenant Jeremiah described doesn't center on rules and standards but on heart change. Jesus ushered in this new covenant with His atoning work on the cross. The tearing of the temple curtain at the time of Jesus' death shows that through Him all people have access to God and that their hearts are permanently changed by the Holy Spirit's presence. Thankfully, because of Jesus, obedience to the new covenant is possible. God's love and grace can change our hearts forever.

HIGHLIGHT · EXPLAIN · APPLY · RESPOND

156//HEBREWS 9

MEMORY VERSES
OPTION 1: **Psalm 67:1-2**
OPTION 2: **Proverbs 20:1**
OPTION 3: **Matthew 6:19-21**

In chapter 9 the writer of Hebrews continued his contrast between the old covenant and the new covenant. The writer described Jesus as the Priest of the true tabernacle and the Mediator of a better covenant. From God's original design, the tabernacle and its rituals were symbols that pointed forward to Jesus and the redemption from sins His sacrifice would bring. He offered the perfect, once-and-for-all sacrifice—Himself. This superior sacrifice can cleanse us and make us fit to serve God.

To ratify the old covenant, Moses sprinkled the blood of sacrifices on "the tabernacle and all the articles of worship" (v. 21). To ratify the new covenant, Jesus offered His own blood. The permanence and power of Jesus' sacrifice to atone from sin reach far beyond what a ritual sacrifice could accomplish. With His death Jesus offered us permanent forgiveness for sins and eternal life in the presence of God.

Verses 23-28 remind readers that the work of Jesus on our behalf is finished, just as He proclaimed from the cross (see John 19:30). Jesus suffered on the cross to ensure that we don't have to suffer for eternity. Now Jesus continues to do the work of a priest by interceding for us in God's presence. Because our relationship with God is rooted in Jesus and sustained by Him, we're secure in Him forever.

HIGHLIGHT · EXPLAIN · APPLY · RESPOND

157//HEBREWS 10

MEMORY VERSES
OPTION 1: **Psalm 67:1-2**
OPTION 2: **Proverbs 20:1**
OPTION 3: **Matthew 6:19-21**

The writer of Hebrews was convinced that the Jewish sacrificial system was powerless to completely cleanse people of their sins. These sacrifices provided forgiveness, but they had to be repeated. They were insufficient to cleanse the worshiper's heart and conscience. The writer emphasized the system's inability to make anyone right with God and to bring them to spiritually maturity. The repeated sacrifices only reminded the Jews of their sins and of the fact that the sacrifices were ineffective. The writer used the Old Testament to demonstrate that Jesus accomplished what the old covenant's sacrificial system couldn't. Through Jesus' perfect sacrifice, people of faith are made right with God and are set on a path to spiritual maturity.

In verse 19 the author moved from theological to practical teaching by giving direction on the way people live out their faith in Jesus and His sacrifice. Our behavior should reflect our belief that Jesus is the sinless, eternal High Priest who offered Himself as the perfect, once-for-all-time sacrifice for our sins. The writer urged his audience to draw near to God in faith and purity, holding firmly to their confession of hope with the assurance of God's faithfulness. He challenged them to encourage one another to love and do good works while consistently meeting together. He warned them against the danger of sin and the threat of persecution. The instructions in Hebrews 10 remind us that the pursuit of God and the acceptance of sin can't coexist in the Christian life.

HIGHLIGHT · EXPLAIN · APPLY · RESPOND

158//HEBREWS 11

Often referred to as the hall of faith, Hebrews 11 catalogs men and women who displayed exceptional faith in God. First the writer defined *faith* as trusting God to the extent of having assurance in His promised blessings. Noting that a person can't please God without faith, the writer pointed to Noah and Abraham as examples of men who demonstrated faith by their actions.

A major component of faith is trusting God when we don't experience the fulfillment of all His promises, as Abraham and Sarah modeled. Sometimes we experience tests of our faith, like Abraham and Moses. Numerous other Old Testament saints demonstrated faith in God; Rahab, the judges, David, and Samuel are a few the writer named. They didn't see God's ultimate promise fulfilled in Jesus, but through their faith God bore witness to its fulfillment.

All of these examples show us that genuine faith is demonstrated in our obedience to God's promises. The writer also used each hero of the faith to remind readers that sustaining faith is possible throughout any and all circumstances. Genuine faith is trusting God with our lives, including our future. God is looking for this kind of faith in His people.

HIGHLIGHT · EXPLAIN · APPLY · RESPOND

159//HEBREWS 12

MEMORY VERSES

OPTION 1: **Psalm 67:1-2**

OPTION 2: **Proverbs 20:1**

OPTION 3: **Matthew 6:19-21**

In Hebrews 11 the writer had described what faith looks like for Christ followers, as modeled by Old Testament saints. In chapter 12 he compared the life of faith to a marathon that requires great endurance. Along the way we'll face difficulties, some of which come as discipline from God. We can endure these seasons by growing spiritually through them. Like an earthly father's discipline, which may be painful though it yields positive results, God's chastisement of His children is difficult to receive. However, it reminds us of our identity as children of God, and its purpose is always redemption, not condemnation.

In addition, this chapter challenges us to strive for spiritual health and holiness while encouraging us to greater service. When we truly understand the sacrifices God has made to draw us to Himself, as the writer described earlier, we'll desire to show gratitude to Him, primarily through serving and worshiping Him. Through Christ we're also united with one another in deeper community.

Chapter 12 closes with the writer's final warning. He cautions us not to reject God's grace when He pursues us. God's offer of grace is available only until Jesus returns, a day we can't predict, so postponing this decision makes no sense. We aren't guaranteed another opportunity, and the consequence of missing God's grace is eternal. This warning should also motivate believers to a greater sense of urgency to share the message of God's grace with others.

HIGHLIGHT · EXPLAIN · APPLY · RESPOND

160//HEBREWS 13

MEMORY VERSES
OPTION 1: **Psalm 67:1-2**
OPTION 2: **Proverbs 20:1**
OPTION 3: **Matthew 6:19-21**

The Book of Hebrews closes with a series of practical instructions and reminders for people who want to live lives of faith and spiritual maturity like the men and women mentioned in Hebrews 11. The writer's specific challenges in this chapter are themes that repeatedly appear throughout Hebrews and the New Testament as a whole: love, hospitality, compassion, sexual morality, contentment, generosity, trust and confidence in God, gratitude for spiritual leaders, a reminder that Jesus is the fulfillment of Judaism, a call to worship, and obedience to authority. The fact that these themes are emphasized time and again teaches us that they're foundational to living the Christian life. Each theme is rooted in love for God and the desire to make His love evident to those around us.

The closing verses of Hebrews remind us that who we are and how we live ultimately reflect Jesus' work in our lives. He's the One who deserves glory and who equips us to live the life of faith to which we're called. That's good news because God's expectation for us is high; it's not easy to be the type of person these teachings challenge us to be. However, God's new covenant makes it possible. The Spirit of God is working in us, molding us into the image of Jesus day by day.

HIGHLIGHT · EXPLAIN · APPLY · RESPOND

161//1 TIMOTHY 1

MEMORY VERSES

OPTION 1: **Psalm 68:5**
OPTION 2: **Proverbs 20:19**
OPTION 3: **Matthew 6:22-24**

In addition to the letters Paul wrote to churches, he also wrote letters to individuals whom he discipled to be leaders and pastors. Timothy was one of those individuals. Acts 16 records the beginning of their ministry partnership and gives insight into Timothy's spiritual heritage.

Timothy was from Lystra and was likely raised Jewish by his mother, who then converted to Christianity and undoubtedly influenced Timothy in his faith. He most likely became a Christian during or as a result of Paul's time there. Paul began investing in Timothy's life when Timothy was probably still a teenager, and Timothy accompanied Paul on his missionary journeys. The letters of 1–2 Timothy reveal the close bond the two shared in life and ministry. From the beginning Paul referred to Timothy as "my true son in the faith" (1 Tim. 1:2).

Paul began his first letter to Timothy by warning him about false teachers and instructing him on the importance of sound Christian doctrine to combat heresies. Next Paul humbly reminded Timothy of his own sinfulness and need for Christ's forgiveness. Paul's letters to Timothy include several sayings that Paul deemed "trustworthy" (v. 15), and a reminder of Jesus' grace for sinners is the first of those. Paul knew in order to be an effective minister of the gospel, Timothy needed to continually remind himself of the power and extent of God's grace in his own life and in the lives of those to whom he would minister.

HIGHLIGHT · EXPLAIN · APPLY · RESPOND

162//1 TIMOTHY 2

MEMORY VERSES
OPTION 1: **Psalm 68:5**
OPTION 2: **Proverbs 20:19**
OPTION 3: **Matthew 6:22-24**

After Paul gave Timothy instructions for combating false teaching and claiming the truths of the gospel, he gave Timothy specific instructions about church and worship practices. Chapter 2 focuses on general worship practices. Paul began with the importance of congregational prayer. Corporate prayers of intercession and thanksgiving should be made on behalf of all people, including kings and people in authority. The mission of the church is to spread the gospel, and one of the most influential ways to do that is through the salvation of people in authority.

In verse 8 Paul shifted his focus to appropriate responsibilities and behaviors during worship services. The way people conduct themselves in worship matters because it reflects their relationships with God and the state of their hearts. Paul's instruction for men to "pray, lifting up holy hands" has less to do with posture and more to do with purity of heart. Paul called them to be prayer warriors, free from anger and arguments that could divide the church.

Paul's instructions to women had a similar purpose. The world may be impressed by the way women dress, but what matters to God is women with pure hearts, dedicated to loving Him and serving others. These teachings may seem foreign to readers today, but Christianity granted many rights and privileges to first-century women they didn't previously have. New to the faith, they were easily swayed by false teaching and needed the solid teaching that Paul, Timothy, and other male leaders could provide. All of these reminders prove that our character and actions matter to God and have a direct impact on the quality of our worship.

HIGHLIGHT · EXPLAIN · APPLY · RESPOND

163//1 TIMOTHY 3

MEMORY VERSES

OPTION 1: **Psalm 68:5**
OPTION 2: **Proverbs 20:19**
OPTION 3: **Matthew 6:22-24**

Paul continued his instructions on church practice in chapter 3, which shifts the focus from congregants to leaders. Paul began with another trustworthy saying: church leadership is noble work. He focused his instructions on two groups of church leadership: elders (or overseers) and deacons. Godly character is at the heart of the qualifications for both groups, ranging from self-controlled and hospitable to monogamous and sober. It's also important that they manage their households well because they're responsible for managing the local body of Christ.

Speaking specifically to elders, Paul noted that they shouldn't be new to the faith. Elders are the leaders of the church, so it's important that they have strong, tested, steadfast relationships with God, as well as a deep, personal knowledge of Scripture.

While elders are the leaders and overseers of the church, deacons are the servant leaders. The same godly character is expected of them, although they don't have the added burden of church oversight. Their leadership is more narrow in its focus.

Verse 15 reminds readers of the reason these instructions about church practice matter: the church is "God's household," and its mission is to share the gospel of Jesus Christ with the world. This task should never be taken lightly, and nothing is to get in its way.

HIGHLIGHT • EXPLAIN • APPLY • RESPOND

164//1 TIMOTHY 4

In 1 Timothy 4 Paul focused his pastoral instructions on Timothy's personal ministry. At the time Paul wrote this letter, Timothy was leading the young church in Ephesus, a church Paul had started. When the church came under the influence of false teachers who were leading people away from the basic tenets of the gospel, Paul sent Timothy to lead the church back to its roots.

Paul called Timothy to be a leader who stood in contrast to these false teachers. His message and actions should point people to Jesus rather than away from Him. Paul reminded Timothy that he had been placed in a position of responsibility to be a good example to other believers. Paul challenged him to be a strong Christian role model. Most important for a Christian leader is for his life to be firmly rooted in godliness. Another of Paul's trustworthy sayings appears here: our hope is in the living God. Leaders must believe this truth and teach it to others.

Paul also encouraged Timothy not to be discouraged by his youth; spiritual maturity is what matters for church leadership. Recognizing this spiritual maturity in Timothy, Paul tasked him with leading the church in Ephesus, a job that involved preaching and teaching the Scriptures and modeling the life of a disciple. The instructions in these verses are as relevant for pastors today as they were for Timothy in Ephesus.

HIGHLIGHT · EXPLAIN · APPLY · RESPOND

165//1 TIMOTHY 5

MEMORY VERSES

OPTION 1: **Psalm 68:5**
OPTION 2: **Proverbs 20:19**
OPTION 3: **Matthew 6:22-24**

Paul's letter to Timothy continues with more detailed instructions about how Timothy should interact with the widows and elders in his church. Paul wanted Timothy to understand that an exemplary Christian leader should respect people in different life stages, including compassion and admonition to those who need it.

Paul first focused on the widows of the church. He prioritized service to those with the greatest needs, beginning with widows who didn't have children or grandchildren to take care of them. These women should be the church's priority. However, Paul stated that the church's investment in these women was to go hand in hand with their commitment to the church.

Next Paul focused on the elders of the church. He gave Timothy the responsibility to protect and advocate for the elders, as well as to hold them accountable to their calling. Paul knew the elders would be in a position to receive the criticism and complaints of the church, so he encouraged Timothy to defend them as needed.

This chapter is clear that the call to church leadership is a serious calling. God holds church leaders to a higher standard than anyone else because they have the responsibility to shepherd His children. For those who aren't in church leadership, this chapter enhances the need to blanket their leaders with prayer and support.

HIGHLIGHT • EXPLAIN • APPLY • RESPOND

166 //1 TIMOTHY 6

MEMORY VERSES
OPTION 1: **Psalm 81:10**
OPTION 2: **Proverbs 20:27**
OPTION 3: **Matthew 6:25-26**

In chapter 6 Paul drew his letter to a close with more practical advice for Timothy and a final pastoral charge. Paul hadn't addressed the issue of money with Timothy, but it was one that was important for Timothy to handle from a godly perspective. It's also evident from verses 3-5 that the false teachers were preaching for financial gain. They exploited people by accepting a profit in exchange for their teaching.

Paul wanted Timothy to understand the foolishness of greed and the wise pursuit of godliness. To make this point, he contrasted the eternal benefit of godliness and contentment with the temporal benefit of material wealth. The love of money is a terrible trap, but people whom God has blessed with riches are expected to use them for the good of God's kingdom. Rather than focus time and energy on getting rich, Paul told Timothy to flee from greed and other sins and to spend his days pursuing "righteousness, godliness, faith, love, endurance, and gentleness" (v. 11).

This teaching was the culmination of Paul's letter to Timothy. The pursuit of god-liness is essential to the Christian life; it's the way we ensure that we're following God and growing in our faith. When we're devoted to our relationship with God and invested in making disciples, He uses us to make a difference in the world, just as He used Timothy and Paul.

HIGHLIGHT · EXPLAIN · APPLY · RESPOND

167//2 TIMOTHY 1

MEMORY VERSES

OPTION 1: **Psalm 81:10**

OPTION 2: **Proverbs 20:27**

OPTION 3: **Matthew 6:25-26**

The exact amount of time that passed between Paul's first and second letters to Timothy is unknown, but it's clear that Paul's circumstances had drastically changed. Second Timothy is thought to be Paul's last letter, and he wrote it from a prison cell in Rome just prior to his execution. The apostle's sense of urgency is evident throughout this letter.

From Acts and 1 Timothy we know that Paul and Timothy were very close as ministers of the gospel, so we shouldn't be surprised that Timothy was one of the last people Paul wrote to before his death. The opening words of this letter also highlight that close bond. Their gospel partnership was an ongoing encouragement to Paul, and he wrote about the strength of Timothy's faith. It's interesting to note how influential Timothy's mother and grandmother had been in Timothy's spiritual growth. Nurturing and strengthening the seeds of faith they had planted in Timothy, Paul also trained him in ministry.

Paul further reminded Timothy of the content of the gospel message, which is built on Jesus. Just as Jesus immensely suffered to bring the gospel to us, sharing the gospel with others may bring us suffering, as it had for Paul. That reality should only strengthen our ministry efforts, however, because it means the power of the gospel is evident in and through our lives.

Using himself as the model, Paul reminded Timothy that discipleship should be paramount in his ministry. At its core, discipleship is about sharing the "sound teaching" (2 Tim. 1:13) of Scripture with others in order to help them grow in their faith. This was the ministry to which God had called Timothy in Ephesus, and He fully equipped Timothy to live out that calling. Discipleship is the calling we all share as followers of Jesus today.

HIGHLIGHT · EXPLAIN · APPLY · RESPOND

168//2 TIMOTHY 2

MEMORY VERSES

OPTION 1: **Psalm 81:10**
OPTION 2: **Proverbs 20:27**
OPTION 3: **Matthew 6:25-26**

Paul began 2 Timothy 2 with a series of commands that challenged Timothy in his ministry and faith: be strong, commit, share in suffering, and remember (see vv. 1-8). Effectiveness in ministry would be determined by how well Timothy would take what Paul had entrusted to him and commit that to faithful men, who were to invest it in others (see v. 2).

Paul warned Timothy that the days of ministry ahead of him would be difficult and that he could expect to suffer in ways similar to Paul. To help Timothy understand what to expect as a gospel servant, Paul used several illustrations of people who endure hardship to achieve a worthwhile goal: soldiers, athletes, and farmers. Each group must make sacrifices to do its work well.

Unlike those groups, however, the ultimate sacrifice had already been made for believers. Nothing Christians suffer can compare to the suffering of Jesus. Paul followed up with another trustworthy saying, the first in 2 Timothy: because of Jesus' victory over death, we know our future is secure. No amount of suffering on earth can change the fact that we're God's children and that we'll spend eternity with Him.

The various teachings that make up verses 14-26 were intended to spur on Timothy and the church toward holy living. Paul's teaching points out that God calls us to regularly practice repentance both by turning away from sin and by actively submitting our lives to Christ.

HIGHLIGHT · EXPLAIN · APPLY · RESPOND

169//2 TIMOTHY 3

MEMORY VERSES

OPTION 1: **Psalm 81:10**

OPTION 2: **Proverbs 20:27**

OPTION 3: **Matthew 6:25-26**

In the second half of 2 Timothy, Paul shifted his focus to the days that lie ahead for Christians, days of persecution and godlessness. Having already encouraged Timothy to stand strong in his faith, Paul identified nineteen sinful behaviors that will characterize unbelievers living in the last days, from ingratitude and unholiness to abusiveness and greed. The issue at the root of all these behaviors is placing love of self over love of God. Verse 5 indicates that even seemingly religious people will be among those Paul described.

Timothy was to avoid these behaviors and the people practicing them. Instead, Timothy's responsibility was to emphasize God's truth. Because of the degradation of the world around him, persecution for his faithfulness was all but guaranteed. Paul encouraged Timothy not to give up the fight, though, because he had the power of God and His Word on his side. The truth of Scripture would stand up against anything Timothy faced because it's the Word of God, breathed out by God Himself. God's Word convicts of sin and teaches us how to pursue righteousness. Scripture reveals who God is and how to live for Him. Timothy was a student of the Word, as all Christians should be, because it's the tool we need to live out the mission God has given us. Through Scripture we learn how to be disciples of Jesus who make disciples, the goal of the Christian life.

HIGHLIGHT · EXPLAIN · APPLY · RESPOND

170//2 TIMOTHY 4

MEMORY VERSES

OPTION 1: **Psalm 81:10**
OPTION 2: **Proverbs 20:27**
OPTION 3: **Matthew 6:25-26**

In chapter 4 Paul continued to warn Timothy about the last days, emphasizing the need to be prepared for persecution and equipped for right living. Timothy's guide through all these difficulties must be the inspired Word of God, which would profit him in all areas of belief and behavior.

Because of the power of God's Word and the prevalence of sin in society, Paul reminded Timothy to preach the Word at all times and in all seasons. To preach includes more than standing behind a pulpit to deliver a sermon. We all have opportunities to make known the truth of God's Word. We must live the faith and witness to the truth all the time.

Paul's image of pouring himself out as a drink offering (see v. 6) was his way of telling Timothy that he was about to make the ultimate sacrifice for God: he was going to die for his faith. To do so was to live life to the fullest, in Paul's mind. He had faithfully committed his life to the mission Jesus had given him on the road to Damascus, and he couldn't wait to spend eternity in God's presence.

In closing his letter to Timothy, Paul included personal notes and final wishes to see people before his death. The letter of 2 Timothy challenges readers to faithfully and wholeheartedly serve God and live out the mission to which He has called us. There will be seasons when our faith will be stretched further than we can imagine, but we must stand firm in the Lord because eternity is at stake.

HIGHLIGHT · EXPLAIN · APPLY · RESPOND

171//TITUS 1

MEMORY VERSES

OPTION 1: **Psalm 82:3-4**

OPTION 2: **Proverbs 21:1**

OPTION 3: **Matthew 6:27-28**

The letter to Titus is another letter Paul wrote to an individual, along the lines of 1–2 Timothy. Like Timothy, Titus was most likely introduced to Christianity by Paul, and he accompanied Paul on part of his missionary journey, traveling to Crete, the largest Greek island, located in the Mediterranean Sea.

Titus was Greek, so when Paul decided someone needed to stay and oversee the new churches in Crete, it made perfect sense for Titus to be that person. Evidently, he had learned enough from Paul that Paul trusted him with this responsibility. Paul never forgot his partners in ministry, and Titus was no exception. This letter was one way Paul continued to equip and encourage Titus after they parted ways.

Chapter 1 reminded Titus of the work Paul wanted him to accomplish in Crete, namely bringing leadership and structure to the new churches on the island. He was to appoint elders, and verses 6-9 reminded him of characteristics essential to that role: blameless, monogamous, humble, self-controlled, hospitable, holy, and so on. This list is very similar to the one in 1 Timothy 3.

In Titus 1:10-16 Paul gave the reason behind the need for structure and clear leadership: young Christians in Crete were in danger of believing the lies of false teachers. Strong leadership in the church would help protect the growing faith of these new believers.

HIGHLIGHT · EXPLAIN · APPLY · RESPOND

172//TITUS 2

In Titus 1 Paul had introduced the problem of false teachers in Crete. He began chapter 2 by identifying the clearest way to offset the dangers of false teaching: teach the Bible. A faith rooted in God's Word alone is the surest way to avoid being led astray from the gospel. This is why it was so important for Titus and the other leaders of the church to "proclaim things consistent with sound teaching" (v. 1).

Paul dedicated the next section of his letter to specific instructions that showed Titus how to lead specific groups in the church, including older men, older women, younger women, younger men, and slaves. Although each group received specific instructions, the themes of godliness, self-control, reverence, and commitment to the gospel applied to each group.

Verses 11-14 summarize Paul's instructions with a word for all believers. Christians are to behave in the manner Paul described because God's grace has been made known to them. When we understand and accept God's gift of grace, it transforms us from people who are worldly and self-consumed to people who pursue lives of godliness as we wait for Jesus' return. When we exhibit the traits of spiritual maturity and selflessness that Paul described, our lives look markedly different from the world around us. Our lives begin to look more and more like Jesus, and this resemblance draws other people to Him.

HIGHLIGHT · EXPLAIN · APPLY · RESPOND

173//TITUS 3

MEMORY VERSES

OPTION 1: **Psalm 82:3-4**
OPTION 2: **Proverbs 21:1**
OPTION 3: **Matthew 6:27-28**

While Titus 2 focused on being grounded in the gospel and relating to one another in the church, chapter 3 broadens that instruction to include the way believers conduct themselves in the world. This teaching includes being submissive to governmental leaders and having an attitude marked by obedience, kindness, peace, and humility.

Why does a Christian's attitude matter? Paul explained in verses 3-8 that knowing Christ dramatically changes a person's life, and that change should be evident in behaviors and attitudes as well. The traits Paul encouraged the Christians in Crete to express are characteristics Jesus modeled while on earth. They're also fruit of the Spirit that should mark the life of every believer. Paul presented a stark contrast between who these believers were before knowing Jesus and who they were in Him; the same comparison defines the life of every Christian today.

These verses constitute another of Paul's trustworthy sayings, an important reminder of the power of the gospel at work in a person's life. Paul wanted Titus to remind those to whom he ministered that Christ had changed them and that their lives should give evidence of that transformation.

As with all of his letters, Paul closed his letter to Titus with a personal note. The letter to Titus reminds us of the importance of sound doctrine and godly living as the foundations of healthy church life and of our witness to the world.

HIGHLIGHT · EXPLAIN · APPLY · RESPOND

174//1 PETER 1

MEMORY VERSES
OPTION 1: **Psalm 82:3-4**
OPTION 2: **Proverbs 21:1**
OPTION 3: **Matthew 6:27-28**

Included among the books of the New Testament are two letters the apostle Peter wrote to groups of Christians. In his first letter Peter addressed both Jewish and Gentile Christians who were experiencing violent persecution. He encouraged his readers to persevere in their faith and to brace for future attacks.

Peter began his letter with a statement of praise to God for Jesus and the hope and security available in Him. Peter also addressed head-on the sufferings his readers were experiencing. Interestingly, though, he did more than acknowledge their suffering; he described suffering as a faith builder. Verse 8 is a testimony to the faith of the early Christians. Through faith they loved Jesus and were whole-heartedly and joyfully committed to living for Him, no matter what they faced.

Verses 13-25 called readers to an active faith that has the pursuit of holiness as its goal. These teachings have implications for our lives as Christ followers today. The basis for Christian hope is Jesus' resurrection and the promise of eternal life. In light of eternity, our trials are temporary and serve to refine our faith. As we await Jesus' return, we're to live holy lives. In obedience to God, we're to reflect His holiness in our behavior. All this is possible because Jesus has redeemed us from our old, sinful way of life.

HIGHLIGHT • EXPLAIN • APPLY • RESPOND

175//1 PETER 2

MEMORY VERSES
OPTION 1: **Psalm 82:3-4**
OPTION 2: **Proverbs 21:1**
OPTION 3: **Matthew 6:27-28**

In chapter 2 Peter used several images to help us understand how Christ has changed us.

1. We've received a new diet, which Peter described as spiritual milk, that helps us grow in Christlikeness (see vv. 1-3). When we pursue Christ through the study of His Word, discipleship with other believers, and other disciplines, God empowers us to live godly lives that are set apart from the characteristics of the world, like those listed in verse 1: malice, deceit, hypocrisy, envy, and slander.

2. The second image Peter used was a new spiritual house (see vv. 4-8). This image refers to the church, which Peter described as a group of people growing into Christlikeness together.

3. The third image Peter included was a new family (see vv. 9-10), described by such phrases as "a chosen race, a royal priesthood, a holy nation, a people for his [God's] possession" (v. 9).

Each phrase reminds us that we're children of God, brothers and sisters united in His mercy and grace. God made us His children so that we'll tell the world about who He is and what He has done to redeem us.

In the second half of this chapter, Peter shifted his emphasis from a reminder of who his readers were in Christ to instructions on how they were to live. Because of the suffering they faced for their faith, his teaching on respecting authority would have been hard to obey. But that was his call, and he used Jesus as the ultimate example of someone who suffered in a God-honoring way.

HIGHLIGHT · EXPLAIN · APPLY · RESPOND

176//1 PETER 3

Peter continued his instruction on believers' behavior amid persecution by turning his attention to Christian marriages. He began with counsel for wives, whom he challenged to submit to their husbands, to focus on inner purity rather than on outer attire, and to extend goodwill toward others. One motivating factor was to win over spouses who weren't yet Christians, a common situation among the first converts to Christianity. Peter's hope was that the women would behave in a way that pointed their husbands to Christ with both words and actions, and he used the Old Testament example of Sarah for support.

Peter challenged husbands to honor their wives, who had an equal spiritual status but needed spiritual leadership from their husbands. Beginning in verse 8, Peter broadened his instructions to all Christians. He encouraged believers to get along with one another, blessing one another through sympathy, compassion, love, and humility.

Repeatedly throughout his letter Peter returned to the topic of suffering. In this chapter he used the reality of suffering as a reminder to live in a way that witnesses to other people. When Christians respond to suffering with hope and increased faith, they put God's power and love on display. This is why it was so important for Peter's audience to be fully prepared to share the gospel, the "reason for the hope that is in you" (v. 15). Our lives and our speech should always glorify God, even in our trials.

HIGHLIGHT • EXPLAIN • APPLY • RESPOND

177//1 PETER 4

MEMORY VERSES

OPTION 1: **Psalm 84:10**
OPTION 2: **Proverbs 21:15**
OPTION 3: **Matthew 6:29-30**

Chapter 4 emphasizes sharing in Christ's suffering and resting in the promises that come through His victory over sin and death on the cross. With Christ as our example, we're to demonstrate the same resolve with which Jesus obeyed God's will and loved and served others, with our focus always on the promise of eternity. Peter reminded his readers of their lifestyle before they met Christ, and he warned that many people would tempt them to fall back into their previous sins. Because this temptation would be great, it was important for them to keep the gospel at the forefront of their minds. Peter reminded them that the wicked would have to give an account to the Lord, who judges "the living and the dead" (v. 5).

Verses 7-11 return to a brief series of commands for Christian living. Jesus promises to return soon, a time we won't know and can't predict, so the way we live in the meantime matters. Peter emphasized prayer, love, hospitality, service, and faithfully using our spiritual gifts.

Peter returned to the issue of suffering in verse 12, this time emphasizing suffering for our faith. This type of suffering shouldn't come as a surprise. Jesus endured this type of suffering, and He repeatedly warned His followers that it would be a part of their experience too. Because of the Holy Spirit's active presence in our lives, we're empowered both to endure suffering and to live for Christ. There's good news in suffering for the faith. It indicates that we're faithfully living for God and that other people notice our faithfulness to Him.

HIGHLIGHT · EXPLAIN · APPLY · RESPOND

178//1 PETER 5

Peter closed his first letter with final thoughts on suffering for faith, directed first to specific groups in the church and then to the church as a whole. Peter encouraged church leaders to take their spiritual calling seriously. They were to be active shepherds who protected and cared for the people entrusted to them. They were also to serve with humility and compassion. Shepherding people through such tumultuous times wouldn't be easy, but church leaders could find strength and motivation in the future glory of Christ.

The theme of humility runs through the rest of Peter's instructions in this chapter. In verse 5 he turned his attention to those who were younger, urging them to respect and submit to their leaders. Peter warned against the rise of pride in a person's life and expected all believers to relate to one another and to God in humility. Peter's exhortation is especially important in light of the presence of the devil, who still actively targets Christians today. The image of Satan as "a roaring lion, looking for anyone he can devour" (v. 8) paints a vivid picture of his predatory, deadly behavior. The only appropriate response to him is to resist him through faith in Jesus.

Peter concluded his letter by encouraging Christians with the promise that the sovereign God would help them endure any trial that came their way. Then, like the writers of many New Testament letters, he closed with a few personal remarks. The letter of 1 Peter can be summed up by the author's counsel to stand firm in the gospel (see v. 12).

HIGHLIGHT · EXPLAIN · APPLY · RESPOND

179//2 PETER 1

MEMORY VERSES

OPTION 1: **Psalm 84:10**
OPTION 2: **Proverbs 21:15**
OPTION 3: **Matthew 6:29-30**

While Peter's first letter was meant to encourage believers in the midst of persecution, his second letter was directed to the general body of believers. Believing his life would soon end (see 1:14), Peter wrote this letter to provide urgent instructions and warnings he wanted to give to the early church. It primarily emphasizes warnings against false teaching (a theme in most of the New Testament letters), practical Christian living, and growing in the knowledge of God.

In chapter 1 Peter described the power of God, which transforms the Christian heart. Through His power we're able to flee sinfulness and pursue godliness. Peter went on to list characteristics of godliness the Holy Spirit produces in our lives. They include (but aren't limited to) goodness, knowledge, self-control, endurance, godliness, brotherly affection, and love. The motivation for these qualities is usefulness in the kingdom of God; they motivate us to pursue God more deeply and to share His love with others.

The remainder of this chapter emphasizes the validity of Scripture and the eyewitness testimony of Peter and other apostles. Peter wanted his readers to firmly plant their faith in Scripture and believe it could be trusted as the primary source and guide for their spiritual lives. Believers' lives are to be rooted in their faith in God, which will grow as they practice it and seek God as He has revealed Himself in Jesus Christ. The gospel the apostles preached is a trustworthy source for this knowledge, and it remains as true today as it was when they spoke it.

HIGHLIGHT • EXPLAIN • APPLY • RESPOND

180//2 PETER 2

MEMORY VERSES

OPTION 1: **Psalm 84:10**
OPTION 2: **Proverbs 21:15**
OPTION 3: **Matthew 6:29-30**

In chapter 2 Peter explained why his readers needed to base their faith in God on the truth of the gospel: because there were counterfeiters among them. Coming at the church from the outside world was a barrage of heretical, blasphemous teachers and doctrine that had been disguised to look like Christianity. Peter painted a scathing picture of these teachers. They were primarily motivated by greed, which led them to teach any lie they thought would bring them the most money.

At its extreme this false teaching denied Jesus and His work on the cross altogether. However, the judgment of God was waiting for these false teachers. Peter reminded his readers of God's wrath against sinful angels, the people of Noah's day, and the cities of Sodom and Gomorrah. The same judgment awaited the false teachers of Peter's day.

In contrast, Peter called to mind Noah and Lot as examples of people who pursued righteousness in the midst of unrighteousness and, as a result, received God's grace rather than judgment. Peter encouraged his readers to be like Noah and Lot, remaining committed to God and His truths, no matter how people tried to influence them. Peter implored his readers to avoid these teachers at all costs and to hold firm to the truth of the gospel that came from those who actually lived with Jesus and witnessed His teachings.

HIGHLIGHT · EXPLAIN · APPLY · RESPOND

181//2 PETER 3

MEMORY VERSES
OPTION 1: **Psalm 85:6-7**
OPTION 2: **Proverbs 21:23**
OPTION 3: **Matthew 6:31-32**

Peter's examination of the false teachers reached a climax in chapter 3, in which he reminded his readers to remember what the prophets and apostles had spoken. He implored his readers to bear in mind the imminent return of the Lord. It's clear that a chief argument of the false teachers was that Jesus wasn't coming back, and they used the delay since His ascension as proof for their case.

Peter, however, reminded readers of the power of God to act swiftly whenever He chooses, as He did with creation and again with the flood. Jesus' return will be the precursor to God's final judgment of the world, so any delay of that return is an act of mercy and patience on God's part, not evidence that He has failed to keep His promises or that He doesn't exist at all. Because God is patient, He wants everyone to come to know Him through repentance and faith (see v. 9).

Jesus will come back "like a thief" (v. 10)—unexpectedly—which means a day will come when His offer of grace and salvation will no longer be available. Rather than watching the clock for Jesus to return, we should share the gospel and help Him draw people everywhere into a relationship with Him while time remains. This theme recalls the beginning of the letter, in which Peter implored believers to live upright, moral lives in full devotion to the teachings of Jesus Christ as they expectantly await His return.

HIGHLIGHT · EXPLAIN · APPLY · RESPOND

182//JOHN 1

MEMORY VERSES
OPTION 1: **Psalm 85:6-7**
OPTION 2: **Proverbs 21:23**
OPTION 3: **Matthew 6:31-32**

John, one of Jesus' apostles, wrote his Gospel to prove that Jesus is God incarnate, the divine Son of God who came to earth as a man. John 1 focuses on Jesus' divinity and role in creation, as well as the start of His earthly ministry. The Word, Jesus, is divine, distinct from God the Father but one with Him. God created everything through the Word. Nothing came into being without His direct involvement. Life came through Jesus, who provided the light of God's love and guidance. As the creation of physical light dispelled the darkness on the first day of creation (see Gen. 1:3), Jesus' light pierced the darkness of sin to provide eternal salvation for those who believe in Him. Although the Word created the world, people didn't recognize or respond to Him. Despite that rejection, some people accepted Jesus, believing in Him as Savior.

John's Gospel also emphasizes the humanity of Jesus. By coming in human form, Jesus allowed us to see the glory of God. John the Baptist's witness proved true as Jesus' life, ministry, death, and resurrection revealed God's grace and truth. In Jesus we find grace, truth, and salvation. Once Christ changes our lives, we, like the first disciples who answered Jesus' call to follow Him, are compelled to live in a way that demonstrates the power of the gospel, pointing other people to Jesus.

HIGHLIGHT · EXPLAIN · APPLY · RESPOND

182//JOHN 1 191

183//JOHN 2

After establishing Jesus' identity as the Son of God and describing the formation of His group of disciples, John marked the beginning of Jesus' earthly ministry with the account of the first miracle Jesus performed. Jesus and His mother, Mary, were attending a wedding celebration, and the hosts ran out of wine. Mary asked Jesus to help them. Jesus used the opportunity to give the people closest to Him a glimpse of who He was and of His power. They didn't know it yet, but the Jesus who created wine from water is the same Jesus who created the world from nothing by speaking it into existence. John noted that this miracle solidified His disciples' faith in Him and first revealed His glory to the world.

Following this miracle, Jesus traveled to Jerusalem for the Passover. When He went into the temple and found it overrun by vendors and money changers, He cast them out. His reference to the temple as "my Father's house" (v. 16) was a clear statement of His divinity and of His relationship with God the Father. The temple, which should have been devoted to worshiping God, had been turned into a marketplace where people attempted to turn worship into profit. Jesus' action made the point that one reason He came was to draw people and their worship back to God. This event also established His religious authority and initiated the tensions that would escalate between Himself and the Jewish religious leaders, a tension that would eventually lead to the cross.

HIGHLIGHT · EXPLAIN · APPLY · RESPOND

184//JOHN 3

MEMORY VERSES
OPTION 1: **Psalm 85:6-7**
OPTION 2: **Proverbs 21:23**
OPTION 3: **Matthew 6:31-32**

John's Gospel includes more of Jesus' conversations than the other Gospels, which focus more on His actions. John 3–4 include two of those important conversations. John 3 recounts Jesus' encounter with a man named Nicodemus, who was a Pharisee, a religious leader during Jesus' day. Having witnessed some of Jesus' miracles and having seen the authority with which He spoke and acted, Nicodemus was curious enough to seek out Jesus at night and discover what else He could learn about Him.

Nicodemus believed God had sent Jesus, but he didn't know Jesus was the promised Messiah, the Savior the Jews were waiting for. Jesus' conversation with Nicodemus sheds light on what's required for a person to enter the kingdom of God: a relationship with Jesus. At the heart of Jesus' teaching is the concept of being born again, which describes the life-changing effect of the Holy Spirit in a person's life. This change takes place as people confess their belief that Jesus is the Son of God, who died to pay the price for their sins. That confession makes way for the forgiving power of God's grace.

John 3:16-18 gives Jesus' first concise explanation of why He came to earth. Jesus, the Son of God, came to save people from their sins. Though we don't immediately learn how Nicodemus responded to what he heard from Jesus that night, verses 22-30 show that John the Baptist clearly knew who Jesus was and why He came. When questioned about Jesus' baptizing work, John acknowledged that his role as the forerunner of the Messiah was complete, and now it was time for Jesus to take over the work of calling people to repentance and faith.

HIGHLIGHT · EXPLAIN · APPLY · RESPOND

185//JOHN 4

MEMORY VERSES

OPTION 1: **Psalm 85:6-7**
OPTION 2: **Proverbs 21:23**
OPTION 3: **Matthew 6:31-32**

In John 4 we read about another important conversation Jesus had early in his ministry. During His travels Jesus passed through Samaria. While in the town of Sychar, Jesus stopped to rest at a well when a woman came to draw water. The woman Jesus met that day couldn't have been more different from Nicodemus, the Pharisee. Although she had no idea who Jesus was when she met Him, she knew He was a Jew, and as a Samaritan woman, she wasn't supposed to associate with Him.

Jesus used this opportunity to figuratively describe who He was and what He had to offer her. Jesus depicted the new life available in Him as "living water" (v. 10). The image of living water that forever satisfies a person's spiritual thirst represents eternal life with God, one benefit of salvation from sin through Jesus. Intrigued, the woman asked more questions, and the knowledge Jesus revealed about her and her personal life opened her eyes to who He was.

When the woman mentioned the Messiah, Jesus affirmed that she was speaking to Him. The woman's belief in Jesus is evident in verses 28-29,39-42, in which we read that she told everyone she met about her conversation with Jesus and that those people sought out Jesus too.

Both of the spiritual conversations in John 3–4 give us insight into salvation and remind us that Jesus is central to salvation. Only a relationship with Him brings the spiritual satisfaction and fulfillment we desire.

HIGHLIGHT · EXPLAIN · APPLY · RESPOND

186//JOHN 5

MEMORY VERSES
OPTION 1: **Psalm 86:5**
OPTION 2: **Proverbs 22:1**
OPTION 3: **Matthew 6:33-34**

John was very selective in the miracles he chose to include in his Gospel. John 5 presents another miracle that highlights Jesus' role as the divine Son of the Trinity. In order to heal the lame man beside the pool of Bethesda, Jesus did nothing more than speak, telling him to get up and walk. Jesus didn't touch him, and the words He spoke weren't necessarily words of healing, just a command. But because the Creator of the universe spoke these words, they had the power to heal and restore this man.

The controversy surrounding this miracle was that Jesus healed on the Sabbath, violating the pharisaical law. However, Jesus was the Lord of the Sabbath, and His response to the critics, "My Father is still working, and I am working also" (v. 17), was both a statement of His authority as the Son of God and a point of great contention with the Pharisees. Instead of fleeing the scene when the Jews grew angry with Him, Jesus took the opportunity to describe in great detail who He was and His relationship to God the Father.

This testimony about Jesus' identity and mission teaches us that as the Son, Jesus followed the Father's instructions and obeyed the Father's commands. In obedience to His Father, Jesus said He would fulfill His roles as both Savior and Judge. Jesus also affirmed that the messianic prophecies of John the Baptist and the Old Testament prophets were spoken about Him.

HIGHLIGHT · EXPLAIN · APPLY · RESPOND

187//JOHN 6

MEMORY VERSES

OPTION 1: **Psalm 86:5**
OPTION 2: **Proverbs 22:1**
OPTION 3: **Matthew 6:33-34**

While the four Gospels have many points of similarity, they also have considerable differences because each Gospel writer wanted to communicate a unique message to a particular audience. Among the teachings and content unique to John's Gospel are the "I am" statements of Jesus, the first of which appears in John 6. John had just recorded Jesus' testimony that He was the Son of God, and with each of these "I am" statements, Jesus revealed some of His attributes and functions as the Son, using images that would be easy for listeners to understand.

John 6 begins with Jesus' feeding miracle, when He produced abundant food for the multitude from a young boy's five loaves of bread and two fish. Following that miracle, Jesus said, "I am the bread of life" (v. 35). By meeting the people's physical need for food and then declaring Himself to be the Bread of life, Jesus helped the people see that He alone could satisfy their spiritual hunger.

Everyone is born with spiritual hunger, whether or not they recognize it, and people attempt to substitute many things to fill this spiritual void, including religion, materialism, and relationships. But the only thing capable of satisfying a person's spiritual hunger is to know Jesus as his or her loving, all-sufficient Savior.

HIGHLIGHT · EXPLAIN · APPLY · RESPOND

188//JOHN 7

Because of his interest in proving that Jesus was the Son of God, John gave focused attention to the ways various people responded to Jesus. He had already mentioned the growing hatred of the religious leaders, and in John 7 we see that they weren't the only ones. Verse 5 notes that many Jews, including Jesus' own brothers, didn't believe He was the promised Messiah.

The tension in this scene stems from Jesus' brothers' desire for Him to go to the Feast of the Tabernacles in Jerusalem so that He could grow His following, not for the glory of God but for His own glory and fame. As Jesus had explained to Mary at the wedding reception (see John 2:4), Jesus knew the time for the culmination of His ministry hadn't yet arrived.

In contrast, when Jesus went and taught in the temple, He pointed listeners to the glory and honor of God. His teaching also highlighted His authority as the Son of God and His mission to draw people to the Father and bestow the Holy Spirit on them. Not surprisingly, the words Jesus spoke created more controversy, with some people affirming that He was the Christ and others refusing to believe because He didn't fit the image of the Messiah they expected (see 7:40-43).

Jesus continues to be as controversial and divisive today as He was for the Jews. The foundation for faith isn't what we imagine Jesus should do for us or what He should be like but what He has done for us through the cross.

HIGHLIGHT · EXPLAIN · APPLY · RESPOND

189//JOHN 8

MEMORY VERSES

OPTION 1: **Psalm 86:5**
OPTION 2: **Proverbs 22:1**
OPTION 3: **Matthew 6:33-34**

The second of Jesus' "I am" statements is the focus of John 8. In addition to calling Himself the Bread of life, Jesus proclaimed, "I am the light of the world" (v. 12). Darkness versus light is a frequent symbol throughout the Bible, with darkness symbolizing evil and light symbolizing good. By calling Himself "the light of the world" and "the light of life" (v. 12), Jesus claimed that all goodness originates with Him and that He alone is a person's hope to escape the darkness of the world. This was a symbolic way of describing the gospel, the salvation from sin and death available to all people through belief in Jesus.

Claims like this increased the tension between Jesus and the Jewish religious leaders, who couldn't bring themselves to believe this was their Messiah. In the dialogue that continued throughout this chapter, Jesus condemned the Jews for their lack of belief in Him, saying they would die in their sins and be eternally separated from God because of their unbelief in Him.

In contrast, Jesus affirmed the faith and eternal security of people who believed in Him. To those people He spoke the encouraging words "You will know the truth, and the truth will set you free" (v. 32). Jesus made it clear that people are either united with God through belief in Him or are God's enemies through disbelief. The same remains true today. This reality reminds us of the importance of telling others about the hope we have in the Light of the world.

HIGHLIGHT · EXPLAIN · APPLY · RESPOND

190//JOHN 9

MEMORY VERSES
OPTION 1: **Psalm 86:5**
OPTION 2: **Proverbs 22:1**
OPTION 3: **Matthew 6:33-34**

The text of John 9 continues to explore the implications of Jesus' identity as the Light of the world by recording another of Jesus' healing miracles. The chapter begins by describing an encounter Jesus and His disciples had with a blind man. The disciples asked a common question in Jesus' day: "Who sinned, this man or his parents, that he was born blind?" (v. 2). In that day people often blamed sin as the reason for a person's physical ailments. Jesus challenged this belief by stating the opposite: this man was blind so that God's glory and works would be displayed. Jesus, the light of the world, would bring this blind man out of both physical and spiritual blindness by restoring His sight. The symbolism is striking.

Again, the hope Jesus brought to this man's life stood in direct contrast to the doubt and disbelief of others Jesus encountered. With each chapter of John's Gospel, the gap between belief and unbelief widened. While the blind man was able to proclaim, "One thing I do know: I was blind, and now I can see!" (v. 25) and "I believe, Lord!" (v. 38), the Pharisees became increasingly more blind in their disbelief (see v. 41). Jesus didn't come to save people who are sinless; Scripture makes it clear that such a person doesn't exist. Jesus came to save sinners who recognize their sinfulness and their need for a Savior. These are the blind people for whom Jesus offers sight.

HIGHLIGHT · EXPLAIN · APPLY · RESPOND

191//JOHN 10

MEMORY VERSES

OPTION 1: **Psalm 90:12**
OPTION 2: **Proverbs 22:6**
OPTION 3: **Matthew 7:1-2**

In John 10 the Gospel writer's image shifts from light to sheep. Two "I am" statements by Jesus appear in this chapter, and both use the culturally relevant illustration of a shepherd and his sheep to help readers better understand Jesus' identity and mission.

The first "I am" declaration appears in verses 7-9, in which Jesus stated, "I am the gate for the sheep" (v. 7). Like the image of the Light of the world, this statement also describes Jesus as the only access to God and the life available in Him. Salvation comes through Him, and He protects His sheep (anyone who believes in Him) from harm.

Furthermore, Jesus described Himself as the Good Shepherd (see v. 11). As the Shepherd, Jesus provides food and comfort for the sheep, protects them from predators, knows them personally, looks for more sheep to take care of, and even dies for His sheep. With this picture Jesus told us that He loves us and considers us His own children whom He protects and provides for.

The sheep recognize their Shepherd's voice and can even distinguish it from the voices of other shepherds. They obey their Shepherd's commands because they know He's working for their good and is always looking out for them. This knowledge allows them to fully trust His love and give them control of their lives. This is how Jesus wants us to live in a relationship with Him. He wants us to know that He loves us and will always take care of us, and He wants us to trust Him with our lives.

HIGHLIGHT · EXPLAIN · APPLY · RESPOND

192//JOHN 11

John 11 records one of Jesus' greatest miracles: the resurrection of Lazarus from the grave. Lazarus was the brother of Mary and Martha, two women who prominently figured in Jesus' life and ministry. When Lazarus grew sick, his sisters turned to Jesus. Having seen Him heal many people before, they knew He could save their brother's life. Although Jesus affirmed that like the affliction of the blind man, Lazarus's sickness was for God's glory, He didn't rush to heal him. Instead, Lazarus died and was buried. When Jesus arrived four days later, the sisters questioned His lack of action, but their belief and faith in Him didn't waver.

Lazarus's death presented Jesus with the opportunity to further establish His authority by showing that He had authority even over death, something only God Himself could claim. Jesus physically raised Lazarus from the dead, an action that paralleled the spiritual resurrection He offers to all of us who are dead in our sin.

Another "I am" statement in John's Gospel is found in this account. Jesus said, "I am the resurrection and the life" (v. 25). Only through a relationship with Jesus is eternal life in God's presence possible. After this miracle the threat against Jesus' life intensified, and the cross drew nearer.

HIGHLIGHT · EXPLAIN · APPLY · RESPOND

193//JOHN 12

MEMORY VERSES
OPTION 1: **Psalm 90:12**
OPTION 2: **Proverbs 22:6**
OPTION 3: **Matthew 7:1-2**

John 12 serves as the transitional chapter between Jesus' earthly ministry and the events surrounding His death. Opposition to Him rapidly increased after He raised Lazarus from the dead, and His own death was approaching. Jesus' knowledge of his impending death made the scene in which Mary publicly anointed Him with burial oils even more symbolic. In John's account of this scene, readers learn more about Jesus' understanding of the upcoming events and gain insight into the greed that would lead to Judas's betrayal.

Throughout John's Gospel the writer made the case for Jesus' divinity, and his account of Jesus' triumphal entry into Jerusalem was no different. Although John didn't go into many details, he included two Old Testament passages that drew attention to Jesus' fulfillment of prophecies about the Messiah.

The remainder of John 12 is a final public call to believe in Jesus, the Light of the world. Jesus referred to the events that would come, His death and resurrection, as His time to be glorified and the reason for His coming to earth. Jesus left the crowds with the call to believe in Him while they had the chance. The benefits of belief described in this chapter remain the same for those who believe in Jesus today: we become "children of light" (v. 36) and gain eternal life with the Father.

HIGHLIGHT • EXPLAIN • APPLY • RESPOND

194//JOHN 13

MEMORY VERSES

OPTION 1: **Psalm 90:12**
OPTION 2: **Proverbs 22:6**
OPTION 3: **Matthew 7:1-2**

Jesus' sacrificial death occupies a central focus in John's Gospel as the events moved toward a climax at the cross and Jesus' triumph through the resurrection. The first twelve chapters of John's Gospel focus on Jesus' life, teachings, and ministry. In chapter 13 the focus shifts to Jesus' final meal with His disciples before His arrest, death, resurrection, and appearances to believers. At this moment in Jesus' ministry, He turned His attention to His disciples, both to prepare them for the coming events and to teach them the kingdom qualities of humility, service, and love. They would be called to embody these traits when they took on Jesus' ministry after His ascension to heaven.

In spite of His foreknowledge of Judas's betrayal, Peter's denial, and the disciples' general unfaithfulness, Jesus demonstrated a servant attitude toward His disciples on the evening prior to His arrest. He washed the feet of His disciples and used that experience to teach them about loving, humble service. Even today Jesus continues to call His followers to imitate His example, even when serving is uncomfortable and inconvenient.

HIGHLIGHT · EXPLAIN · APPLY · RESPOND

195//JOHN 14

MEMORY VERSES

OPTION 1: **Psalm 90:12**
OPTION 2: **Proverbs 22:6**
OPTION 3: **Matthew 7:1-2**

After Jesus washed the feet of the disciples, He continued to outline expectations for them after His death. Chapter 13 closed with Peter's question and Jesus' knowledge of Peter's future betrayal. Anticipating additional questions and the sorrow His disciples would experience at His departure, Jesus offered a message of comfort and consolation to enable them to live confidently. Jesus called them to trust in Him by reminding them of their belief in Him and their eternal security in heaven.

In another of Jesus' "I am" statements, He referred to Himself as "the way, the truth, and the life" (14:6). Jesus is the single, reliable source of redemptive revelation. Apart from Him, no means of knowing God and no hope of abundant, eternal life exist.

Another means of comfort for Jesus' disciples would be the presence of the Holy Spirit, whom Jesus promised to send in His place. The Holy Spirit serves as a Counselor and a Teacher. He brings peace and comfort to a believer's soul, and He increases our understanding of God and His will for our lives.

In this teaching Jesus also included a call to obedience, which He linked with faith. The person who believes in Jesus is the one who listens to Him and does what He says. Obedience to God doesn't guarantee a person's salvation, which comes through belief in Jesus alone, but if Jesus has truly changed a person's heart, obedience to Him follows.

HIGHLIGHT · EXPLAIN · APPLY · RESPOND

196//JOHN 15

MEMORY VERSES
OPTION 1: **Psalm 96:2-3**
OPTION 2: **Proverbs 23:13-14**
OPTION 3: **Matthew 7:3-4**

After encouraging His disciples with words of hope and comfort, Jesus taught them more about their relationship with Him. The final "I am" statement is found in John 15, when Jesus said, "I am the true vine" (v. 1). The images in this chapter describe Jesus' relationship with believers in two ways: (1) Vine and branches and (2) Master and friends.

As branches, we have the responsibility of abiding, or actively trusting and remaining, in Him in order to experience a productive life of faithfulness and obedience that yields much fruit for the kingdom of God. The images of the Vine and branches also include a description as God the Father as the Master Gardener, who cuts off branches that show no signs of life and who prunes, or trims, fruitful branches to help them yield even greater crops. The point of this image is clear: our growth in our relationship with God depends on our abiding connection to Jesus, the Vine.

The image of the Master and friends expands on this concept. As friends of Jesus, we have the privilege of participating in His mission for us and through us as we obey His commands.

One important point Jesus wanted His disciples to understand about His mission is that it will undoubtedly put us at odds with the world, just as He experienced. Rather than being a point of discouragement, however, persecution shows we're bearing the fruit that comes from abiding in Him.

HIGHLIGHT • EXPLAIN • APPLY • RESPOND

197//JOHN 16

MEMORY VERSES

OPTION 1: **Psalm 96:2-3**
OPTION 2: **Proverbs 23:13-14**
OPTION 3: **Matthew 7:3-4**

In the final instructions Jesus gave to His disciples on the night before His crucifixion (see John 13–16), Jesus promised that He would ask the Father to send the Holy Spirit to His disciples (see 14:16). He revealed that the Holy Spirit would be their Counselor (see 14:26), testify about Jesus Christ (see 15:26), and enable believers to testify also (see 15:27).

In chapter 16 Jesus gave His disciples more insight into the function of the Holy Spirit in their lives and in the world. The Spirit's ministry to the world would be to convict people of sin, righteousness, and judgment in His efforts to bring them to faith and salvation in Jesus Christ. The Spirit would guide believers into all truth. Genuine spirituality involves growing in a personal knowledge of and experience with the person and ministry of the Spirit in our daily lives. Only through the Spirit's strength are we able to find the hope and confidence Jesus encouraged at the close of this chapter with the words "Be courageous! I have conquered the world" (v. 33).

At the same time, Jesus never abandons His followers. He described His ongoing work as our intermediary. While the Holy Spirit is at work in our lives, Jesus sits with His Father in heaven, interceding on our behalf as the One through whom we're made right with God.

HIGHLIGHT • EXPLAIN • APPLY • RESPOND

198//JOHN 17

MEMORY VERSES

OPTION 1: **Psalm 96:2-3**
OPTION 2: **Proverbs 23:13-14**
OPTION 3: **Matthew 7:3-4**

John 17 is often referred to as Jesus' High Priestly prayer. Jesus' prayer on the eve of His arrest and trials included a prayer for Himself, a prayer for His disciples, and a prayer for future believers of every age.

Jesus prayed that He would glorify His Father through His death. These verses (vv. 1-5) summarize His mission in coming to earth. Jesus came to glorify God by offering salvation from sin and eternal life to all who believed in Him as the Messiah, God's Son. That mission culminated at the cross.

Jesus then prayed that His disciples would glorify the Father by preserving the unity they had with Jesus. Jesus petitioned the Father to protect His disciples from the evil one. He also asked God to grow them in Christlikeness as they continued His mission of drawing people to the Father.

Finally, Jesus prayed for all who would come to believe in Him in the future. He wanted these believers to experience unity with the Father and the Son and to grow in knowledge and love. As believers demonstrated unity, unbelievers would respond to the proclamation of the gospel, bringing glory to the Father. Jesus' selfless prayer in a time of great personal danger is a model for all of us.

HIGHLIGHT · EXPLAIN · APPLY · RESPOND

199//JOHN 18

MEMORY VERSES

OPTION 1: **Psalm 96:2-3**
OPTION 2: **Proverbs 23:13-14**
OPTION 3: **Matthew 7:3-4**

John 18 begins the narrative of Jesus' final days on earth. His prayer for believers in John 17 marked the end of His teaching, and John's writing shifted to the events of Jesus' betrayal, arrest, and crucifixion.

Unlike the other Gospel writers, John didn't describe Jesus' prayer in the garden of Gethsemane. Instead, he began with Judas's betrayal and Jesus' surrender to the soldiers and religious leaders. From the beginning of this narrative, John highlighted the fact that Jesus knew what was happening to Him and allowed it to happen. As the divine Son of God, Jesus was always in control, even when He was betrayed and put to death. He willingly gave His life to save ours.

John next recorded a portion of Jesus' trial, beginning with His appearance before Annas, one of Israel's high priests. This scene also included the first two of Peter's denials of Jesus. While Jesus was defending His identity as the Messiah before Israel's leaders, Peter cowered, denying any relation to Him. The contrast is striking and intentional on John's part.

After Jesus appeared before the religious leaders, He was sent to Pilate, the Roman governor. John highlighted in detail the conversation between these two men, in which Jesus defended His kingship. Although Pilate seemed to believe Jesus, He didn't defend Him. Pilate chose not to be on the side of truth, a choice with devastating, eternal consequences.

HIGHLIGHT · EXPLAIN · APPLY · RESPOND

200//JOHN 19

MEMORY VERSES

OPTION 1: **Psalm 96:2-3**
OPTION 2: **Proverbs 23:13-14**
OPTION 3: **Matthew 7:3-4**

In chapter 18 John had described Jesus' arrest and trials before the high priest and before Pilate. Pilate had found no basis for the charges brought against Jesus, but he wasn't willing to sacrifice himself and his political interests to set Him free. Therefore, he yielded to the religious leaders' demands for Jesus' death.

Though Pilate handed Jesus over to the Jews to be crucified, it's important to note that Jesus willingly gave Himself to die a sacrificial death for the sins of the world. John emphasized Jesus' control of these events. Throughout the account, Jesus willingly gave Himself so that we could receive salvation through Him. John also recorded many unique elements of the crucifixion that gave further evidence of Jesus' divinity, including fulfillments of Old Testament prophecy and Jesus' declaration "It is finished" (19:30).

Jesus' crucifixion occurred during the season of the Passover celebration, and He died as the Lamb of God (see 1:29,36). The blood of lambs had spared the Israelites when the destroyer invaded the land of Egypt before the Israelites left for the promised land (see Ex. 12:13). John wrote in 1 John 1:7 that "the blood of Jesus his Son cleanses us from all sin." Jesus died for us.

HIGHLIGHT · EXPLAIN · APPLY · RESPOND

201//JOHN 20

MEMORY VERSES
OPTION 1: **Psalm 100:4-5**
OPTION 2: **Proverbs 24:16**
OPTION 3: **Matthew 7:5-6**

In John 17:1-5 Jesus had referred to a time when He would be glorified. That glorification came to fruition in chapter 20 with John's description of Jesus' resurrection from the dead. For John, this was the ultimate proof that Jesus was the Son of God. Though all the Gospel writers included the resurrection, John's account highlights specific conversations Jesus had with His disciples afterward. We see ways His resurrection affected their faith and should affect ours as well.

Mary discovered the empty tomb, and hers is the first conversation highlighted. The evening after Mary found the tomb empty, Jesus appeared to the disciples, who were huddled behind locked doors. To these disciples Jesus brought words of peace, comfort, and commission.

Jesus appeared a week later to the disciples, including Thomas, who had difficulty believing the news, having been absent during Jesus' first appearance. Again, Jesus brought words of peace and blessing, as well as a call to everyone to believe in Him. He invited Thomas to see and touch His scars, but Thomas responded in faith without touching His wounds.

John closed this chapter by echoing Jesus' call to believe in Him. John's purpose in writing his Gospel was to call people to believe in Jesus as the Son of God who offers the gift of eternal life, and it should be the purpose of every believer's life as well.

HIGHLIGHT · EXPLAIN · APPLY · RESPOND

202//JOHN 21

MEMORY VERSES

OPTION 1: **Psalm 100:4-5**

OPTION 2: **Proverbs 24:16**

OPTION 3: **Matthew 7:5-6**

John could have ended his Gospel with chapter 20, but he included one more chapter that completed Peter's story and provided all of Jesus' disciples a clear sense of their mission. Jesus' final appearance was to Peter and six other disciples on the seashore as they were fishing. To make His presence known, Jesus performed a miracle similar to the one He had done when He first called His disciples, bringing their experience with Him full circle.

During that time Jesus also had a personal conversation with Peter. Three times Peter had denied knowing Jesus, just as Jesus had predicted. In this scene Jesus asked Peter three times to declare his love for Him. In response to each question, Peter emphatically affirmed His love for Jesus. Jesus followed each affirmation with a call to minister to His people, His sheep.

From this dialogue, followers of Jesus gain much insight into what Jesus expects of His disciples. Love is essential for being a faithful disciple. Believers exemplify love for Jesus by caring for His sheep. If we really love Jesus and want to follow Him, we'll serve Him by caring for other believers. Peter became one of the most influential apostles in the early church, and his life exemplified wholehearted, selfless faithfulness to Jesus' mission. John's Gospel consistently reminds us that Jesus is the Son of God, and like Peter, we're to love and serve Him wholeheartedly.

HIGHLIGHT · EXPLAIN · APPLY · RESPOND

203//1 JOHN 1

MEMORY VERSES

OPTION 1: **Psalm 100:4-5**
OPTION 2: **Proverbs 24:16**
OPTION 3: **Matthew 7:5-6**

In addition to the Gospel of John, the apostle wrote four other books that are included in the canon of Scripture: the Letters of 1 John; 2 John; 3 John; and Revelation. John wrote his Gospel to call people to believe in Jesus as the Son of God, but he wrote 1 John to people who were already Christians.

Like Peter's first letter, John's first letter is one of assurance and comfort to Christians. He began with a description of Jesus that emphasized both His humanity and His divinity. Like Peter, John described the life of a follower of Christ, but continuing the image of light versus darkness from his Gospel, he used the image of walking in the light to help believers understand what the Christian life looks like. John described people who walk in the light of Christ as those who have fellowship with God and one another.

At the heart of fellowship, or unity, with God is confession of sin. John reminded his readers that a repentant heart, not sinlessness, is the aim of a Christian's life. Sinning is inevitable on our side of eternity, but a heart that Jesus has truly changed confesses sin and accepts God's forgiveness. John finished chapter 1 by encouraging us to reflect the light of our Heavenly Father through a morally pure lifestyle.

HIGHLIGHT • EXPLAIN • APPLY • RESPOND

204//1 JOHN 2

First John 2 picks up where chapter 1 left off, with John's comments on sin in the Christian life. At the end of chapter 1, John had noted the importance of confession of sin. Next he encouraged his readers to avoid sin altogether. Jesus' grace in a person's life isn't a license to sin more; rather, it should motivate the believer to pursue a sinless life modeled on the life of Jesus. That pursuit can feel defeating because of the inevitability of sin, but Jesus' atoning work on our behalf should encourage us. Because of Jesus, God doesn't count our sin against us.

John's Gospel included Jesus' challenge to obey His commands, and John continued that message in 1 John 2. We display evidence of a genuine relationship and fellowship with God by obeying His commands, walking as He walked, and loving others as He did. These themes appear again and again in John's letter. For John, the clearest indicator of a person's relationship with Jesus is love for others. Our love for others is modeled on Jesus' love for us, which is always sacrificial and costly.

Another theme in John's letter is his repeated warnings against false teachers. People had infiltrated the church with teachings that seemed to be Christian in nature but in fact led people away from Christ. The prevalence of false teaching is why it's so important for people to test what they hear against the words of Scripture and the prompting of the Holy Spirit. God's truth will never contradict His Word and the basic truths of the gospel.

HIGHLIGHT · EXPLAIN · APPLY · RESPOND

205//1 JOHN 3

MEMORY VERSES

OPTION 1: **Psalm 100:4-5**
OPTION 2: **Proverbs 24:16**
OPTION 3: **Matthew 7:5-6**

John returned to the themes of love and obedience in chapter 3. He began by empha-sizing God's love for us, which motivates our obedience to His commands. God's love shapes our identity, making us His children and conforming us to His image. His love also encourages us to pursue sinlessness.

John communicated to his readers the weight and danger of sin by reminding them that Jesus died to take away sin's power over us. False teachers in John's day were likely trying to convince believers that their sin wasn't a grave matter, but John emphatically stated that position couldn't be further from the truth. Unrepentant sin and godliness can't coexist.

Jesus' sacrifice for our sin exemplified love and selflessness, and at the close of chapter 3, John challenged Christians to model Jesus' love in their relationships with others. We display our love for others when we meet people's needs and share God's truth with them. In this way our lives are consistent with Jesus' life on earth. Jesus expressed His love for others by meeting their physical and spiritual needs.

HIGHLIGHT · EXPLAIN · APPLY · RESPOND

206//1 JOHN 4

The dual emphases of John's letter continue to be evident in chapter 4, the first half providing additional warnings against false teachers and the second half returning to teachings on love. Like Peter and Paul, John addressed the issue of false teachers who were interfering with the spread of the gospel. This was a serious problem for the early church. Because of the dangerous threat false teachings posed to the believers' faith, John urged his readers to use the Word of God to test all human teachers who claimed to speak with spiritual authority. The mark of genuine faith is the confession that Jesus Christ came in the flesh, an all-important belief the false teachers denied. The truth about the nature of Christ is so basic to Christianity that it can never be compromised. Jesus was both fully God and fully man.

John abruptly turned from a discussion of true and false spirits to an appeal for believers to love one another. Christians should love one another because God loved them first. Again John reminded readers that God's love was supremely demonstrated when He sent His Son to be a sacrifice for our sins. The false teachers were trying to undermine this foundational truth of the gospel.

HIGHLIGHT • EXPLAIN • APPLY • RESPOND

207//1 JOHN 5

MEMORY VERSES

OPTION 1: **Psalm 103:1-2**

OPTION 2: **Proverbs 25:11-12**

OPTION 3: **Matthew 7:7-8**

In chapter 5 John summarized by calling readers to lives of belief, love, and obedience. Verse 1 states the gospel as plainly as possible: belief is rooted in Jesus, who is the Christ, the Son of God. When we believe in Jesus, the natural result is that we love one another and obey God's commands. In the event that his readers felt overwhelmed by the call to obedience, John reminded them that God's law brings freedom rather than burden. Christ frees us from the bondage of sin and empowers us to live for God alone.

Like John's Gospel, 1 John closed with a call to believe in Jesus. John did everything he could to help people know Jesus as the Son of God and receive the gift of eternal life that comes through knowing Him. In addition to eternal life, a Christian gains the gift of answered prayer, which John brought to the forefront in verses 14-15. Prayer is one way we articulate our love for God and act on our love for one another. A Christian can have confidence in prayer, in victory over sin, and in eternal security. These are key truths of the faith John wanted every believer to claim.

HIGHLIGHT · EXPLAIN · APPLY · RESPOND

208//2 JOHN

MEMORY VERSES
OPTION 1: **Psalm 103:1-2**
OPTION 2: **Proverbs 25:11-12**
OPTION 3: **Matthew 7:7-8**

The Letter of 2 John shares its main themes with the Letter of 1 John, but the two letters are very different in nature. Like Paul's letters to Titus and Philemon, 2 John is a personal letter John wrote to a narrow audience. John addressed his letter to "the elect lady and her children" (v. 1). There's much debate about whether this address refers to a specific person or to a specific church that John referred to in female terms, like the bride of Christ. Whichever interpretation is true, John's main points remain the same.

False teachers were a problem in the early church, as John had noted at length in 1 John. To combat the dangers they posed, John emphasized the importance of walking in the truth of God's Word and loving one another. When these two pillars of the Christian faith are upheld in the local church, false teachers and their lies hold no power over the people. False teachers seek to undermine the authority of Jesus, the Truth, and to strip the church of its power by pitting its members against one another. The best way to guard against these dangers is to love God and obey His commands. The Book of 2 John is a short, succinct letter on the foundation of the Christian faith.

HIGHLIGHT · EXPLAIN · APPLY · RESPOND

209//3 JOHN

MEMORY VERSES

OPTION 1: **Psalm 103:1-2**
OPTION 2: **Proverbs 25:11-12**
OPTION 3: **Matthew 7:7-8**

Like 2 John, 3 John is another personal letter by John the apostle. In each of John's letters and in his Gospel, he stressed the importance of showing obedience to God by loving one another. In this letter, which he wrote to a man named Gaius, he commended a specific person for doing just that. John knew Gaius, likely from visiting his town, and he also knew other people who continued to interact with this man. John affirmed Gaius's actions in showing hospitality and love to traveling preachers and missionaries who came through his town.

As people traveled throughout the region spreading the gospel in its early days, they relied on the housing, food, and financial support of the people in the towns they visited. Gaius's hospitality was so important and meant so much to John because it showed other Christians a clear way they could put Jesus' command to "love one another" (John 13:34) into practice. By loving people this way, Gaius partnered with them in their gospel work.

Gaius's example stands in direct contrast to that of Diotrephes, whose actions showed that he didn't walk in the truth or love others. It's clear from this comparison that actions speak more clearly than words about the condition of a believer's heart. God values a heart that loves Him and puts that love into action by loving others.

HIGHLIGHT · EXPLAIN · APPLY · RESPOND

210//JUDE

The final personal letter in the New Testament is the Letter of Jude. This is the only book in the biblical canon written by Jude, the brother of Jesus and James. Jude's primary audience was Jewish Christians, but his letter is relevant to believers in every time and place.

In its broadest sense this letter warns believers to stand firm in their faith. Many New Testament writers warned against the dangers of false teachers, and Jude was no exception. Readers can discern from the letter how seriously the writer took this issue and how desperately he wanted fellow believers to cling to the truth of the gospel. The specific issue Jude addressed is identified in verse 4: teachers who tried to downplay sin and presume on God's grace. Some teachers argued that because of grace, people could behave in whatever way they wanted. However, this teaching stood in direct contrast to Jesus' call to an obedient life and a pursuit of holiness. Jesus' grace is a wonderful gift that should push us toward Him rather than toward sin.

Jude referred to three Old Testament examples of this dangerous slippery slope: the Israelites whom God rescued from Egypt and who then turned against Him in the wilderness; angels who joined Satan's army; and the cities of Sodom and Gomorrah, which were completely overrun by sinfulness. These examples would have been very familiar to Jude's Jewish audience, and each one ended in God's judgment and condemnation of sin.

Although Jesus changed the way God deals with our sin, He didn't lessen its severity. That's why sanctification, the process of growing in Christlikeness, is an essential part of the Christian faith. Once we're united with God through salvation, it's essential that we continue to grow in our knowledge of Him and strive toward ever greater obedience, ensuring that our faith is solid so that we can't be swayed by anyone who seeks to undermine it.

HIGHLIGHT · EXPLAIN · APPLY · RESPOND

211//REVELATION 1

The Bible begins in Genesis 1 with a picture of creation, when God gave shape and life to the world and established His relationship with humanity. After sin entered the world, that relationship was broken. The rest of Scripture describes the great lengths God went to in order to draw people back to Himself.

In the Book of Revelation, the final book of the Bible, we get a glimpse of the end days: the time when Jesus will return, God will complete His redemptive work, and people who believe in Him will receive final victory over sin and eternal life with Him. The apostle John, who wrote the Gospel of John and the Letters of 1–3 John, was also the author of Revelation. John shared in the opening verses of this book that the words to follow would record a vision God gave him as a prophecy of the events that will happen when Jesus returns and God completes His redemptive work in the world.

Revelation 1 includes a vision of Jesus that proves He's alive, portraying a glory far beyond what we could ever imagine. John's response to this vision shows us that Jesus deserves our worship. The better we understand who He is, the better we'll understand how to worship Him.

HIGHLIGHT · EXPLAIN · APPLY · RESPOND

212//REVELATION 2

MEMORY VERSES
OPTION 1: **Psalm 103:3-4**
OPTION 2: **Proverbs 26:20**
OPTION 3: **Matthew 7:9-10**

Before Jesus showed John a vision of the last days, He gave him messages for seven churches located in present-day Turkey. Chapters 2–3 contain those letters. John had been the pastor of the church of Ephesus, one of the seven, and had probably traveled extensively throughout the entire region to visit the people of those churches. His rapport with them would have likely encouraged them to listen to the words of the letters, even though they were sometimes harsh.

The first letter was to the church in Ephesus. In it Jesus affirmed several qualities about the church, including their faithfulness to God, perseverance through persecution, and testing of false prophets. His criticism of this church was "You have abandoned the love you had at first" (2:4), meaning love for God and others was no longer their primary focus. To love God and others is the greatest commandment, in Jesus' own words (see Matt. 22:37-40), so no other Christian work matters if we aren't expressing that love.

The church in Smyrna received the second letter from Jesus. Evidently, they found themselves in the midst of intense persecution for their faith, because Jesus had only words of hope and encouragement for them. He acknowledged their circumstances and encouraged them not to fear but to trust in Him and place their hope in the glory of eternity that awaited.

For the churches in Pergamum and Thyatira, Jesus had words of praise and warning. Both churches were faithful in persevering through persecution, but both embraced false teaching. Warning against false teaching that leads us away from the one true faith is a common theme in the New Testament. God alone is worthy of our worship. He won't tolerate false teaching in His church.

HIGHLIGHT • EXPLAIN • APPLY • RESPOND

213//REVELATION 3

MEMORY VERSES
OPTION 1: **Psalm 103:3-4**
OPTION 2: **Proverbs 26:20**
OPTION 3: **Matthew 7:9-10**

Revelation 3 contains the last three church letters from Jesus, including the two most critical ones. The church in Sardis didn't receive any encouragement or praise from Jesus, only criticism. Jesus declared them dead inside, meaning their faith was lifeless, and He called them to repent of their sins or face eternal judgment. Jesus' praise for a few faithful individuals in Sardis stands in stark contrast to His criticism of the church as a whole.

In contrast to the church in Sardis, the church in Philadelphia received only praise from Jesus because of their faithful endurance through suffering.

The final letter, to the church in Laodicea, is arguably the most uncomfortable to read because it can hit close to home with contemporary Christians. Jesus accused this church of being lukewarm in their faith. Cold water is refreshing, and hot water is useful in many ways, such as bathing, cleaning, and medical purposes. Lukewarm water, however, is neither refreshing nor useful. Wealthy and self-sufficient, the church in Laodicea failed to realize their daily need for Jesus. Jesus urged them to repent of their sins and renew their trust in Him alone.

At the center of each of the seven letters is a call that's still important to the body of Christ today: remain true to the risen Christ regardless of present circumstances. In each letter Jesus dictated to John, it's evident that He knew the people in these churches well. He knew their motivations, their strengths, and their weaknesses. In the same way, Jesus knows us well. When we become aware of His knowledge of us and His lordship over us, we're forced to confront our sins and rejoice in His mercy and grace.

HIGHLIGHT • EXPLAIN • APPLY • RESPOND

214//REVELATION 4

MEMORY VERSES

OPTION 1: **Psalm 103:3-4**

OPTION 2: **Proverbs 26:20**

OPTION 3: **Matthew 7:9-10**

After John received the letters to the seven churches, his vision shifted to a detailed picture of heaven and prophetic revelations about the end times. This vision begins in chapter 4 with a glimpse into the throne room of heaven, and it ends in chapter 22 with Jesus' promise that He will return to set in motion the events detailed between those chapters. The goal of the entire vision was to establish hope and confidence in God's victory over sin and in the completion of His redemptive work that began with the incarnation of His Son.

According to chapter 4, the setting of this vision is the throne room of heaven, which John described in intricate detail. Each character represented in the vision is vividly portrayed and is shown to be worshiping the One who's on the throne forever. Rich in allusions to the Old Testament, particularly Ezekiel 1:5-10 and Isaiah 6:1-4, the picture of the throne room validated the events John would describe next.

The description of the creatures and the elders who day and night never stop praising God is a humbling, convicting picture of the worship God deserves. Like the twenty-four elders, we should continually lay our crowns at God's feet in an act of worship and surrender to the only One who deserves our praise.

HIGHLIGHT · EXPLAIN · APPLY · RESPOND

215//REVELATION 5

MEMORY VERSES
OPTION 1: **Psalm 103:3-4**
OPTION 2: **Proverbs 26:20**
OPTION 3: **Matthew 7:9-10**

In chapter 5 John moved from the general scene in heaven to specific events that unfolded as he watched. The One on the throne, God the Father, was holding a scroll in His right hand, but John wept because nobody was worthy even to look at what it said. His tears didn't last long, however, for the Lion of the tribe of Judah, who had the appearance of a slaughtered Passover lamb, proved His worthiness to take the scroll and open it.

That Lion and Lamb was Jesus, described in His postresurrection glory. With the appearance of Jesus, the object of heavenly worship shifted from focusing solely on the throne to including the Lamb as well. The description of Jesus is rich in symbolism that represents both His humility and His power. The entire company of the throne room fell down and worshiped Him just before He was to open the seals one by one. The scroll described here represents the events of the end times, as the following chapters of Revelation reveal.

Much debate is given to the literal versus figurative elements of John's vision, but the main point transcends both aspects: God knows how His story will end, and He remains in control of His world until the end. Jesus is the main character of this vision, as He is for the whole of Scripture, so we know God's story will end triumphantly for everyone Jesus calls His own.

HIGHLIGHT · EXPLAIN · APPLY · RESPOND

216//REVELATION 6

Revelation 6 begins a new section of John's vision as Jesus opened God's scroll and began to reveal its contents. This section of the vision emphasizes the stages of God's judgment that are coming on the world. The acts described in this chapter aren't exclusive to John's vision; similar end-time prophecies are included in the Book of Daniel and in Jesus' teachings in Matthew 24 and Mark 13.

The seals opened in chapter 6 were the first in a three-phase judgment process that also included the trumpets (see chaps. 8–9) and the bowls (see chap. 16). Not until each of these periods of judgment had passed would God's victory over sin and Satan be complete. Each seal Jesus opened was unique in its content. Bible commentators greatly differ on what the specific details of John's vision mean, but in general, these seals speak to an increasing degree of judgment by God. The first four seals opened to reveal riders on horses that enacted judgments against the earth, with images that represented global threats like war and famine, followed by the rider of death. The fifth seal revealed a scene from heaven in which Christian martyrs awaited their glorification for their suffering. The sixth seal opened to reveal an earthquake of global magnitude and a universal acknowledgment of God's glory and wrath. The final seal that completed this phase of judgment wasn't opened until Revelation 8:1.

The words at the close of chapter 6 serve as a warning to everyone who rejects Jesus today and as motivation for believers to work tirelessly to bring people to Jesus. No one can stand in the face of God's wrath except those in Jesus.

HIGHLIGHT · EXPLAIN · APPLY · RESPOND

217//REVELATION 7

MEMORY VERSES

OPTION 1: **Psalm 103:11-12**
OPTION 2: **Proverbs 27:17**
OPTION 3: **Matthew 7:11-12**

Revelation 7 pauses the drama of the seals of judgment to include a vision of two groups of people who weren't affected by the events described in chapters 6 and 8. Verse 1's description of angels holding back the winds of the earth provides a beautiful picture of God's restraining His judgment to protect those who belong to Him. God marked as His own 144,000 people, described as servants of God, who would be protected from God's judgment during the end-time events. Even in the midst of great judgment, we're reminded that God cares for and protects His own.

The scene of the multitude of people in heaven gives a similar picture of protection and hope for those who turn to God. This group is described as people who were faithful to God through their suffering. Two important emphases in their description are the recognition that salvation occurs only through God (see 7:10) and the promise of redemption in verses 15-17. God must judge sin, and He must hold Satan and his followers accountable for their wrongs, but even then God will continue to draw people to Himself until the end. God promises enduring care for those who follow Him.

HIGHLIGHT · EXPLAIN · APPLY · RESPOND

218//REVELATION 8

After the hope and optimism of Revelation 7, chapter 8 returns with the opening of the final seal of judgment. Now that God's people had been sealed for Him, judgment was no longer withheld. The contents of this seal included seven angels with seven trumpets, the second wave of God's judgment. Verses 3-5 suggest that this judgment came in response to requests for justice from God's people. The images of the incense burner and the altar remind readers of the function of incense in the Old Testament temple, which represented the prayers of God's people rising to Him with the smoke. Many readers of John's words had questioned God's justice as they had watched suffering take place for a long time. This scene reassured them that God heard their prayers and would act justly against evil in the world.

While the seals enacted judgment on the people of earth in moderation, the trumpets describe scenes of more global, permanent destruction as aspects of creation were destroyed. With each trumpet one-third of creation was destroyed in the following order: the ground; the sea; the rivers and streams; and the sun, moon, and stars. With the fourth trumpet one-third of day and night was gone as well.

The image of the reversal of creation's days is striking. God promised to fully redeem His broken creation, but that redemption wouldn't come without great cost. When we see the pains God must go to in order to right His world, we're humbled by the catastrophic nature of our sin.

HIGHLIGHT • EXPLAIN • APPLY • RESPOND

219//REVELATION 9

MEMORY VERSES

OPTION 1: **Psalm 103:11-12**
OPTION 2: **Proverbs 27:17**
OPTION 3: **Matthew 7:11-12**

God's judgments grew more severe with each stage. The vision John saw with the sounding of the fifth trumpet is one of great physical torment. God demanded the release of demonic forces from hell that resembled locusts. For five excruciating months they tormented everyone on earth except people marked by God's seal. The torment was so great that people sought death, but God forbade it. The sixth trumpet released four horsemen, who killed one-third of the earth's population.

Amid such a grave picture of future events, readers can't miss John's note in verses 20-21. Even with God's judgment raining down around them, some people still refused to repent of their sins and turn to God. This is a tragic reflection on the depravity of the human condition. We interact with many people today who feel the same way. They're so immersed in themselves and their sin that they fail to see the ways God is at work around them, as well as their own desperate need for Him. The job of every follower of Jesus is to do everything we can to help people see the reasons they need Him and the hope He can bring to their lives.

HIGHLIGHT · EXPLAIN · APPLY · RESPOND

220//REVELATION 10

The visions recorded in Revelation 8–9 gave readers a sobering picture of God's future judgment. In chapter 10 John's vision paused the prophecies of the trumpet judgments to give an aside, as chapter 7 had paused the seals. Unlike the hope and encouragement in chapter 7's description of people marked by God, chapters 10–11 dramatically set the stage for the final, most severe judgments.

The angel in this part of John's vision announced that the end was at hand and that the blowing of the seventh trumpet would set its events in motion. This angel also carried with him a little scroll, which he told John to eat. The description that the scroll would turn his stomach sour reveals the difficulty John would have in warning people about the final judgments.

We also learn from this chapter that John heard about particular end-time events that he was instructed not to write down. God has prepared us in large part for what the future holds, but He has withheld some details we don't need to know. Even though we can't know all the hows, whens, and whys of God's plan for the future, we can trust Him in the present and can eagerly anticipate the victory and rewards He promises.

HIGHLIGHT • EXPLAIN • APPLY • RESPOND

221//REVELATION 11

MEMORY VERSES

OPTION 1: **Psalm 106:1**
OPTION 2: **Proverbs 27:19**
OPTION 3: **Matthew 7:13-14**

Revelation 11 continues the break from the trumpet judgments with a description of two witnesses, prophets sent by God. It's clear from the description of these men that God would protect them so that their message could be communicated. God also promised His care and protection of the people John counted worshiping in the inner sanctuary of the temple.

In a shocking scene God allowed His prophets to be killed by "the beast that comes up out of the abyss" (v. 7). This creature plays a prominent role throughout the remainder of Revelation. Its first act was to murder God's prophets and leave their dead bodies exposed for the sport of the world. The gloating and celebrating that followed the death of God's servants showed just how far the world had fallen from Him. However, God resurrected His prophets, and their ascension to heaven marked the beginning of the end.

The earthquake that followed killed another seven thousand of the people left on earth. These cumulative events left no doubt about God's power and glory, and some of those left finally responded to Him. With that the seventh trumpet of judgment was blown, and John heard the declaration that the time for God's final judgment was at hand.

HIGHLIGHT · EXPLAIN · APPLY · RESPOND

222//REVELATION 12

As John's vision continued to unfold, he witnessed the culmination of the conflict between God and Satan. John described two signs he saw in heaven. The first sign was that of a woman in labor. She may represent all of God's people or the Israelites in particular. The fact that the woman was pregnant and wore a crown with twelve stars makes Israel the more likely option.

The second sign John saw was a red dragon. John gave a detailed description of the dragon, whom he later identified as Satan. John's vision gives readers a behind-the-scenes look into the conflict between God and Satan at the time of Jesus' birth (see v. 5). Although God continues to permit Satan to have some power today, Jesus defeated Satan when He conquered death by rising from the dead. The quotation in verses 10-12 reveals the eternal impact that Jesus' resurrection had on Satan. He was defeated once by the empty tomb, and he was permanently cast out of God's presence by the conflict John described in this chapter. The hope of these verses is followed by the recognition that for a time Satan would take out the anger of his defeat on the earth.

As with much of Revelation, the timing and literal nature of the events described in this chapter are much debated, but the message is clear: Jesus established His power over Satan when He died on the cross for our sins. While we wait for Jesus to return, we cling to the promise of definitive victory in the future to help us endure our trials today.

HIGHLIGHT · EXPLAIN · APPLY · RESPOND

223//REVELATION 13

MEMORY VERSES
OPTION 1: **Psalm 106:1**
OPTION 2: **Proverbs 27:19**
OPTION 3: **Matthew 7:13-14**

The conflict John described in Revelation 12 continued to escalate in chapter 13. Here we see the dragon on earth, joined by two additional evil forces: the beast of the sea and the beast of the earth. From the time Satan entered the biblical narrative in Genesis 3, he directly opposed God. Here we see that conflict extend so far as to directly oppose the holy Trinity.

The vision John received shows Satan and his two beasts as an evil trinity bent on deceiving the people of earth by leading them away from the one true God. The beast of the sea had become known as the antichrist because his authority stood in direct contrast to Jesus. Having been given power over all peoples and nations and having become the object of many unbelievers' worship, he turned many more people away from following God in an already tumultuous time.

The second beast was the beast of the earth. Later referred to as the false prophet, this beast opposed the Holy Spirit. As the Holy Spirit points to Jesus, the false prophet pointed people to the antichrist as their object for worship, leading them astray by impressive miracles that could easily be confused for miracles of God. This beast also placed the mark of the beast on people, pitting followers of Satan against the 144,000 sealed by God.

Amid the conflict and terror of this scene, a couple of verses bring readers great hope. In Revelation 13:9-10 John reminded readers that those who oppose God will get what they deserve. It may not happen as soon as we would like, but John reminded us that God is faithful to His Word, and in the meantime we must endure in the faith, trusting God to bring His justice and to redeem His world.

HIGHLIGHT · EXPLAIN · APPLY · RESPOND

224//REVELATION 14

MEMORY VERSES

OPTION 1: **Psalm 106:1**
OPTION 2: **Proverbs 27:19**
OPTION 3: **Matthew 7:13-14**

Revelation 13 contained a brief word of hope for God's people, but the chapter didn't end on an encouraging note. John's readers might have wondered what was in store for people who remained faithful to God during such great persecution. Chapter 14 is a more encouraging part of John's vision.

The chapter begins with a vision of the Lamb and the 144,000 who had been sealed by God. Unlike those marked by the beast, these individuals bore the names of the Father and the Son, eternally linking them with God. These faithful followers of Christ joined in the eternal worship John had described in Revelation 4–5. What better motivation could there be to faithfully endure the persecution and trials we must face during this life?

In the next part of his vision, John saw three angels who each declared different aspects of the events about to unfold.

1. The gospel was proclaimed with the final call to obedience before God's great judgment.
2. Babylon (possibly the actual city, a symbol of Rome, or the world as a whole) had fallen.
3. People marked by the beast would fall into eternal torment, but those who died as Christians would receive a special blessing.

Again John took the opportunity to call his readers to faithful, patient endurance while they waited for Jesus' return. The image of the harvest that closes the chapter provided a symbolic look at God's final judgment, the details of which were about to be revealed. At this point in John's vision, the time had come for God to rid the world of evil and to complete the victory Jesus had guaranteed on the cross.

HIGHLIGHT · EXPLAIN · APPLY · RESPOND

225//REVELATION 15

MEMORY VERSES
OPTION 1: **Psalm 106:1**
OPTION 2: **Proverbs 27:19**
OPTION 3: **Matthew 7:13-14**

Since Revelation 6 the drama depicting God's judgment of the world had been building. It began with John's vision of the seven seals and was followed by the seven trumpets. With each new seal and trumpet, God's judgment grew in severity and scope. Everything had been escalating to chapters 15–18, which describe God's final judgments and victory over evil.

In chapter 15 John gave readers another glimpse into heaven when he saw seven angels who held the seven bowl judgments. Before the first bowl was poured out, however, John described the victorious saints he witnessed before the throne of God. These saints sang a worship song that proclaimed God's glory, sovereignty, justice, holiness, and righteousness. It's important to remember each of these attributes of God as we read about the wrath and judgment that follow.

God was right to judge the evil in the world. He had created the world to reflect Him and His glory. Ever since the world had been broken by sin, God had been on a mission to redeem it and restore it to its original glory, but that couldn't happen without destroying the evil that had originally broken it. After this reminder of God's righteousness and glory, John's vision reached the climactic unveiling of the seven bowls of God's wrath.

HIGHLIGHT · EXPLAIN · APPLY · RESPOND

226//REVELATION 16

MEMORY VERSES

OPTION 1: **Psalm 119:9-10**

OPTION 2: **Proverbs 28:13-14**

OPTION 3: **Matthew 7:15-16**

Revelation 16 focuses entirely on the seven bowl judgments. Readers will catch many similarities between these and the previous judgments mentioned in Revelation, as well as some of the ten plagues in Exodus. However, the bowl judgments were poured out on the entire earth instead of thirds as in the trumpet judgments.

The first bowl resulted in a plague of painful sores on anyone who bore the mark of the beast. The second bowl turned the oceans to blood, and everything living in them died. The third bowl had the same effect on the rivers and streams, so all of the earth's water had now turned to blood. After the third bowl was poured out, an angel explained this plague as God's justice for the shed blood of His people. The fourth bowl turned the sun to a beam of fire, and the fifth bowl resulted in global darkness and pain. At this point all of the earth was plagued by God's judgments, and even though the people were living in agony, they still refused to acknowledge God's holiness and turn to Him. The sixth bowl described Satan's preparation for Armageddon, the great battle between good and evil. He gathered his army as God prepared the earth for battle. The seventh and final bowl judgment produced an earthquake and a hailstorm greater than any the world had ever seen.

The people left on the earth cursed God because it was clear who was to blame for what was happening. Similarly today we meet many people who believe God exists but refuse to trust Him with their lives. Revelation gives us a sobering reminder of why belief in Jesus is so important and why we should devote ourselves to the mission of the gospel while people still have time to repent and believe in Him.

HIGHLIGHT · EXPLAIN · APPLY · RESPOND

227//REVELATION 17

MEMORY VERSES

OPTION 1: **Psalm 119:9-10**
OPTION 2: **Proverbs 28:13-14**
OPTION 3: **Matthew 7:15-16**

Revelation 17–18 provides readers with greater detail and symbolism related to the fall of Babylon. John received this vision from one of the angels present for the seven bowl judgments. Although these two chapters also use rich symbolism, the angel gave John some clarity into what the images represented.

The primary images in this chapter are the prostitute and the beast. The prostitute most likely represents the corrupt world powers that stand in opposition to God until the end. Throughout Revelation, Babylon refers to the system of the world that has organized to rebel against God. Many interpreters also refer to a rebuilding of the literal city of Babylon or to Rome, the center of world power in John's day.

Regardless of the specifics, the symbol of the prostitute refers to forces that tempted people away from God through false teaching, persecution, and worldly temptations. The lures of power, wealth, and self-gratification have always pulled people away from God. The connection between this woman and the beast, Satan, makes it clear that the angel was describing a time when immorality will reign and people will align themselves with the beast, setting themselves up in opposition to Jesus, the Lamb.

Verses 14-17 hold the key to Revelation 17: the powers of the world and of Satan are no match for the Lamb, and God is the One who will orchestrate the world's events up to the very end.

HIGHLIGHT • EXPLAIN • APPLY • RESPOND

228//REVELATION 18

MEMORY VERSES

OPTION 1: **Psalm 119:9-10**
OPTION 2: **Proverbs 28:13-14**
OPTION 3: **Matthew 7:15-16**

Chapters 18–19 continue John's vision of the fall of Babylon and the defeat of the beast and his armies. Babylon remains the subject of chapter 18, but whereas chapter 17 addressed the religious state of the world in the end times, chapter 18 focuses more on commerce. This great city built for itself immense wealth and conducted itself with blasphemous arrogance in the face of God.

In language that echoes Jeremiah 50–51, John recorded the song of victory over the beast who rose up against God, sung by an angel whose splendor illuminated the earth. This angel announced the fall of Babylon, an event prophesied throughout Scripture. John also recorded another voice, likely Jesus or God the Father, calling for God's people to turn their backs on Babylon, which represents the world's idolatrous pursuits and sinful living. The lusts of the world have a strong, tempting pull on our lives, but God wants His people to completely separate from them in order to avoid being caught up in the world's sins and therefore its judgments.

In contrast to the angel's victorious song and God's encouragement to flee sin, the world mourned for its great city that was laid to waste (see Rev. 18:9-19). These verses remind readers that none of the things that appeal to us in our world, such as money, power, and lust, will go with us into eternity. To pursue them is to place our hope in something that has no lasting value. Only a relationship with God has eternal worth.

HIGHLIGHT • EXPLAIN • APPLY • RESPOND

229//REVELATION 19

MEMORY VERSES

OPTION 1: **Psalm 119:9-10**

OPTION 2: **Proverbs 28:13-14**

OPTION 3: **Matthew 7:15-16**

Chapter 19 continues the celebration begun by the magnificent angel in chapter 18, and a vast multitude in heaven rejoiced at God's victory over "the notorious prostitute who corrupted the earth with her sexual immorality" (19:2). Our God avenges injustice. In this chapter we again see the great multitude, elders, and creatures from chapters 4–5 who worship at the foot of God's throne. Their praise now included celebration of God's victory over sin.

John then witnessed the announcement of a wedding ceremony between the Lamb and His bride as He rode in on a white horse, clothed in brilliant white. This was the second coming of Jesus, the event for which all Christians live in great anticipation. John's description of Jesus includes many titles that capture His character: Faithful and True, just Judge, Word of God, King of kings, and Lord of lords.

With Jesus' entry to claim victory over Babylon and the beast, John witnessed the final defeat of the beast and his armies. As Christians, we find strength and hope for life by realizing that when Jesus comes again, He will defeat the forces of evil. This truth should also compel us to share our hope in Christ with everyone we know so that they can share in the same promise.

HIGHLIGHT · EXPLAIN · APPLY · RESPOND

230//REVELATION 20

The final three chapters of Revelation focus on Satan's final push and ultimate defeat and on a look ahead at our eternal future with God. Chapter 20 is divided into three sections: the millennium, the final defeat of Satan, and the great-white-throne judgment. John's vision describes a thousand-year period after Jesus returns when He will reign on the earth. During this time Satan will be bound and held captive.

The interpretation of these verses is one of the most popular debates in Christian theology, with most people falling into one of three theological camps: premillennialism, postmillennialism, and amillennialism. The differences among these views center on whether the thousand-year time period will be literal and when it will occur. John recorded that after Jesus' thousand-year reign, Satan will make one last push against God. He'll again build an army in an attempt to overthrow Jesus, but they won't even reach the point of battle before God will defeat them and throw them into hell forever. With that God's judgment of evil will be complete.

The final scene in this chapter is often called the great-white-throne judgment, which refers to God's judgment of all humankind. People who have faith in Jesus will dwell with God for eternity; those who don't will join Satan in eternal torment. The Book of Revelation constantly draws us back to God's sovereignty and to the promise of His ultimate victory over sin, death, and hell.

HIGHLIGHT · EXPLAIN · APPLY · RESPOND

231//REVELATION 21

MEMORY VERSES

OPTION 1: **Psalm 119:11**

OPTION 2: **Proverbs 28:18**

OPTION 3: **Matthew 7:17-18**

Chapter 21 begins a description of the new heaven; new earth; and new Jerusalem, a holy city. Verses 3-4 affirm the great hope of every Christian: eternally dwelling with God in a place devoid of sin, pain, and death. The redemptive plan God had initiated in Genesis 3 will be complete. Time and again in Scripture we've seen that both creation and humanity were broken by sin, and here we see that God will once and for all make all things new, just as He promised.

The description of the city in Revelation 21:9-21 is strikingly detailed, although we can only imagine how far human words fall short in capturing this glorified state. In verses 22-27 John commented on the absence of a temple in the holy city. This is the most important detail about our future home. We'll live in the presence of God forever. His glory will shine so brightly that we won't need a sun or a moon. Everything in the city will reflect His glory, holiness, and purity, and we'll spend all our days worshiping and serving Him.

HIGHLIGHT · EXPLAIN · APPLY · RESPOND

232//REVELATION 22

MEMORY VERSES

OPTION 1: **Psalm 119:11**
OPTION 2: **Proverbs 28:18**
OPTION 3: **Matthew 7:17-18**

John closed his book by describing the river of life, which symbolizes the eternal life Jesus makes available to us. Just as the Bible began with a description of Eden, which fell, it ends with this description of a new Eden, which will endure forever because of Jesus' redemptive work. The curse from Genesis 3 will be gone.

As Jesus concluded His vision to John, He issued an urgent call to faith. He promised to return, and He's always faithful to keep His promises. The names Jesus included in His final statement to John reinforce His faithfulness: the Alpha and the Omega, the First and the Last, the Beginning and the End. His faithfulness is clear, from the account of creation in Genesis to the promise of the new creation in Revelation.

Jesus wants all people to know Him, but as the vision in Revelation makes clear, a time is coming when unbelievers will no longer have the hope of redemption from their sin and the offer of eternal life with God. Until then God wants to use you to guide those around you to know Him personally, just as He used John. Jesus offers living water to satisfy the spiritual thirst of all people. John concluded the Book of Revelation with Jesus' promise to return soon and with a phrase that can become our personal prayer: "Amen! Come, Lord Jesus!" (Rev. 22:20).

HIGHLIGHT · EXPLAIN · APPLY · RESPOND

233//MATTHEW 1

MEMORY VERSES
OPTION 1: **Psalm 119:11**
OPTION 2: **Proverbs 28:18**
OPTION 3: **Matthew 7:17-18**

Each of the Gospels gives a detailed account of Jesus' life on earth; however, each Gospel writer had a unique purpose for writing, and that purpose shaped the encounters and teachings he included. It also determined the way the writer began and ended his Gospel. John wanted to prove Jesus' divinity, Mark emphasized Jesus' servant nature, and Luke wrote primarily to Gentiles to highlight their need for a Savior and Jesus' identity as that Savior.

The Gospel of Matthew, on the other hand, was written to a Jewish audience to demonstrate that Jesus was the fulfillment of the Old Testament Scriptures. This fact explains why Matthew began with Jesus' genealogy. The genealogy affirms that Jesus descended from Abraham, Judah, and David, fulfilling various Old Testament prophecies about the Messiah.

Following the genealogy, Matthew focused on events surrounding Jesus' birth. He began with the angel's appearance to Joseph. Matthew was the only Gospel writer to include this interaction. The angel shared with Joseph the message of the miraculous conception, a detail of Jesus' birth that underscores His divine nature— Immanuel, "God is with us" (v. 23). This scene also gives insight into Joseph's faithfulness to God and therefore his faithfulness to Mary. From the beginning of Matthew's Gospel, the faithfulness of God's chosen people was on display.

HIGHLIGHT · EXPLAIN · APPLY · RESPOND

234//MATTHEW 2

MEMORY VERSES

OPTION 1: **Psalm 119:11**
OPTION 2: **Proverbs 28:18**
OPTION 3: **Matthew 7:17-18**

Matthew 2 continues the story of Jesus' birth, but instead of sharing about the angel's visit to Mary, Mary's visit to Elizabeth, the census, and Jesus' birth in Bethlehem—details included in other Gospels—Matthew skipped to events that followed Jesus' arrival: the wise men's visit and the family's escape to Egypt.

The visit from the wise men is another detail only Matthew included. The exact identity of these men isn't known, but it's interesting that word of Jesus' birth had spread to "the east" (v. 1), likely Babylon, and that these kings believed the prophecy that Jesus would be the King of the Jews. The wise men's search, discovery, and subsequent worship of Jesus further confirmed His identity as the Messiah.

Herod's reaction to the wise men's questions was an early indicator of the effect Jesus' presence would have on political and religious leaders of His day. Herod felt threatened enough by the birth of this child that he plotted to have Him killed. This reaction highlighted both Herod's insecurity as a leader and Jesus' profound impact on the world around Him, even from His infancy.

Even the family's escape to Egypt, eventual return to Israel, and settling in the city of Nazareth were prophetic fulfillments. Reading the birth and infancy narratives in Matthew, we're reminded that God keeps His promises. We also learn that Jesus was God's unique Son and that He alone was positioned to change the world.

HIGHLIGHT • EXPLAIN • APPLY • RESPOND

235//MATTHEW 3

MEMORY VERSES
OPTION 1: **Psalm 119:11**
OPTION 2: **Proverbs 28:18**
OPTION 3: **Matthew 7:17-18**

Before Jesus began His public ministry, John the Baptist prepared the way for Him by proclaiming a message of repentance and calling people to baptism as a symbol of their heart transformation. Matthew pointed out that John also fulfilled Old Testament prophecy, quoting Isaiah 40:3:

A voice of one crying out:
Prepare the way of the LORD in the wilderness;
make a straight highway for our God in the desert.

Matthew 3:11-12 gives John's own prophecy about Jesus, whom he described as being anointed by the power of the Holy Spirit and as coming to judge sinners and call people to a right relationship with God. When Jesus arrived on the scene, He did just that.

John's baptism of Jesus marked the beginning of Jesus' earthly ministry in Matthew's Gospel. Jesus traveled to the river for John to baptize Him. By being baptized, Jesus identified Himself with John's message and with the people He came to save. It's interesting to recognize that all three Persons of the Trinity were present at this important moment in Jesus' ministry, affirming that Jesus was the Son of God and that His mission was anointed by the Holy Spirit.

HIGHLIGHT • EXPLAIN • APPLY • RESPOND

236//MATTHEW 4

After His baptism Jesus endured a period of temptation in the desert. Matthew stated that the Holy Spirit led Jesus into the wilderness for this time of temptation, signifying that God remained in control of the situation, even though Satan may have thought otherwise.

Satan tempted Jesus in three specific ways, each one bringing into question God's goodness and trustworthiness: (1) Satan tempted Jesus to make bread, appealing to Jesus' hunger from His time of fasting. (2) The devil tempted Jesus to throw Himself off the temple to learn whether God would rescue Him. (3) By trying to appeal to a desire for power and glory, Satan tempted Jesus to turn away from God and to worship Satan instead.

To each temptation Jesus responded by quoting Scripture (see Deut. 8:3; 6:16; 6:13, respectively). Satan's efforts to tempt Jesus away from God and His plan were futile.

This exchange reveals the reality of the spiritual battle raging around us and provides for us a concrete example of how God equips us to withstand temptation. When we face temptation, we, like Jesus, can trust in the character of God and the promises of Scripture, no matter how appealing the temptation might be.

After His time in the desert, Jesus launched His public ministry by proclaiming the message that the kingdom of God was at hand, choosing His disciples, and preaching to and healing the crowds.

HIGHLIGHT · EXPLAIN · APPLY · RESPOND

237//MATTHEW 5

MEMORY VERSES

OPTION 1: **Psalm 119:105**

OPTION 2: **Proverbs 29:18**

OPTION 3: **Matthew 7:19-20**

In Matthew 5 the Gospel shifts to Jesus' Sermon on the Mount, in which He taught citizens of the kingdom of God how to conduct themselves. The sermon begins with the Beatitudes, blessings God gives to people who cultivate certain spiritual attributes. Jesus emphasized inner motives rather than mere outward conformity to the law. From the Beatitudes we learn that Jesus wants His followers to depend on Him, to grieve over their sin, to be kind to others and love them, and to patiently endure persecution for the faith.

Jesus then addressed the issue of behavior, giving two word pictures that described what it means to be His follower. Disciples of Christ are to be salt and light, meaning we should have a positive impact on the world around us and draw people to Him.

Jesus next responded to several Jewish laws to help His disciples understand that right behavior is never the ultimate indicator of a life that pleases God. A person must have the right heart motive too. The commands of God remind us that He has a plan for the way we ought to live our lives, based on His character and His gracious redemptive work on our behalf. The God who demands perfection has provided a means of living a life of holiness through the sacrifice of His perfect Son, Jesus.

HIGHLIGHT · EXPLAIN · APPLY · RESPOND

238//MATTHEW 6

MEMORY VERSES

OPTION 1: **Psalm 119:105**
OPTION 2: **Proverbs 29:18**
OPTION 3: **Matthew 7:19-20**

As Jesus continued His Sermon on the Mount, He taught that religious behaviors—specifically, giving, praying, and fasting—can be carried out with healthy or unhealthy motives. Inappropriate motives focus on recognition and attention, while appropriate motives focus on sacrifice and the worship of God. Included in this teaching is Jesus' well-known Model Prayer, which highlights prayer as a means of worshiping God, aligning ourselves with His will, and depending on Him to meet our daily physical and spiritual needs.

The rest of Matthew 6 addresses our priorities from a kingdom perspective. Jesus particularly emphasized ways anxiety and worry can prevent us from receiving the full benefit of God's blessing. His teaching is important for believers because our priorities demand the bulk of our time and attention and reveal our level of trust in God. Kingdom people should aspire to a singular focus on God and loyalty to Him. Worry is the opposite of trust in God.

HIGHLIGHT · EXPLAIN · APPLY · RESPOND

239//MATTHEW 7

MEMORY VERSES
OPTION 1: **Psalm 119:105**
OPTION 2: **Proverbs 29:18**
OPTION 3: **Matthew 7:19-20**

The next section of the Sermon on the Mount focuses on relationships. Jesus taught that His kingdom people aren't to be judgmental and condemning. Rather, the loving relationship we enjoy with God sets the standard for our relationships with others.

Jesus also taught that prayer is the primary way we function in relationship with God, who wants us to continually approach Him with our requests. He delights to give us what we need. Jesus further taught that our prayers are powerful when we're persistent, when we believe God's promise, and when we trust God's heart.

Jesus' sermon built to a climactic conclusion in which He challenged His listeners to make a choice. Would they follow Him through the narrow gate into the kingdom, or would they choose the wide gate that many people enter, which leads to ultimate destruction? A true Christian's life is marked by obedience that flows from a committed, personal relationship with Jesus Christ.

HIGHLIGHT · EXPLAIN · APPLY · RESPOND

240//MATTHEW 8

MEMORY VERSES

OPTION 1: **Psalm 119:105**
OPTION 2: **Proverbs 29:18**
OPTION 3: **Matthew 7:19-20**

After the Sermon on the Mount, Matthew's Gospel returns to Jesus' ministry, which was marked by miraculous healings and wonders. Matthew 8 records three miracles of healing that demonstrated slightly different aspects of Jesus' power. The cleansing of the leper demonstrated Jesus' power over one of the worst maladies of the day. The healing of the centurion's servant showed that Jesus didn't need to be physically present to heal. At Capernaum Jesus cast out demons, demonstrating His sovereign power over evil.

After those healings Jesus illustrated the true nature of discipleship. True discipleship is defined by trust in Jesus, no matter what the circumstances are. The next two miracles, the calming of the storm and the two men possessed by multiple demons, revealed Jesus' power over nature itself and over the most extensive, entrenched evil. The complete picture of Jesus' power on display in Matthew 8 shows that, through Christ, the God of the universe transforms individual lives.

HIGHLIGHT • EXPLAIN • APPLY • RESPOND

241//MATTHEW 9

MEMORY VERSES
OPTION 1: **Psalm 127:1**
OPTION 2: **Proverbs 29:22-23**
OPTION 3: **Matthew 7:21-23**

Chapter 9 continues to focus on Jesus' earthly ministry, specifically His miraculous works and His teachings. Other Synoptic Gospels (Matthew, Mark, and Luke) record many events described in these chapters, but Matthew chose these specific examples to further highlight Jesus' authority and identity as the Messiah.

Matthew followed this account with another that caused controversy with the religious leaders: Jesus' call of Matthew, a tax collector, to be a disciple and His dining with other tax collectors and sinners at Matthew's house. Tax collectors were considered some of the lowest of the low in Jesus' time because the Roman government employed them and because they made a living by cheating people out of money. That reputation didn't matter to Jesus. He saw in Matthew someone willing and ready to follow Him. In Jesus' own words, "It is not those who are well who need a doctor, but those who are sick" (Matt. 9:12). Sin is spiritual sickness.

After additional accounts of healing and conflicts with the Pharisees, Matthew included a scene unique to his Gospel (see vv. 35-38). In a behind-the-scenes look into Jesus' heart, the Savior described the world around Him as a field that needed to be harvested but lacked the workers to do so. This analogy continues to be relevant today. People all around us are ready to hear the gospel and believe in Jesus, but they need us to share this good news with them. This call to discipleship and missions is an ongoing theme throughout Matthew's Gospel.

HIGHLIGHT · EXPLAIN · APPLY · RESPOND

242//MATTHEW 10

MEMORY VERSES

OPTION 1: **Psalm 127:1**
OPTION 2: **Proverbs 29:22-23**
OPTION 3: **Matthew 7:21-23**

Matthew 9 had closed with the image of a harvest field full of people who needed to know about Jesus. That harvest is the focus of chapter 10, which recounts Jesus' sending of the twelve disciples. Up to this point they had shadowed Jesus as He traveled throughout the region preaching the call to repentance and performing miracles that highlighted His authority. Now, however, Jesus sent out the disciples on their own to actively participate in His mission work in His power and authority as the Son of God. He instructed them to "go to the lost sheep of the house of Israel" (v. 6). The Jews were God's chosen people, but they had fallen away from Him. Jesus sent the disciples to call Jews to repent of their sins and turn back to a relationship with God.

Knowing the disciples would encounter persecution for their message, Jesus prepared them. His message of repentance, as well as the authority with which He shared it, was controversial, and the people who rejected Jesus would reject His disciples as well. Jesus said they could expect to be persecuted by religious leaders and councils, by governors and kings, and even by their families. Though His prediction was troubling, Jesus assured the disciples that the work He sent them to do was worth whatever it cost them. Their work carried the weight of eternity.

HIGHLIGHT · EXPLAIN · APPLY · RESPOND

243//MATTHEW 11

MEMORY VERSES
OPTION 1: **Psalm 127:1**
OPTION 2: **Proverbs 29:22-23**
OPTION 3: **Matthew 7:21-23**

In Matthew 11 the Gospel narrative shifts from Jesus' travels and miracles to His teaching. This chapter begins with an exchange between Jesus and John the Baptist's disciples. Matthew's account of this interaction follows Luke's account almost verbatim. Jesus confirmed for John that He was the Messiah. He also affirmed John's faithfulness and commitment to the mission God had given him, a mission that had landed him in prison.

The teaching in the second half of this chapter is unique to Matthew's Gospel. As Jesus and His disciples traveled throughout the region, the majority of people they encountered didn't respond positively to Jesus' message and repent of their sins. Therefore, Jesus pronounced a word of judgment against these cities. Unless they turned from their sin to God, they would face a judgment worse than the judgments against some of the most sinful cities mentioned in the Old Testament. Hearing Jesus teach isn't enough; a person's heart must be truly changed in order to experience His grace.

After that word of judgment, Jesus invited people into the rest He offered. Jesus was referring to freedom from the law that comes with belief in Him. The Jews were bound to their religious systems and rules, which blinded them to the Messiah when He came. A relationship with Jesus brings peace because we're freed from our efforts to earn God's favor; instead, we can rest in Jesus' work on our behalf.

HIGHLIGHT · EXPLAIN · APPLY · RESPOND

244//MATTHEW 12

MEMORY VERSES
OPTION 1: **Psalm 127:1**
OPTION 2: **Proverbs 29:22-23**
OPTION 3: **Matthew 7:21-23**

Matthew 12 provides more details about the growing conflict between Jesus and the Jewish religious leaders. This tension highlighted the divide between Jesus' identity and mission as the Jews' Messiah and their failure to see Him for who He really was.

As the conflicts in this chapter reveal, the central problem was that Jesus didn't behave the way the Pharisees thought their Messiah should behave. He broke their rules, such as all the laws associated with the Sabbath (see vv. 1-14), and He helped people they deemed unworthy of help, like the demon possessed (see vv. 22-37). The Pharisees were too distracted by their own priorities and expectations to see God's plan unfolding before them. Jesus used these conflicts as opportunities to confront them about their hard hearts and spiritual blindness. They thought they were holy and righteous because they rigorously obeyed the law, but Jesus described them as a "brood of vipers" (v. 34) and "an evil and adulterous generation" (v. 39).

In this chapter Matthew also included a quotation by the prophet Isaiah that gives insight into the purpose of Jesus' messianic mission. The Pharisees wanted a Messiah who would powerfully overthrow Rome and elevate the Israelites to a place of political power. But as Isaiah foretold, God's Messiah would humbly and peacefully serve as a beacon of God's hope and justice. The same humility, hope, and peace should characterize believers today as we continue to live out Jesus' redemptive mission.

HIGHLIGHT · EXPLAIN · APPLY · RESPOND

245//MATTHEW 13

MEMORY VERSES

OPTION 1: **Psalm 127:1**
OPTION 2: **Proverbs 29:22-23**
OPTION 3: **Matthew 7:21-23**

After His conflict with the Pharisees over their misunderstanding of the Messiah, Jesus gave His disciples and the crowds insight into what God's kingdom looks like and how a person enters it. To present these truths, Jesus used His favorite teaching method, the parable.

Matthew included seven kingdom parables in this chapter. The first one, the parable of the four soils, was also included in Mark's and Luke's Gospels. It teaches that a kingdom person is first and foremost someone who listens to and obeys God's Word.

The parable of the weeds in verses 24-30 was later explained by Jesus in verses 36-43. For now God's kingdom is present on earth, where God's people (the wheat) intermingle with unbelievers (the weeds). But a time is coming when God will separate the weeds from the wheat—unbelievers from believers—and will judge both according to their relationships with Jesus. This parable reminds believers that while we wait for that day of judgment, it's critical for us to reach as many people as we can with the good news of the gospel.

The next two parables, mustard seed and yeast, illustrate that the presence of God's kingdom on earth started out small—in a manger in Bethlehem—but would eventually overtake the entire world. The final three parables describe the kingdom as being invaluable, worth sacrificing everything for, and available only for those who believe in God through Jesus. It's clear from each parable in this chapter that the kingdom of God is present on earth even now and that entrance into the kingdom depends on a relationship with Jesus.

HIGHLIGHT · EXPLAIN · APPLY · RESPOND

246//MATTHEW 14

MEMORY VERSES
OPTION 1: **Psalm 139:23-24**
OPTION 2: **Proverbs 30:5**
OPTION 3: **Matthew 7:24-25**

As Jesus' ministry quickly moved closer to Jerusalem and the cross, the reactions to Him grew stronger. Jesus' following continued to grow, but the anger of those who opposed Him intensified. All of the events recorded in Matthew 14 appear elsewhere in the Synoptic Gospels, highlighting their importance to Jesus' mission.

This chapter begins with Herod's killing of John the Baptist. This news saddened Jesus, so He withdrew to a boat in order to grieve in private. After he returned to shore, the crowds had grown larger, and even in the midst of His grief, their needs moved His heart. He performed additional miracles of healing, as well as the miraculous feeding of the thousands.

Those miracles and the one that followed, when Jesus walked on water, gave His disciples further insight into Jesus' authority and power as the Messiah, the Son of God. They also revealed the disciples' insufficient faith. The disciples had been traveling with Jesus for a while, had witnessed all of His miraculous works and teachings, and had even been sent out with His authority in their lives. However, sometimes they still questioned the limits of His power. They never imagined He could create food where there was none or had the power to walk on water. The Jesus they served was the Son of God, the One who created everything. As the cross drew near, it was critically important for the disciples to understand who Jesus was so that they would understand what He had to do.

HIGHLIGHT · EXPLAIN · APPLY · RESPOND

247//MATTHEW 15

MEMORY VERSES

OPTION 1: **Psalm 139:23-24**
OPTION 2: **Proverbs 30:5**
OPTION 3: **Matthew 7:24-25**

Opposition to Jesus continued to grow, and by this point in His ministry, the religious leaders were looking for an opportunity to have Him arrested and put to death. They continued to attack His and His disciples' breaking of the law, even though in Matthew 5:17 Jesus had pointed out that He had come to fulfill the law. In 15:2 they questioned Jesus about why the disciples didn't participate in ritual cleansing. In response, Jesus pointed out the hypocrisy of the Pharisees, who used their own laws to skirt obedience to God's commands. They were guilty of the same sin they accused the disciples of committing.

This incident gave Jesus another opportunity to emphasize the heart change brought about by genuine obedience to God. Heart change was the greatest difference between the old and new covenants. With the old covenant (the Mosaic law), faith was attributed to people who lived in obedience to God's laws. With the new covenant, initiated by Jesus, faith is attributed to those who believe in Him, and obedience is a fruit of that belief. Our words and actions overflow from our hearts, which Jesus has cleansed and changed.

Although opposition to Jesus increased, so did belief in Him. The remaining verses in this chapter show Jesus performing more miracles and illustrate the growing belief of the crowds who followed Him: "The crowd was amazed when they saw those unable to speak talking, the crippled restored, the lame walking, and the blind seeing, and they gave glory to the God of Israel" (v. 31).

HIGHLIGHT · EXPLAIN · APPLY · RESPOND

248//MATTHEW 16

MEMORY VERSES

OPTION 1: **Psalm 139:23-24**
OPTION 2: **Proverbs 30:5**
OPTION 3: **Matthew 7:24-25**

In another attempt to trap Jesus, the religious leaders again asked Him for a sign that would prove He was the Messiah. Ironically, everything Jesus had done up to this point in His ministry proved just that. He had already fulfilled many Old Testament messianic prophecies, healed the sick, raised the dead, calmed the seas, and granted forgiveness of sins. All of these miraculous acts revealed His true identity. Because the Jews refused to believe Jesus was the Messiah, He knew no additional signs would convince them otherwise.

"The sign of Jonah" Jesus mentioned in verse 4 was a hint about His death and resurrection. As Jonah was in the belly of the fish for three days before being spit out onto land, Jesus would be dead in the tomb for three days before rising from the dead.

After that brief exchange with the religious leaders, Jesus warned His disciples about being negatively influenced by their teaching. He used an image He had used before—the power of yeast to affect its surroundings—to illustrate that even a little false teaching about the Messiah could lead them astray. He wanted His disciples to trust in Him and not be influenced by the loud, critical voices around them. He wanted all of them to join Peter in confidently, unapologetically believing that Jesus was "the Messiah, the Son of the living God" (v. 16). Their firm belief and commitment to this truth would become even more important once Jesus was no longer with them, a time He alluded to at the close of this chapter.

HIGHLIGHT · EXPLAIN · APPLY · RESPOND

249//MATTHEW 17

MEMORY VERSES
OPTION 1: **Psalm 139:23-24**
OPTION 2: **Proverbs 30:5**
OPTION 3: **Matthew 7:24-25**

In chapter 17 Jesus continued to prepare His disciples for His death and their responsibility after He was gone. The first scene in this chapter is the transfiguration. Jesus had taught the disciples about the realities of His kingdom, both its present reality and its future fulfillment. What they witnessed on the mountain that day confirmed those truths. Jesus was the Messiah, the Son of God, and although His birth initiated His kingdom on earth, the full reality of that kingdom wasn't yet visible. When these three disciples got a glimpse of its glory, they didn't want to leave.

What the disciples witnessed on the mountain and their failure to heal the demon-possessed boy were humbling reminders of their need for increased faith in Jesus. He wanted them to be ready to carry on His ministry after He was gone, and He knew they would need bold faith in Him and in His power at work through them. Their faith needed to be strong enough to see them through the persecution, suffering, and challenging days of ministry that awaited them.

This chapter ends with a conversation between Jesus and Peter that's unique to Matthew's Gospel. When Jesus and His disciples went to the temple in Capernaum, the collectors of the temple tax questioned them about paying their taxes. Jesus taught Peter that although their allegiance should always be to God and His kingdom, God expects His followers to live as responsible citizens in their earthly kingdoms as well.

HIGHLIGHT · EXPLAIN · APPLY · RESPOND

250//MATTHEW 18

MEMORY VERSES
OPTION 1: **Psalm 139:23-24**
OPTION 2: **Proverbs 30:5**
OPTION 3: **Matthew 7:24-25**

The teachings in Matthew 18 continue where chapter 17 ended: with an emphasis on how to live as disciples of Jesus. Like the Sermon on the Mount earlier in this Gospel, Jesus' teaching focused on traits and behaviors of kingdom citizens rather than on characteristics of the kingdom itself. Jesus' teaching was prompted by a dispute among the disciples about who would be greatest in the kingdom; in other words, who was the best disciple? This incident again highlighted the disciples' slowness to understand the true nature of God's kingdom. Jesus reminded them that humility, dependence on God, and childlike faith are traits that the greatest disciples embody.

In the series of teachings that followed, Jesus warned against the danger of temptation and emphasized the need to proactively fight against it. Next He challenged His disciples to value children—and by default, everyone—by reminding them how much every life, no matter how young, matters to God.

It's also important for disciples to know how Jesus wants us to respond to fellow Christians when they sin against us. Rather than react selfishly to being sinned against, we're to respond in a way that pushes the offender toward Jesus through repentance. Similarly, the parable of the unforgiving debtor in Matthew 18:21-35 reminds us that forgiveness is a defining characteristic of disciples of Christ. God has shown us unfathomable forgiveness by sacrificing Jesus for our sin. We must always pursue forgiveness with anyone who offends or wrongs us, because it's one of the clearest ways we can reflect Jesus' love and grace in that relationship.

HIGHLIGHT · EXPLAIN · APPLY · RESPOND

251//MATTHEW 19

Because Matthew wrote his Gospel primarily for a Jewish audience, much of his writing focuses on Jesus' conflict with the Jewish religious leaders, primarily the Pharisees and Sadducees. By the time Jesus left Galilee for Judea *en route* to Jerusalem and the cross, that conflict had reached a boiling point. This conflict became central to Matthew's account of the events that led to the crucifixion. In chapter 19 Jesus' conversations with the religious leaders focused on two contentious points: grounds for divorce and the way people gain eternal life. When the Pharisees tried to back Jesus into a theological corner over the question of divorce, He responded by articulating God's design for marriage.

Verses 16-30 recount Jesus' conversation with the rich young ruler. This man approached Jesus while He was teaching and inquired about the requirements for eternal life with God. In response, Jesus told the man to sell all of his possessions and give the money to the poor. Although the man was faithful to obey the law, he refused to give up everything to follow Jesus, and he remained outside the kingdom of God.

Jesus' instruction to this man highlighted his idols; his money and possessions greatly mattered to him. They were his whole identity. In contrast, Jesus taught time and again that nothing should have a greater priority in our lives than following Him, and our faith in God should be the source of our identity. Through both conversations in this chapter, Jesus reminds us that rules don't matter as much as a heart changed by God. When hearts are truly changed, obedience and service naturally follow.

HIGHLIGHT · EXPLAIN · APPLY · RESPOND

252//MATTHEW 20

MEMORY VERSES

OPTION 1: **Psalm 145:8**
OPTION 2: **Proverbs 31:8-9**
OPTION 3: **Matthew 7:26-27**

The parable at the beginning of chapter 20 is unique to Matthew's Gospel. Closely following Jesus' conversation with the rich young ruler, it gives another perspective on the difference between life in Jesus' kingdom and life in the world. In Matthew 19:30 Jesus had declared, "Many who are first will be last, and the last first." One reason the religious leaders hated Jesus is that He undermined their feelings of religious superiority. They thought they would have a place of prominence in God's kingdom because of their obedience to the law, but unless they recognized Jesus as the Messiah, they would have no place in the kingdom at all.

The parable in Matthew 20 makes the same point. As the landowner was generous in his pay, God is generous in His grace to sinners. That grace is the same for everyone. It's available to all people, no matter how righteous or sinful, through belief in Jesus Christ.

Later in this chapter Matthew wrote about Jesus' interaction with the mother of two of His disciples, James and John. When she asked for her sons to be shown favor in His kingdom, Jesus again took the opportunity to clarify that kingdom people are to be servants. In addition, following Jesus means a life of sacrifice, as Jesus would demonstrate by giving His life. True disciples of Jesus love others more than they love themselves and are willing to sacrifice everything to lead others to Jesus.

HIGHLIGHT · EXPLAIN · APPLY · RESPOND

253//MATTHEW 21

MEMORY VERSES

OPTION 1: **Psalm 145:8**

OPTION 2: **Proverbs 31:8-9**

OPTION 3: **Matthew 7:26-27**

Matthew 21 begins with Jesus' triumphal entry into Jerusalem and the cleansing of the temple, which further highlighted His authority and identity as the Messiah, the promised Son of God. The triumphal entry also marked the beginning of the end of Jesus' earthly ministry, as the time for His death on the cross grew near. Matthew focused his account of this scene on Jesus' fulfillment of Old Testament prophecy and His identity as the King of the Jews, themes that would continue throughout the Passion Week events.

The remainder of chapter 21 draws attention to the failure of the Jewish religious leaders to recognize Jesus as the Messiah. They doubted and questioned His authority, and they refused to believe God had truly sent Him. Clearly seeing their unbelief, Jesus directly rebuked them in the parable of the two sons (see vv. 28-32). The religious leaders knew God's Word, but when both John the Baptist and Jesus called them to repent of their sins and believe in Him as the Messiah, they refused.

Jesus went further by telling a parable that foreshadowed the Passion Week events. The parable of the vineyard owner in verses 33-46 describes Jesus' rejection and eventual murder at the hands of the Jews. Jesus also revealed that God's kingdom was being given to the Gentiles because of the Jews' rejection. Matthew made it clear to his Jewish readers that their religious leaders were no longer the voice of authority for God's people. That responsibility belonged to Jesus during His time on earth. Then it would shift to His apostles and to the leaders of the church.

HIGHLIGHT • EXPLAIN • APPLY • RESPOND

254//MATTHEW 22

MEMORY VERSES

OPTION 1: **Psalm 145:8**
OPTION 2: **Proverbs 31:8-9**
OPTION 3: **Matthew 7:26-27**

Matthew included the parable of the wedding feast as the third in a series of parables Jesus directly addressed to the Jews. Like the two that came before it, this one also highlights the Jews' failure to recognize Jesus as their Messiah and the consequences of their blindness.

Throughout Israel's history God had sent many prophets who foretold the coming of the Messiah, but Israel didn't listen. When the Messiah arrived, they failed to recognize Him and didn't believe His claims. They were like the invited guests who didn't attend the wedding banquet. Consequently, God invited everyone into His kingdom. However, He stipulated one condition, highlighted in the parable by the man who wasn't wearing wedding clothes: belief in Jesus and acceptance of His grace. Regardless of national heritage or religious upbringing, anyone who believes in Jesus will be saved.

Following this parable, Matthew recorded four more interactions between Jesus and the Jewish religious leaders, all part of their continued efforts to have Jesus arrested. In an effort to expose a lack of authority, the leaders questioned Jesus about paying taxes, the resurrection, and the greatest commandment in the law. Jesus answered all of their questions in a way only God Himself could, and the chapter ends with His own question about the identity of the Messiah, another reminder that they were missing the most important truth that can be known.

HIGHLIGHT · EXPLAIN · APPLY · RESPOND

255//MATTHEW 23

The conflict between the religious leaders and Jesus reached its climax in Matthew 23. Although the leaders had ample opportunity to see Him for who He really was, they refused to believe. As a result, Jesus spoke out against them, exposing their hypocrisy, religious burdens, and self-righteous behavior. Their behavior directly contradicted the kingdom principles He had presented, primarily peace, humility, and servanthood.

After warning the crowd about their leaders, Jesus proclaimed seven woes against the leaders. At the heart of Jesus' denunciation was the fact that these leaders bore the responsibility to shepherd God's people and point them to His truth, but they were actually leading people away from God. Their job was to teach the Scriptures, but they manipulated and distorted God's Word to the point that salvation seemed exponentially more complicated than it actually was.

God takes the shepherding of His people very seriously, and He won't allow His people to be led astray by false teachings or misinterpretations of His Word. The Bible tells us everything we need to become a part of God's kingdom, and whether or not we're in roles of spiritual leadership, we must value Scripture highly and interpret it accurately.

HIGHLIGHT · EXPLAIN · APPLY · RESPOND

256//MATTHEW 24

MEMORY VERSES

OPTION 1: **Psalm 150:6**

OPTION 2: **Proverbs 31:29-30**

OPTION 3: **Matthew 7:28-29**

Matthew 24 contains several teachings by Jesus about the future. As His death drew closer, Jesus knew the disciples needed to be prepared for the suffering and persecution that would eventually come, and He also knew they needed a reason to maintain hope when circumstances grew challenging.

Jesus prophesied about the fall of the temple, which would take place in AD 70. To the disciples' question about signs of the end, Jesus replied that we shouldn't misinterpret the signs. Persecutions of various types are to be expected. False messiahs will arise. People will be deceived. All of these events are preludes to the end of the age, when Jesus Himself will return and make all things right once and for all.

Scripture repeatedly teaches us that the end times will be a time of judgment. This is good news for people who know Jesus as their Savior and Lord, but it's bad news for people who don't have a personal relationship with Him. In Matthew 24 Jesus illustrated the certainty of judgment with the parable of the fig tree and warned against trying to predict the time of His return. Understanding and applying teachings about the end times can be difficult, but the most important lesson is that Jesus will return again. We must serve Him faithfully until He comes.

HIGHLIGHT · EXPLAIN · APPLY · RESPOND

257//MATTHEW 25

Matthew 25 continues Jesus' teachings on His second coming and the way His followers should live in the meantime. Unlike the teachings in Matthew 24, the ones recorded in this chapter are unique to Matthew's Gospel.

The parable of the ten virgins stresses the importance of being watchful and ready for Jesus to return. Like the five virgins who carried extra oil for their lamps, we need to spend our days faithfully living for Him and anticipating His return. We can't rely on the faith of someone else, such as a parent or a spouse, to substitute for our own.

The parable of the talents highlights the gifts and responsibilities God has given each of us and our need to steward them wisely. Faithful followers of Jesus spend the days before His return serving Him and investing in His kingdom.

The final parable in this chapter, the parable of the sheep and the goats, provides a picture of Jesus' judgment in the last days, when He will separate His faithful followers from those who don't know Him. Jesus made it clear from His description of the sheep that people who love Him will love and serve others. This parable portrays the great commandment from Matthew 22:37-39 in action.

The teachings in Matthew 25 remind readers that the real need isn't for insight to interpret signs of the times but perseverance to remain faithful to the mission of drawing more people to Christ. While we wait for Jesus to return, we must diligently spread the gospel so that as many people as possible can have the hope and promise of eternal life with Him.

HIGHLIGHT · EXPLAIN · APPLY · RESPOND

258//MATTHEW 26

MEMORY VERSES

OPTION 1: **Psalm 150:6**
OPTION 2: **Proverbs 31:29-30**
OPTION 3: **Matthew 7:28-29**

Jesus' teaching on His second coming in Matthew 25 brought His years of teaching and ministry to a close. In chapter 26 Matthew shifted his focus to Jesus' arrest, trial, and crucifixion. The content Matthew included in this chapter is represented in the other Synoptic Gospels, but as in the rest of his book, Matthew emphasized Jesus' identity as the Messiah.

The name Son of man, which occurs several times throughout these events, was a Jewish title associated with the coming Messiah and the suffering He would endure. Matthew wanted His Jewish readers to understand that the prophecies about the suffering and sacrifice of the Messiah were about to be fulfilled.

Prior to Jesus' arrest, Matthew included an account of the woman (addressed elsewhere as Mary) who anointed Him with burial oil, Judas's betrayal, and the disciples' preparations for and participation in the last supper. During the Passover meal Jesus directly connected the symbolism of their meal with the sacrifice He was about to make. He described the breaking of the bread as the breaking of His body and the drinking of the cup as the pouring out of His blood for the forgiveness of sins. This meal, the first Lord's Supper, quickly became an integral part of church practice to commemorate and reflect on the sacrifice Jesus made on behalf of humankind.

Following that significant meal, Matthew included Jesus' prediction of Peter's denial; Jesus' prayer, suffering, betrayal, and arrest in the garden of Gethsemane; and the initial phase of His trial. Through all of these events, Jesus, the Son of man, surrendered to the will of His Heavenly Father in order to bring the hope of redemption to all people.

HIGHLIGHT · EXPLAIN · APPLY · RESPOND

259//MATTHEW 27

MEMORY VERSES
OPTION 1: **Psalm 150:6**
OPTION 2: **Proverbs 31:29-30**
OPTION 3: **Matthew 7:28-29**

Matthew 27 primarily concentrates on Jesus' trial and death, but it begins with the death of Judas. Another detail only Matthew included, it's in part a fulfillment of Old Testament prophecies about the Messiah's death. Judas felt remorse over his betrayal of Jesus, but his remorse led to despair and suicide rather than repentance.

After this scene Matthew returned to Jesus' trial. Through injustice and persecution Jesus remained humble and steadfast in His obedience to the will of the Father. Jesus' interrogation ended with Pilate's granting the religious leaders' request to sentence Jesus to crucifixion in place of Barabbas, a guilty criminal. With that verdict Jesus, though innocent, was delivered over to death, as had been prophesied.

Crucifixion was the most painful, barbaric form of capital punishment in the ancient world. The Romans at first used it only for slaves, then later for enemies of the state, and by the first century as a deterrent against criminal activity. Jesus was none of those. However, His sacrificial death had always been God's plan.

Jesus' crucifixion produced different responses from the people who saw it. The religious leaders and soldiers mocked Him, but a Roman centurion professed Jesus' identity as the Son of God. Regardless of people's responses, Jesus' blood covered the sins of all who place their faith in His name.

HIGHLIGHT · EXPLAIN · APPLY · RESPOND

260//MATTHEW 28

MEMORY VERSES
OPTION 1: **Psalm 150:6**
OPTION 2: **Proverbs 31:29-30**
OPTION 3: **Matthew 7:28-29**

The record of the resurrection is surprisingly short in all of the Gospels. The writers weren't necessarily trying to prove the resurrection, because it was largely considered indisputable in the early church. They were satisfied with sharing only a few of Jesus' appearances.

The postresurrection events Matthew recorded are particularly significant for the assignment Jesus gave to all of His disciples throughout history. Matthew included Jesus' appearance to the women who found the empty tomb and His appearance to the eleven remaining disciples. It was then that Jesus issued the Great Commission, commanding the disciples to replicate His gospel ministry by going to the world and making disciples.

Sharing Christ and bringing people into the kingdom are ongoing lifestyle commitments, ones we should live out with the same sense of urgency that characterized the first disciples. As we continue to live out the Great Commission today, we must remember that we aren't working in our own strength. Our task isn't to be clever, motivational, or exciting. We're to be obedient, humbly claiming the promise that Jesus is with us always.

HIGHLIGHT · EXPLAIN · APPLY · RESPOND

SAMPLE HEAR ENTRY

Read: Philippians 4:10-13
Date: 12-22-18
Title: The Secret of Contentment

H // Highlight

"I am able to do all things through Him who strengthens me" (Phil. 4:13).

E // Explain

Paul was telling the church at Philippi that he had discovered the secret of contentment. No matter the situation in Paul's life, he realized that Christ was all he needed, and Christ was the One who strengthened him to persevere through difficult times.

A // Apply

In my life I will experience many ups and downs. My contentment isn't found in circumstances. Rather, it's based on my relationship with Jesus Christ. Only Jesus gives me the strength I need to be content in every circumstance of life.

R // Respond

Lord Jesus, please help me as I strive to be content in You. Through Your strength I can make it through any situation I must face.

SAMPLE PRAYER LOG

Date Asked	Prayer Request	Date Answered

SAMPLE SCRIPTURE-MEMORY CARD

You, therefore, my son, be strong
in the grace that is in Christ Jesus.
And what you have heard from me
in the presence of many witnesses,
commit to faithful men who will
be able to teach others also.

2 Timothy 2:1-2

F-260 NT BIBLE-READING PLAN

WEEK 1

- ☐ Luke 1
- ☐ Luke 2
- ☐ Luke 3
- ☐ Luke 4
- ☐ Luke 5

MEMORY VERSES

OPTION 1: Psalm 1:1-2
OPTION 2: Proverbs 1:7
OPTION 3: Matthew 5:1-2

WEEK 2

- ☐ Luke 6
- ☐ Luke 7
- ☐ Luke 8
- ☐ Luke 9
- ☐ Luke 10

MEMORY VERSES

OPTION 1: Psalm 1:3-4
OPTION 2: Proverbs 2:6-7
OPTION 3: Matthew 5:3-4

WEEK 3

- ☐ Luke 11
- ☐ Luke 12
- ☐ Luke 13
- ☐ Luke 14
- ☐ Luke 15

MEMORY VERSES

OPTION 1: Psalm 1:5-6
OPTION 2: Proverbs 3:5-6
OPTION 3: Matthew 5:5-6

WEEK 4

- ☐ Luke 16
- ☐ Luke 17
- ☐ Luke 18
- ☐ Luke 19
- ☐ Luke 20

MEMORY VERSES

OPTION 1: Psalm 3:3-4
OPTION 2: Proverbs 3:9-10
OPTION 3: Matthew 5:7-8

WEEK 5

- ☐ Luke 21
- ☐ Luke 22
- ☐ Luke 23
- ☐ Luke 24
- ☐ Acts 1

MEMORY VERSES

OPTION 1: Psalm 8:4-5
OPTION 2: Proverbs 3:11-12
OPTION 3: Matthew 5:9-10

WEEK 6

- ☐ Acts 2
- ☐ Acts 3
- ☐ Acts 4
- ☐ Acts 5
- ☐ Acts 6

MEMORY VERSES

OPTION 1: Psalm 9:9-10
OPTION 2: Proverbs 3:33-34
OPTION 3: Matthew 5:11-12

WEEK 7

- ☐ Acts 7
- ☐ Acts 8
- ☐ Acts 9
- ☐ Acts 10
- ☐ Acts 11

MEMORY VERSES

OPTION 1: Psalm 13:5-6
OPTION 2: Proverbs 4:23
OPTION 3: Matthew 5:13-14

WEEK 8

- ☐ Acts 12
- ☐ Acts 13
- ☐ Acts 14
- ☐ James 1
- ☐ James 2

MEMORY VERSES

OPTION 1: Psalm 16:11
OPTION 2: Proverbs 5:20-21
OPTION 3: Matthew 5:15-16

WEEK 9

- ☐ James 3
- ☐ James 4
- ☐ James 5
- ☐ Acts 15
- ☐ Acts 16

MEMORY VERSES

OPTION 1: Psalm 18:2
OPTION 2: Proverbs 6:10-11
OPTION 3: Matthew 5:17-18

WEEK 10

- ☐ Galatians 1
- ☐ Galatians 2
- ☐ Galatians 3
- ☐ Galatians 4
- ☐ Galatians 5

MEMORY VERSES

OPTION 1: Psalm 19:14
OPTION 2: Proverbs 9:9-10
OPTION 3: Matthew 5:19-20

WEEK 11

- ☐ Galatians 6
- ☐ Acts 17
- ☐ Acts 18
- ☐ 1 Thessalonians 1
- ☐ 1 Thessalonians 2

MEMORY VERSES

OPTION 1: Psalm 23:1-2
OPTION 2: Proverbs 10:9
OPTION 3: Matthew 5:21-22

WEEK 12

- ☐ 1 Thessalonians 3
- ☐ 1 Thessalonians 4
- ☐ 1 Thessalonians 5
- ☐ 2 Thessalonians 1
- ☐ 2 Thessalonians 2

MEMORY VERSES

OPTION 1: Psalm 23:3-4
OPTION 2: Proverbs 10:27-28
OPTION 3: Matthew 5:23-24

WEEK 13

- [ ] 2 Thessalonians 3
- [ ] Acts 19
- [ ] 1 Corinthians 1
- [ ] 1 Corinthians 2
- [ ] 1 Corinthians 3

MEMORY VERSES

OPTION 1: Psalm 23:5-6
OPTION 2: Proverbs 11:24-25
OPTION 3: Matthew 5:25-26

WEEK 14

- [ ] 1 Corinthians 4
- [ ] 1 Corinthians 5
- [ ] 1 Corinthians 6
- [ ] 1 Corinthians 7
- [ ] 1 Corinthians 8

MEMORY VERSES

OPTION 1: Psalm 24:3-4
OPTION 2: Proverbs 12:2-3
OPTION 3: Matthew 5:27-28

WEEK 15

- [ ] 1 Corinthians 9
- [ ] 1 Corinthians 10
- [ ] 1 Corinthians 11
- [ ] 1 Corinthians 12
- [ ] 1 Corinthians 13

MEMORY VERSES

OPTION 1: Psalm 25:4-5
OPTION 2: Proverbs 13:2-3
OPTION 3: Matthew 5:29-30

WEEK 16

- [ ] 1 Corinthians 14
- [ ] 1 Corinthians 15
- [ ] 1 Corinthians 16
- [ ] 2 Corinthians 1
- [ ] 2 Corinthians 2

MEMORY VERSES

OPTION 1: Psalm 26:2-3
OPTION 2: Proverbs 13:13-14
OPTION 3: Matthew 5:31-32

WEEK 17

- [ ] 2 Corinthians 3
- [ ] 2 Corinthians 4
- [ ] 2 Corinthians 5
- [ ] 2 Corinthians 6
- [ ] 2 Corinthians 7

MEMORY VERSES

OPTION 1: Psalm 27:10
OPTION 2: Proverbs 14:2-3
OPTION 3: Matthew 5:33-35

WEEK 18

- [ ] 2 Corinthians 8
- [ ] 2 Corinthians 9
- [ ] 2 Corinthians 10
- [ ] 2 Corinthians 11
- [ ] 2 Corinthians 12

MEMORY VERSES

OPTION 1: Psalm 30:5
OPTION 2: Proverbs 14:12
OPTION 3: Matthew 5:36-37

WEEK 19

- ☐ 2 Corinthians 13
- ☐ Mark 1
- ☐ Mark 2
- ☐ Mark 3
- ☐ Mark 4

MEMORY VERSES

OPTION 1: Psalm 32:1
OPTION 2: Proverbs 14:26-27
OPTION 3: Matthew 5:38-39

WEEK 20

- ☐ Mark 5
- ☐ Mark 6
- ☐ Mark 7
- ☐ Mark 8
- ☐ Mark 9

MEMORY VERSES

OPTION 1: Psalm 33:4-5
OPTION 2: Proverbs 14:34
OPTION 3: Matthew 5:40-42

WEEK 21

- ☐ Mark 10
- ☐ Mark 11
- ☐ Mark 12
- ☐ Mark 13
- ☐ Mark 14

MEMORY VERSES

OPTION 1: Psalm 34:8
OPTION 2: Proverbs 15:1-2
OPTION 3: Matthew 5:43-44

WEEK 22

- ☐ Mark 15
- ☐ Mark 16
- ☐ Romans 1
- ☐ Romans 2
- ☐ Romans 3

MEMORY VERSES

OPTION 1: Psalm 37:4-5
OPTION 2: Proverbs 15:16-17
OPTION 3: Matthew 5:45-46

WEEK 23

- ☐ Romans 4
- ☐ Romans 5
- ☐ Romans 6
- ☐ Romans 7
- ☐ Romans 8

MEMORY VERSES

OPTION 1: Psalm 37:23-24
OPTION 2: Proverbs 15:22-23
OPTION 3: Matthew 5:47-48

WEEK 24

- ☐ Romans 9
- ☐ Romans 10
- ☐ Romans 11
- ☐ Romans 12
- ☐ Romans 13

MEMORY VERSES

OPTION 1: Psalm 40:1-2
OPTION 2: Proverbs 16:9
OPTION 3: Matthew 6:1-2

WEEK 25

- ☐ Romans 14
- ☐ Romans 15
- ☐ Romans 16
- ☐ Acts 20
- ☐ Acts 21

MEMORY VERSES

OPTION 1: Psalm 42:1-2
OPTION 2: Proverbs 17:27-28
OPTION 3: Matthew 6:3-4

WEEK 26

- ☐ Acts 22
- ☐ Acts 23
- ☐ Acts 24
- ☐ Acts 25
- ☐ Acts 26

MEMORY VERSES

OPTION 1: Psalm 46:10
OPTION 2: Proverbs 18:10
OPTION 3: Matthew 6:5-6

WEEK 27

- ☐ Acts 27
- ☐ Acts 28
- ☐ Colossians 1
- ☐ Colossians 2
- ☐ Colossians 3

MEMORY VERSES

OPTION 1: Psalm 51:10-11
OPTION 2: Proverbs 18:21
OPTION 3: Matthew 6:7-8

WEEK 28

- ☐ Colossians 4
- ☐ Ephesians 1
- ☐ Ephesians 2
- ☐ Ephesians 3
- ☐ Ephesians 4

MEMORY VERSES

OPTION 1: Psalm 51:12-13
OPTION 2: Proverbs 18:22
OPTION 3: Matthew 6:9-11

WEEK 29

- ☐ Ephesians 5
- ☐ Ephesians 6
- ☐ Philippians 1
- ☐ Philippians 2
- ☐ Philippians 3

MEMORY VERSES

OPTION 1: Psalm 51:16-17
OPTION 2: Proverbs 18:24
OPTION 3: Matthew 6:12-13

WEEK 30

- ☐ Philippians 4
- ☐ Philemon
- ☐ Hebrews 1
- ☐ Hebrews 2
- ☐ Hebrews 3

MEMORY VERSES

OPTION 1: Psalm 55:22
OPTION 2: Proverbs 19:17
OPTION 3: Matthew 6:14-15

WEEK 31

- ☐ Hebrews 4
- ☐ Hebrews 5
- ☐ Hebrews 6
- ☐ Hebrews 7
- ☐ Hebrews 8

MEMORY VERSES

OPTION 1: Psalm 63:1
OPTION 2: Proverbs 19:21
OPTION 3: Matthew 6:16-18

WEEK 32

- ☐ Hebrews 9
- ☐ Hebrews 10
- ☐ Hebrews 11
- ☐ Hebrews 12
- ☐ Hebrews 13

MEMORY VERSES

OPTION 1: Psalm 67:1-2
OPTION 2: Proverbs 20:1
OPTION 3: Matthew 6:19-21

WEEK 33

- ☐ 1 Timothy 1
- ☐ 1 Timothy 2
- ☐ 1 Timothy 3
- ☐ 1 Timothy 4
- ☐ 1 Timothy 5

MEMORY VERSES

OPTION 1: Psalm 68:5
OPTION 2: Proverbs 20:19
OPTION 3: Matthew 6:22-24

WEEK 34

- ☐ 1 Timothy 6
- ☐ 2 Timothy 1
- ☐ 2 Timothy 2
- ☐ 2 Timothy 3
- ☐ 2 Timothy 4

MEMORY VERSES

OPTION 1: Psalm 81:10
OPTION 2: Proverbs 20:27
OPTION 3: Matthew 6:25-26

WEEK 35

- ☐ Titus 1
- ☐ Titus 2
- ☐ Titus 3
- ☐ 1 Peter 1
- ☐ 1 Peter 2

MEMORY VERSES

OPTION 1: Psalm 82:3-4
OPTION 2: Proverbs 21:1
OPTION 3: Matthew 6:27-28

WEEK 36

- ☐ 1 Peter 3
- ☐ 1 Peter 4
- ☐ 1 Peter 5
- ☐ 2 Peter 1
- ☐ 2 Peter 2

MEMORY VERSES

OPTION 1: Psalm 84:10
OPTION 2: Proverbs 21:15
OPTION 3: Matthew 6:29-30

WEEK 37

- [ ] 2 Peter 3
- [ ] John 1
- [ ] John 2
- [ ] John 3
- [ ] John 4

MEMORY VERSES

OPTION 1: Psalm 85:6-7
OPTION 2: Proverbs 21:23
OPTION 3: Matthew 6:31-32

WEEK 38

- [ ] John 5
- [ ] John 6
- [ ] John 7
- [ ] John 8
- [ ] John 9

MEMORY VERSES

OPTION 1: Psalm 86:5
OPTION 2: Proverbs 22:1
OPTION 3: Matthew 6:33-34

WEEK 39

- [ ] John 10
- [ ] John 11
- [ ] John 12
- [ ] John 13
- [ ] John 14

MEMORY VERSES

OPTION 1: Psalm 90:12
OPTION 2: Proverbs 22:6
OPTION 3: Matthew 7:1-2

WEEK 40

- [ ] John 15
- [ ] John 16
- [ ] John 17
- [ ] John 18
- [ ] John 19

MEMORY VERSES

OPTION 1: Psalm 96:2-3
OPTION 2: Proverbs 23:13-14
OPTION 3: Matthew 7:3-4

WEEK 41

- [ ] John 20
- [ ] John 21
- [ ] 1 John 1
- [ ] 1 John 2
- [ ] 1 John 3

MEMORY VERSES

OPTION 1: Psalm 100:4-5
OPTION 2: Proverbs 24:16
OPTION 3: Matthew 7:5-6

WEEK 42

- [ ] 1 John 4
- [ ] 1 John 5
- [ ] 2 John
- [ ] 3 John
- [ ] Jude

MEMORY VERSES

OPTION 1: Psalm 103:1-2
OPTION 2: Proverbs 25:11-12
OPTION 3: Matthew 7:7-8

WEEK 43

- ☐ Revelation 1
- ☐ Revelation 2
- ☐ Revelation 3
- ☐ Revelation 4
- ☐ Revelation 5

MEMORY VERSES

OPTION 1: Psalm 103:3-4
OPTION 2: Proverbs 26:20
OPTION 3: Matthew 7:9-10

WEEK 44

- ☐ Revelation 6
- ☐ Revelation 7
- ☐ Revelation 8
- ☐ Revelation 9
- ☐ Revelation 10

MEMORY VERSES

OPTION 1: Psalm 103:11-12
OPTION 2: Proverbs 27:17
OPTION 3: Matthew 7:11-12

WEEK 45

- ☐ Revelation 11
- ☐ Revelation 12
- ☐ Revelation 13
- ☐ Revelation 14
- ☐ Revelation 15

MEMORY VERSES

OPTION 1: Psalm 106:1
OPTION 2: Proverbs 27:19
OPTION 3: Matthew 7:13-14

WEEK 46

- ☐ Revelation 16
- ☐ Revelation 17
- ☐ Revelation 18
- ☐ Revelation 19
- ☐ Revelation 20

MEMORY VERSES

OPTION 1: Psalm 119:9-10
OPTION 2: Proverbs 28:13-14
OPTION 3: Matthew 7:15-16

WEEK 47

- ☐ Revelation 21
- ☐ Revelation 22
- ☐ Matthew 1
- ☐ Matthew 2
- ☐ Matthew 3

MEMORY VERSES

OPTION 1: Psalm 119:11
OPTION 2: Proverbs 28:18
OPTION 3: Matthew 7:17-18

WEEK 48

- ☐ Matthew 4
- ☐ Matthew 5
- ☐ Matthew 6
- ☐ Matthew 7
- ☐ Matthew 8

MEMORY VERSES

OPTION 1: Psalm 119:105
OPTION 2: Proverbs 29:18
OPTION 3: Matthew 7:19-20

WEEK 49

- [ ] Matthew 9
- [ ] Matthew 10
- [ ] Matthew 11
- [ ] Matthew 12
- [ ] Matthew 13

MEMORY VERSES

OPTION 1: Psalm 127:1
OPTION 2: Proverbs 29:22-23
OPTION 3: Matthew 7:21-23

WEEK 50

- [ ] Matthew 14
- [ ] Matthew 15
- [ ] Matthew 16
- [ ] Matthew 17
- [ ] Matthew 18

MEMORY VERSES

OPTION 1: Psalm 139:23-24
OPTION 2: Proverbs 30:5
OPTION 3: Matthew 7:24-25

WEEK 51

- [ ] Matthew 19
- [ ] Matthew 20
- [ ] Matthew 21
- [ ] Matthew 22
- [ ] Matthew 23

MEMORY VERSES

OPTION 1: Psalm 145:8
OPTION 2: Proverbs 31:8-9
OPTION 3: Matthew 7:26-27

WEEK 52

- [ ] Matthew 24
- [ ] Matthew 25
- [ ] Matthew 26
- [ ] Matthew 27
- [ ] Matthew 28

MEMORY VERSES

OPTION 1: Psalm 150:6
OPTION 2: Proverbs 31:29-30
OPTION 3: Matthew 7:28-29

NOTES //

Expand your understanding of the Bible with your whole family!

You've made it through the New Testament. But you can read through ALL of the key, foundational passages of the Bible in one year, while still having the flexibility of reading five days each week. Options exist for students and kids too! And each resource uses the HEAR journaling method, allowing for practical application throughout the yearlong plan.

Foundations:
A 260-Day Bible Reading
Plan for Busy Believers
005769893 **$12.99**

Foundations for Students:
A 260-Day Bible Reading
Plan for Busy Teens
005791600 **$14.99**

Foundations for Kids:
A 260-Day Bible
Reading Plan for Kids
005790788 **$14.99**

Let our team help you customize our practical, reproducible strategy founded on biblical principles and launch a disciplemaking movement in your church or ministry.

REPLICATE.ORG/TRAINING

EQUIPPING COHORTS

The REC is a cohort that meets four times over a two-year period for the purpose of building a strategic discipleship plan for your local church.

WHO SHOULD ATTEND?

Senior Pastors
Education Directors
Disciple-Making Pastors
Student Pastors*
Women's Ministry Leaders*

We have dedicated cohorts for Student & Women's ministry.

REPLICATE.ORG/REC

DISCIPLESHIP
BLUEPRINT

Discipleship Blueprint is a weekend experience that allows you to spend time in the context of a local church actively engaging in discipleship.

REPLICATE.ORG/BLUEPRINT

Disciplemaking resources to grow your people.

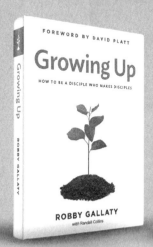  

"An outstanding introduction to the basics of the faith in a manner that will equip Christians to grow into maturity."

THOM S. RAINER

"I want to encourage you as clearly as I possibly can. Please don't read this book. Instead, do it."

DAVID PLATT

"Read this book, be encouraged, and then pass it on to a fellow pilgrim."

RUSSELL D. MOORE

Disciplemaking Resources

Replicate.org

Our Replicate website is packed with tools to help create awareness for
disciplemaking. In addition to downloads and web-based content, the Replicate blog
is a great source of insight and commentary on the current state of disciplemaking.

The Replicate Disciplemaking Podcast

Making Disciples with Robby Gallaty podcast is now available on
iTunes, Spotify, and Google Podcasts. Each week, we'll discuss practical
disciplemaking strategies along with stories from the trenches. If you are a
pastor or lay leader in your church, you won't want to miss this.